PELICAN BOOKS

HOW

D0801140

PAUL EINZIG

HOW MONEY IS MANAGED

*

THE ENDS AND MEANS OF
MONETARY POLICY

PENGUIN BOOKS

First published 1954

*Made and printed in Great Britain
for Penguin Books Ltd
Harmondsworth, Middlesex
by Wyman & Sons Ltd
London, Reading and Fakenham*

CONTENTS

*

CONTENTS

PART THREE
The Means of Monetary Policy

PART FOUR
Conclusion

Preface

MONETARY policy figures prominently nowadays not only in expert discussion but also in Parliamentary debates, in the lay Press, and in everyday conversation. It has an immense literature in every civilized language. There have been, however, very few systematic attempts to describe and examine the entire range of its ends and means. Many books on economics, or on money, deal extensively with questions of monetary policy as part of their broader subject. Other books deal with some particular type of monetary policy, usually the one in which their author happens to be particularly interested or which happens to be of topical interest at the time of writing. For example, scores of books were produced in the early thirties on the suspension of the gold standard in Britain and on President Roosevelt's monetary experiments. No attempt is made in most of such books to view topical problems from the perspective of history or to analyse the principles of monetary policy in general. A description of all present and past methods of managing money is seldom attempted. It is true that some books on money devote entire chapters or even sections to such general treatment of the subject, as distinct from detailed discussion of some particular type of monetary policy. Owing to considerations of space, however, they only present that vast material in a nutshell.

Some textbooks on money give a survey of a wide variety of monetary policies, but few of them aim at covering anything like the entire range over the whole period of monetary history. Not many of them have attempted to classify and analyse methods of managing money employed even in modern times according to their ends and their means. A narrow conception of monetary policy tends to restrict the scope of many works to the treatment of policies relating to the quantity of money. Measures such as price controls, exchange restrictions, or physical controls pursuing monetary ends, are usually considered to be outside their scope.

The above remarks should not be interpreted as implying criticism of the large number of distinguished authors who have made valuable contributions to the subject in the past. A great deal of this literature on monetary policy is of the highest standard and I am greatly indebted to the books enumerated in my Bibliography both for their factual material and their inspiring views. It is for each author to determine the scope of his work, and there is no reason for me to criticize any of them for having dealt with this subject from an angle different from the one I have adopted.

The object of this book is to present a broad picture covering the entire field of monetary policy in the wider sense of the term. It does not attempt a detailed description or analysis of any particular period or of any particular aspect of the subject. Nor does it aim at putting forward any plan of some new monetary policy or at marshalling arguments for or against any of the known policies. What it tries to do is first of all to describe the widest possible variety of monetary policies which have been in operation throughout the ages. There is a great deal to be said for viewing this subject – as indeed most subjects – from the perspective of history. Points of similarity between present-day devices and practices long forgotten – such as exist for instance between modern competitive currency depreciation and competitive currency debasement races in earlier centuries – have more than mere historical interest. It is, of course, outside the scope of this book to present a complete history of monetary policy, but historical and ethnological instances are frequently used in the attempt to trace the origin and evolution of modern policies.

The unusually broad range covered by this book is not the only basis on which I claim to be justified in adding yet another to the large number of existing volumes on monetary policy. I feel there is a strong case for re-examination of the subject at the present stage in view of the fundamental changes that have taken place during the last two decades, both in the ends and means of monetary policy and in its economic and social background. Until recently monetary policy was judged according to whether it was able to maintain monetary stability. More recently the emphasis shifted to the question whether a monetary policy assisted in the increasing utilization of the community's economic resources. Since the Second World War both considerations have come to be subordinated to the social end of securing the highest degree of welfare to the largest number. There is, moreover, a much wider variety of means at the disposal of the authorities in charge of monetary policy. Finally, full employment and perpetual high taxation have changed the background against which monetary policy operates, and this alone calls for a revision of many conclusions reached by monetary economists and practical experts during periods when there was large-scale unemployment and when taxation was much lower.

It is a matter of opinion whether the changes in the objectives of monetary policy have been for the better or the worse. Heated controversy is raging around this question. The majority of traditionalists would like to revert to the system under which monetary policy is guided by purely monetary considerations. According to them the stability and convertibility of money must be the supreme goal to be pursued at all costs. The most they are prepared to concede is that non-monetary economic considerations should be allowed to influence monetary policy to a higher degree than in the past. On the other hand, Socialists and their sympathizers take the line that aims of social welfare must prevail over everything else. At the one extreme we have those who would like to put the clock back and who would be prepared unhesitatingly to sacrifice the livelihood of millions for the sake of upholding the stability of freely convertible currencies. At the other extreme we have those who would like monetary policy to disregard completely not only considerations of monetary stability and convertibility but even considerations of productivity if this is necessary in the interest of achieving an equalitarian distribution of wealth.

Although this book aims at maintaining a neutral attitude regarding the highly controversial questions around various monetary policies, I have felt impelled to depart from neutrality in this fundamental controversy. I do not take sides with either of the extreme schools, but feel very strongly that a compromise must be reached between them. Given the facts of universal suffrage and the menace of Communism, it has become politically impossible to revert to a monetary policy that would disregard considerations of social welfare, even if we wished to do so. Traditionalist monetary experts ought to have sufficient practical sense to realize this, no matter how firmly they may be convinced that the Government's primary duty is to maintain monetary stability and to ensure full convertibility. They must see that in circumstances in which this could be achieved only at the cost of lasting unemployment and a ruthless cutting down of social services their policy, whether right or wrong, would be hopelessly impracticable. On the other hand, their opponents, too, should have a sufficient sense of reality to know that there are limits beyond which it is unwise to disregard monetary or economic considerations in the pursuit of social aims with the aid of monetary policy. They ought to realize that excessive disregard of such considerations is liable to avenge itself sooner or later. The very classes for whose sake such a one-sided point of view is imposed on monetary policy are liable to pay the penalty in the form of instability and insecurity, an increasing cost of living, large-scale unemployment, and a deterioration of the output available for distribution.

Whatever may be the ideal monetary policy from the point of view of one or the other of the extreme schools, in the world in which we have to live some compromise between the two points of view is advisable. Social aims can no longer be disregarded in any democratic country. Monetary policy must take those aims into full account. It must do so, however, in a spirit of realism. Those responsible for shaping our monetary policy must be aware of the limits within which they can disregard monetary and economic considerations with comparative impunity. Thus social considerations may call for an expansion in monetary policy, but

expansion must stop short at the limit beyond which it is liable
to endanger the standard of living and economic security of
the community, including the classes which it tries to help.

I am aware that, in favouring a middle course on a subject that is so overcharged with political controversy as
is monetary policy, my book is fated to be shot at from
both sides. My last book, *Inflation*, was accused by the *New
Statesman* of providing useful ammunition for Tories, and
by the *Yorkshire Post* of being politically biased in favour of
Socialism. I have no doubt that both reviewers would have
been able to produce scores of quotations which, divorced
from their context, might appear to confirm their respective charges. The same is doubtless true of the present book.
Traditionalists can easily find in it passages which, considered in isolation, might appear to endorse the expansionist view. Likewise, Socialists and other shades of monetary
expansionists might feel justified in representing me, on the
strength of certain passages, as a convert to monetary orthodoxy. But I hope the unprejudiced reader will realize that
it would have been easy for me to win the support of one of
the two camps by fully endorsing its attitude. Convinced as
I am that the right solution lies in a compromise, I have no
choice but to take an unpopular and ungrateful course, at
the risk of getting the worst of both worlds.

It is important that Governments, Parliaments, and public opinion in every country should have a clearer understanding of what is at stake. If they are prepared to take
risks in the interests of economic and social progress they
should know the extent of the risks and the sacrifices involved.
There may be justification for taking risks, but monetary
policy must not be a leap in the dark. One of the main objects
of this book is to stress the need for weighing the advantages
and disadvantages of achieving certain ends of monetary
policy at the expense of other ends. Another main object
is to warn against confusing the means of monetary policy
with its end. Both aims can be approached more effectively
by surveying monetary policy from every possible angle.

It is for this purpose that the book follows the method

of dealing with each important end and each important means of monetary policy in separate chapters, each one of which deals with the general subject from the particular angle of its narrower subject. A certain amount of overlapping is inevitable under this treatment, just as photographs taken of the same object from various angles are bound to some extent to overlap. There is, however, no other way of contrasting effectively the alternative ends and means of monetary policy with each other, and of weighing them one against another.

Just one word about the main title of this book – *How Money is Managed*. Conventionally the term 'managed' monetary system is used in economic literature in contradistinction to 'automatic' monetary system. For this reason it is perhaps advisable to point out that its use in the title of my book does not limit its scope to policies relating to the former. As Bagehot remarked, even under an automatic monetary system somebody must take decisions. And any such decisions come within the sphere of monetary management of monetary policy in the broader sense of the term. To avoid confusion, however, in the text of the book I propose to use the term 'managed' in its conventional sense.

It was my original intention to deal with the means of monetary policy before dealing with its ends. I am greatly indebted to Professor Sir Dennis H. Robertson for having advised me, when I discussed with him the general plan of my book, to reverse the order. He made me realize that it is the logical order to analyse the ends before dealing with the means. The change has meant much more than a mere formal rearrangement of the material. I feel it has reinforced to a remarkable degree the emphasis of the principal message my book seeks to convey – that the future welfare of mankind depends on our ability to reconcile the conflicting economic and social ends of monetary policy.

120 Cliffords Inn   PAUL EINZIG
  London, E.C.4
    April, 1954.

PART ONE
Introduction

*

CHAPTER ONE

The Monetary System

OUR task is to define, classify, describe, and analyse monetary policy according to its ends and means. Before embarking on this task it is necessary to give a brief outline of the subject-matter with which monetary policy is concerned – the monetary system.

Money is a most remarkable instrument which can be employed or influenced for many ends and in many ways. Monetary policy is concerned with money in a twofold sense. It is concerned with decisions and measures calculated to affect the monetary situation or the monetary system. And it has to employ the monetary system for the purpose of influencing the non-monetary economic situation, and even the social and political situation. Money may be either the end of monetary policy or its means. It is often both end and means, when monetary devices are used to the end of influencing the monetary situation.

Money, like most other social institutions, has developed gradually over a very long period through trial and error. It appeared in many forms before taking its present form, which, advanced as it may appear to us, cannot be regarded as final. In the course of its evolution the monetary system seldom remained entirely unchanged for a very long period in any given community. From time to time it was uprooted by some major crisis which brought about some important change. Even during prolonged periods of relative economic and political stability it was liable to change from time to time, if not in its fundamental principles at any rate in some of its essential details. Some monetary changes were spectacular in their circumstances and were accompanied by wide publicity. Other changes came about almost imperceptibly, and their significance was not realized by contemporary observers.

Apart from changes over a period of time there have always been marked differences between the systems in operation at any given moment in different communities. The diversity of monetary systems and their relatively frequent changes have between them produced an immense variety of systems. It would take many volumes to describe and analyse all, or even a reasonably representative selection of them. For our present purposes it is sufficient to deal with certain features and characteristics of money that are more or less common to all monetary systems. For it is, broadly speaking, true that the similarities between them are more important than their differences. Sir James Frazer, in a much-quoted passage in his *Golden Bough*, remarked: 'Our resemblances to the savage are still far more numerous than our differences from him.' This observation can well be applied to primitive and modern money. Some of the most important elements contained in the highly sophisticated monetary system of our days can be traced back to the rudimentary systems that were in operation during earlier periods, right at the dawn of history.

Generally speaking, we are justified in saying that there is nothing inherently good or inherently bad in any monetary system as such. Its advantages or disadvantages depend largely on its interpretation and application, and even more on the economic, social, and political background that conditions the operation of any monetary system. Disorganized monetary systems are usually the result of a war, or a major economic crisis, or some political or social upheaval, or gross mismanagement by Governments. Although the remark addressed by Baron Joseph-Dominique Louis, Finance Minister of Louis XVIII, to his fellow-Ministers, '*Faites-moi de bonne politique, je vous ferai de bonnes finances*', referred to public finance, it is fully valid also in the monetary sphere. During a period of political and economic stability it is easy to operate almost any monetary system satisfactorily, while political or economic unwisdom is liable to discredit almost any currency.

There is, for instance, nothing inherently evil and vicious

about inconvertible paper money as such, provided that it is handled sensibly. Writing in the 18th century, Goethe, in his *Faust* (Part II, First Act), represents it as the Devil's own invention. Yet it is only when the printing press is abused that paper money is apt to become a thoroughly bad system. At the other extreme there is nothing fundamentally wrong with the automatic gold standard as such, even though its unduly rigid and dogmatic application is liable to handicap progress and may become from time to time the cause of grave difficulties. The relaxation of the rigidity of the monetary system may be a blessing or a curse, according to the circumstances and the degree to which it is relaxed.

The functions of money may be classified into two broad categories – static and dynamic functions. By its static functions, money serves as a passive technical device ensuring a better operation of the economic system, without actively influencing its trends. By its dynamic functions, money tends to exert a powerful influence on the trends of the price level, on the volume of production, trade and consumption, and on the distribution of wealth. It is capable of stimulating or holding up economic and social progress. It may even exert a decisive influence on the course of history and on the progress of civilization.

Many of the qualities which enable money to fulfil its static functions satisfactorily are substantially the same today as they were many centuries ago. Now as then, money has five main technical functions to fulfil. It is intended to serve as a medium of exchange, a means of non-commercial payments (taxation, fines, gifts, etc.), a standard of value, a standard of deferred payments, and a store of value. In plain English it has to be suitable for use as a means of payment, both commercial and non-commercial; for the measurement of values and their expression in the form of prices; for the determination of future liabilities; and as a medium in which wealth can be accumulated. None of these static functions should normally give rise to any price trends or influence the basic economic trends in other ways.

Admittedly, when money was first adopted, or when a more advanced type of money replaced a less advanced type, such changes necessarily produced a 'once-for-all' dynamic effect. For instance when trading by barter gave way to trading with the aid of a medium of exchange, this change must have caused a substantial increase in production and trade and a marked acceleration of economic progress. It must have produced also some far-reaching social changes. Once, however, money is established it fulfils its technical functions without producing any such dynamic effects. The normal routine rôle of those functions is essentially 'neutral' and static. The use of a medium of exchange or of a standard of value does not in itself give rise to dynamic changes in the operation of the economy – at any rate until another major change occurs in the monetary system. Money does not cause a rise or a fall in the price level, or an expansion or contraction in business activity, by fulfilling the normal functions of a medium of exchange or its other technical functions. Such effects are produced by its dynamic functions. If the rôle of money were confined to its static functions, monetary policy would be a comparatively simple matter. It would have to pursue the single purpose of maintaining a reasonable degree of stability in the value of money, which is by far the most important among the requirements it has to fulfil in order to be able to perform its technical functions satisfactorily.

The functions of money as a medium of exchange imply its free acceptance in payment for goods and services. To that end it is essential that there should be a sufficient degree of confidence in money and that there should be enough of it to go round. Confidence in a currency and its acceptability as a means of payment is apt to be undermined by its rapid depreciation, or by a possibility that it might cease to become acceptable for some other reason. Its depreciation must reach a very advanced stage, however, before it ceases altogether to be usable as a medium of exchange. Long before that stage is reached its depreciation is apt to cause much inconvenience and grave disadvantages, but a depreciating money may continue to act none the less as a medium of exchange. So long as its recipients spend it within a short time after receiving it they do not stand to suffer any unduly heavy losses through a gradual fall in its value. It is only when its depreciation becomes so rapid that it is apt to lose a large part of its value from one day to another and even from one hour to another that it may cease to be freely acceptable as a medium of exchange and may even cease to be suitable as a means of non-commercial payment. A less advanced degree of instability in its value is sufficient to disqualify money from acting as a satisfactory standard of value, store of value, or standard of deferred payments.

A rise in the value of money does not interfere with its technical function as a means of payment for goods and services, or as a means of non-commercial payments. On the contrary an appreciating currency is bound to be much sought after by sellers of goods and services as a medium of exchange and even more as a store of value. An appreciating currency is a good investment even if it bears no interest. On the other hand, any instability in its value tends to make it less suitable for use as a standard of value or as a standard of deferred payments. A measuring rod the length of which is liable to changes is obviously unsuitable for its purpose. Situations have arisen in the past and also in more recent times in which a depreciating money, while remaining a medium of exchange, has ceased to be suitable for other functions. As a result a separation of functions might develop by which one object is used for a medium of exchange and a different one for other monetary purposes. Such a separation of functions characterized some of the primitive monetary systems in the early days of history, and also some recent monetary systems in primitive communities. During troubled periods we are apt to revert to that system, discarded long ago in advanced communities. Many countries in Central and Eastern Europe did in fact revert to it during the chaotic periods that followed the World Wars. While continuing to use paper money extensively as a means of payment, they came to reckon prices and wages in terms of gold or some commodity, or some unit of stable value.

Until recently textbooks on money concentrated on the well-known technical functions – medium of exchange, means of non-commercial payments, standard of value, standard of deferred payments, and store of value – which were regarded as the only essential functions of money. There is, however, at least one additional technical function which is fully as important as the ones mentioned above. It is the function of money as the medium through which the price mechanism operates.

Under a system of free economy – as distinct from a planned economy under which the volume of production of various categories of goods is determined by the State authority – the quantity of goods that is produced is largely determined by the profit earned on them. This in turn is determined by the prices obtained for them, compared with their cost of production. Prices again are determined largely by the relation between supply and demand. Conversely, supply and demand themselves are influenced by cost of production and prices. These tend to adjust themselves according to the quantities available for sale and the number of people who have the desire and the means to buy the goods, but in turn they also tend to effect an increase or reduction of supply or of demand according to the profit margin – if any – they leave to producers. In a free economy movements of individual prices play, therefore, a very important part in determining production, distribution, and consumption. And prices are expressed in terms of money. This means that money does much more than merely serve as a convenient technical device to facilitate the exchanges of goods and as a unit of account by which the values of various objects can conveniently be compared. It is the medium through which the price mechanism in a free economy tends to establish a balance between cost of production and sale price, and between supply and demand.

It may be a matter of opinion whether this is an ideal system or whether the system under which production, distribution, and consumption are planned by the Government instead of being left to the automatic working of the price mechanism is preferable. So long as that mechanism exists, and to the extent to which it continues to operate automatically, money will continue to play a very important part by serving as a medium through which that system operates. The fundamental character of its rôle in this respect is recognized by many modern economists who contrast planned totalitarian economy with automatic money economy, in place of the more conventional contradistinction between capitalist and collectivist economies.

The rôle of money as a medium through which the price system operates is essentially static, in that it merely serves as a passive technical device and does not fundamentally affect the operation of the price system. Admittedly, if the level of prices of certain categories of goods or services should rise or fall substantially, the discrepancy in relation to other prices may give rise to major trends liable to upset the static equilibrium of the economy. But such unsettling influences are not initiated by money in its capacity as a medium through which the price system operates. In that capacity money is an essentially 'neutral' device. It does not determine individual prices: they are merely expressed in terms of money.

Recent literature tends to represent money as something much more than a mere passive technical device to facilitate the exchange of goods and services, to serve as an instrument of their valuation, to provide means for expressing claims and for accumulating wealth, and to act as a medium through which the price system operates. Contemporary writers attribute to it several additional rôles of fundamental importance in the determination of economic trends. These rôles, which may be described as 'dynamic' because they are liable to cause major changes of a fundamental character, are by no means new. But it is only comparatively recently that they have begun to receive the attention they deserve. Foremost amongst them is the influence of money on the national economy through the effects of its depreciation or appreciation – or, what is the same thing, of a rise or a fall in the general price level. While the individual prices of various foods and services can fluctuate in relation to each other even under a barter economy there can be no such thing as a change in the general price level except under a monetary economy.

Money plays a very active, dynamic, and highly important part in the economic system through its function of influencing the general level of prices. The quantity of money and the frequency with which its owners spend it is liable to influence the demand for goods and services. If more money is available for spending while the supply of goods and services offered for sale remains the same, the chances are that higher prices will be asked and paid for the same goods and services. If there is not enough money available for spending, or if the amount available is not spent freely enough, sellers of goods and services may have to accept lower prices. A general rise or fall in the price level is liable to affect, for better or for worse, the welfare of most sections of the community. It may influence the life of every man, woman, and child.

The effect of the trend of the general price level on the economic situation is apt to be very considerable and may have far-reaching social and political consequences. Indeed, it may even affect the course of history. Surely this rôle goes far beyond that of a convenient device with the aid of which goods and services are exchanged. Nor is the influence of the trend of the price level the only way in which money can influence fundamental economic trends. Money is a powerful factor that is liable to stimulate or hinder economic and cultural progress. Intelligent and progressive application of the monetary system tends to result in fuller utilization of natural resources and of technological inventions leading to a higher standard of living. On the other hand a too narrow and rigid application of the monetary system is apt to handicap progress. And the misuse of facilities provided by the monetary system is apt to lead to grave setbacks through the destructive consequences of a runaway inflation or even of a relatively moderate but persistent 'creeping' inflation. The system carries within it the possibility of regulating the trend of trade, encouraging productive activity and commerce when they are in need of stimulus and discouraging them when they appear to be excessive. Monetary conditions are apt to stimulate or discourage consumption as well as production.

According to the conventional 'static' conception money is not supposed to play any such part in the economic system. Its quantity should be just sufficient to meet normal requirements, and therefore it is not supposed to cause a rise in the price level and in business activity through being in excess of requirements, or a fall in the price level and in business activity through being short of requirements. This conception is based on the assumption that the rôle of money is confined to its 'static' technical functions dealt with above. On the basis of that assumption money is supposed to be 'neutral' and does not play an active part in determining the course of our economy. The possibility that it may cause temporary disturbances is admitted, but according to the static theory money is not amongst the fundamental factors by which our economy is influenced. It is a mere intermediary to ensure a more efficient functioning of the factors that really matter, affecting production, distribution, and consumption. In practice, however, money is seldom completely 'neutral' for any length of time. The laws of nature do not provide the means of ensuring that there should be just enough money, neither too much nor too little, under an 'automatic' operation of the system. Nor has human brain yet devised a foolproof 'managed' system under which it could be ensured that the volume of money should be exactly sufficient, neither excessive nor deficient. It is, therefore, inevitable that money should play an important and active part in influencing economic trends through the inadequacy or excess of its quantity compared with the amount required for maintaining the stability of its value and of the volume of economic activities. These are its most important dynamic functions. But there are others.

With the aid of the modern monetary system Governments are in a position to spend well in excess of the amounts they can raise by taxation. It is possible for them to raise very large amounts by borrowing. Thanks to the modern credit system, Treasuries are now able to create monetary conditions in which they can borrow practically any sums they require. The monetary system enables them, therefore, to embark on costly economic, social, political, and military policies which would be out of their reach financially were it not for the dynamic functions of money. Such policies are apt to affect fundamentally the economy of the community concerned. For better or for worse these dynamic functions of money enable the Government to create a public debt running into astronomic figures.

The monetary system also provides the means by which the burden of such excessive indebtedness, public or private, can be reduced in a comparatively painless manner through a depreciation of the monetary unit. This may obviate in given circumstances the necessity for reducing an intolerable burden of indebtedness through wholesale bankruptcy or repudiation. The reduction of the burden of indebtedness is liable to have far-reaching effects in the social as well as in the economic sphere. In other respects, too, money may play an important part in the social sphere as a means for redistribution of wealth.

All these dynamic functions of money are fully as important as its static functions on which earlier monetary economists focused their entire attention. Admittedly money was not adopted or maintained in use in order to bring about changes in the price level, or to regulate the trend of economic activities, or to provide a relatively painless means of reducing indebtedness, or to distribute wealth. Money was adopted and is maintained for meeting the requirements of its technical functions. Indeed it would not be able to fulfil its dynamic functions unless it fulfilled its static technical functions. This is no reason, however, for ignoring or underrating the former.

It is true that in everyday life the static functions of money are usually much more in evidence. Its fundamental functions are well in the background during more or less stable and normal periods. It is only those engaged in shaping monetary policy, and those who wish to be able to form an opinion about the merits or demerits of that policy, who have to take into account all the time the dynamic functions of money as well as its static functions. During periods of crisis or important changes, the dynamic functions force themselves on the attention of the lay public. But from the point of view of monetary policy considerations relating to these functions must always be present in the minds of the monetary authorities.

Admittedly the measures taken to ensure that money is able to fulfil its technical functions satisfactorily are often identical with those required in the interests of its dynamic functions. This, however, need not necessarily be the case. From the point of view of its technical functions it is essential to maintain a stable value of money to the highest possible degree. On the other hand from the point of view of dynamic functions it may appear to be necessary in given circumstances to depart from stability. Situations may arise in which a policy aiming at a rise or a fall in the price level is a necessary evil from the point of view of some dynamic function of money – such as the stimulation of business activity or the discouragement of excessive speculation – however deplorable this may appear from the point of view of its static functions. What matters is that on balance the system as a whole should give the highest possible degree of satisfaction.

CHAPTER TWO

The British Monetary System

WE remarked in the last chapter that there have been in operation in the course of monetary history an infinite variety of monetary systems serving largely the same purposes but differing widely from each other in many material respects. In order to provide at least one detailed instance of a monetary system serving as an objective and an instrument of monetary policy, we propose to describe in this chapter the monetary system in operation in Great Britain at the time of writing – in 1953. That system, even though it differs in many respects from the American and other important monetary systems, may be regarded in its broad outlines as a fairly representative example.

In its existing form the British monetary system is of very recent origin, and is in an essentially fluid state. It is liable to change materially at any moment. Many people of the older generation still remember the totally different system that existed before the first World War, since when a succession of different systems have been adopted and discarded. Sovereigns which were the principal currency in circulation before 1914 have long been replaced, first by Treasury notes and subsequently by Bank of England notes. Subsidiary coinage, for use as token money, consisting of coins of an inferior metallic value in denominations of $\frac{1}{4}$d. to 2s. 6d. is now the only metallic money in use. There were Bank of England notes in circulation long before 1914, but, apart from a brief period during and after the Napoleonic Wars, and again during and after the first World War, these notes were always freely convertible into gold coin or bullion according to the holder's wishes. Since 1931 they are no longer convertible into gold. They are taken in payment for goods or services, or in settlement of liabilities, but not on account of their intrinsic value, which is little more than nothing. Nor are they accepted on the ground of any hope that one day they might become convertible into gold. Such hopes have long been abandoned. The reason why the notes are readily accepted is that those who take them have confidence in them, knowing that they in turn are in a position to use them for payments within the United Kingdom. It is largely for the same reason that token money is accepted as small change even though the silver or bronze or cupro-nickel value of the coins is only a fraction of their face value.

One feature of the British monetary system that has remained substantially the same as it was during the latter part of the nineteenth century is that bank deposits constitute the major part of the monetary supply. To-day their total is around £6,000 million, while that of the note issue is around £1,500 million only. The grand total of notes and of bank deposits is generally regarded as the figure of Britain's monetary supply. It is almost as easy to pay with cheques drawn on bank balances as with notes, and in many instances the former are preferred. Deposit accounts, as distinct from current accounts, are somewhat less mobile, but deposits can be converted either into notes or into current account balances subject to certain formalities and delays, so that they too may be regarded as being part of the supply of money.

Either notes or cheques drawn on current account balances can be used by the holders in payment for goods, services, and in settlement of liabilities of every kind. The unlimited acceptance of notes in payment within the United Kingdom is ensured not only by the confidence of the public but also by law under which they are 'legal tender'. Subsidiary coins are also legal tender up to limited amounts. There is and can of course be no law to enforce the universal acceptance of cheques, but in practice they are accepted to a very considerable degree. Any reluctance of payees to accept cheques in immediate discharge of current liabilities does not prevent the use of this form of money, because it only means that a few days are allowed for the cheques to be cleared before the payment is recognized as such.

Only a small fraction of the quantity of notes and bank deposits in existence is used in payments on any given day. On the other hand, in the course of a year the volume of turnover settled by means of cash or cheques amounts to many times the amount of the note issue *plus* bank deposits. During 1952 the total amount of cheques cleared was about $12\frac{1}{2}$ times the amount of deposits. No corresponding statistics are, of course, available concerning the turnover in notes.

The amount of Bank of England notes and of current account balances is not the only factor that determines monetary conditions in Britain. A great deal depends on the way in which owners of notes and deposits make use of the purchasing power represented by their monetary resources. The mere existence of these resources does not in itself affect production, prices, or consumption. As we shall see later the Government is in a position to increase or reduce these resources. But their increase does not necessarily mean that the additional amounts are spent in full. Nor does their reduction necessarily mean a corresponding curtailment of purchasing power. The public is in a position to take the initiative for causing an increase or reduction in the volume of money. This can be done by reducing or increasing its holding of savings certificates or other short-term or maturing Government securities, or by making more or less extensive use of the credit facilities offered to it by the banks. But in reasonably normal conditions the banks and the monetary authorities between them are in a position to ensure the maintenance of the volume of money around a certain level, or its adjustment to a certain level in accordance with the aims of monetary policy. This will be explained in detail in a later chapter.

In the days of the gold standard before 1914, when the pound was convertible, it was widely assumed that the confidence it inspired was due to the fact that holders of notes and of bank balances could always rely on being able to convert their holdings into sovereigns. When after an interval of eleven years the gold standard was resumed in 1925, it was a different gold standard. The notes were no longer convertible into coins but only into gold bars, and, broadly speaking, only for the purpose of shipment abroad. This limited convertibility into gold was suspended in September 1931. Holders of sterling remained entitled, however, up to the outbreak of the Second World War eight years later, to convert their pounds into dollars or other foreign currencies in the foreign exchange market at the prevailing rates of exchange. In September 1939, the convertibility of sterling into currencies of countries other than those of the Sterling Area was also suspended.

A limited degree of convertibility into certain foreign currencies was gradually resumed after 1945. Nevertheless, the fact remains that at the time of writing sterling is not convertible into any definite quantity of gold, as it was before 1914 and again between 1925 and 1931, nor is it convertible into a fluctuating quantity of dollars at market rates, as it was between 1931 and 1939. The currencies into which sterling can be converted at the time of writing are no more convertible into gold than sterling. In spite of such limitation of convertibility the pound continues to enjoy a high degree of confidence and is unhesitatingly accepted in payment in the United Kingdom. The reason for its acceptability lies partly in the fact that it is legal tender. This in itself would not be sufficient to ensure its acceptability. No law is able to enforce the free acceptance of a rapidly depreciating currency. In Britain inconvertible paper money is accepted by everybody largely because its quantity is relatively limited, and therefore its value remains relatively steady. Even during the 'cheap money policy' of the early period of the Labour Government between 1945 and 1947, there was no runaway inflation. Although sterling was not nearly as scarce as most economists and other critics of that policy would have liked it to be, the increase in the volume of notes and deposits was not so great in extent as to cause a rapid depreciation and to inspire distrust.

It is true, prices in Britain, as in other countries, have been rising almost without a break since 1939. Their rise has been, however, relatively moderate. The constant decline of the purchasing power of sterling may have discouraged saving because it made it appear probable that in fifteen or twenty years' time the amounts saved would buy half or less than half what they would buy if they were to be spent at once. But the extent of the internal depreciation of sterling from one week to another, or from one month to another, or even from one year to another, is barely perceptible. For this reason sterling is accepted in payment, because it retains more or less its value between the time we receive it and the time we spend it.

Another reason why sterling commanded the confidence of the public during the post-War period was that the Government endeavoured to safeguard its international value. Apart from its devaluation in 1949 sterling remained rigidly stabilized in terms of gold and dollars throughout the War and during the post-War period. While in some countries devaluation followed devaluation after 1945, in Britain the Government made a real effort to maintain the gold value of the pound in face of adverse trends and only yielded to sweeping pressure on one isolated occasion. It is true that stability of sterling was maintained largely through preventing unauthorized exchange dealings, cutting down imports in order to improve the balance of payments, and obtaining financial aid from the United States. Nevertheless what matters from the point of view of confidence in sterling is the fact that its international value after the War remained, for no matter what causes, reasonably stable.

Sterling remained acceptable as a means of payment and continued to be used as a standard of value, standard of deferred payments, and store of value. The only substantial change in its use as a unit of account to measure current and future liabilities was in the sphere of collective wages agreements. A large and increasing number of these agreements contain a 'cost of living clause' as a result of which wages are automatically adjusted if the cost of living index changes to a certain extent. Apart from such arrangements deferred liabilities are generally fixed in terms of sterling irrespective of any changes in its purchasing power.

Until the suspension of the gold standard in 1931 the gold value of the pound was fixed by Act of Parliament. At present it is determined in accordance with the Bretton Woods Agreement under which the International Monetary Fund has now the right to veto any alteration of the gold parity of sterling by more than ten per cent, in either direction, of its dollar value fixed in 1946. The Government has undertaken to maintain the exchange rate of sterling within a narrow range of its parity in relation to the dollar. From the point of view of the legal position in Britain there would be nothing to prevent the Government from altering the exchange value of sterling by administrative action. This is prevented, however, by the international agreement under which the Government committed itself in 1945 to carry out the Bretton Woods Agreement.

From the outbreak of the second World War until November 1951 there was no free dealing in most foreign currencies. Importers and others in need of foreign exchanges had to apply through their banks to the Bank of England for the authorization of exchanges they needed, and were granted licences authorizing them to buy the exchanges from their banks at a fixed rate. In November 1951, free dealings in exchanges for commercial requirements were restored, but not for transfers of capital or for speculation. The authorities are under no obligation to intervene in the foreign exchange market except in order to prevent the sterling-dollar rate from going beyond the limits of $2.78 to $2.82 to the pound.

Great Britain is the centre of the Sterling Area, a group of countries the currencies of which are closely linked with sterling. The group includes the whole British Commonwealth and Empire with the exception of Canada, and also a small number of countries outside the Commonwealth. There are practically no exchange restrictions between members of the group, so that money can be transferred from one country to another almost without hindrance. The British gold and dollar reserve serves as a central reserve for the whole Sterling Area, to which the countries of the group – subject to certain exceptions – contribute their gold and dollar surpluses, and out of which their requirements are met. As a general rule if the exchange value of sterling is changed, as it was in 1949, the exchange value of all currencies of the Sterling Area is changed accordingly, so that their value in terms of sterling remains unchanged. There are, however, exceptions to this rule. For instance, in 1949 Pakistan did not devalue her currency in sympathy with sterling.

Partly owing to the fact that London is the centre of the Sterling Area and partly owing to the part sterling continues to play in international trade, large balances are kept in London by overseas countries. Since the War these balances have fluctuated round £3,500 million, largely owing to abnormal war-time accumulations of sterling balances. This amount is considerably above that of the gold and dollar reserve. If sterling were freely convertible a withdrawal of a large proportion of these balances could deprive the Sterling Area of its entire gold and dollar reserve. As it is, the inconvertibility of sterling and the existence of a number of agreements with large holders of sterling balances providing for a temporary blocking and a gradual release of war-time balances safeguards sterling and the Sterling Area from such a disaster.

Gold is not paid out by the authorities either for the benefit of internal holders of pound notes or for that of foreign holders of sterling balances. It is sold only when the authorities consider it expedient – usually when dollars are needed to support sterling to prevent its depreciation below $2.78; and then it is sold only to other Governments.

To sum up, the automatic gold standard was abandoned in 1914, the managed gold bullion standard in 1931. The system of flexible sterling convertible into other currencies but not into gold gave way at the outbreak of the second World War to a system of almost entirely inconvertible, rigidly stabilized and controlled sterling. The present system may be described as one of stabilized and partly controlled sterling of limited convertibility. The internal value of the pound is maintained by keeping the quantity of money relatively scarce. A maximum limit is fixed to the note circulation but this limit is liable to frequent adjustment by administrative action by the Treasury, subject to subsequent approval by Parliament if the fiduciary issue is maintained above its authorized limit over a certain period.

The volume of money represented by bank deposits is kept down by a combination of Government policy and banking tradition. It is not kept down as rigidly as it was under the gold standard when an expansion of the volume of currency and credit was liable to correct itself automatically by causing an outflow of gold leading in turn to a contraction of credit. Under the existing system there is no technical arrangement that would prevent a runaway inflation such as we have witnessed in other countries. In spite of this inflation has been relatively moderate because those responsible for the management of our monetary policy have practised a certain degree of restraint. As Robertson rightly put it in an article appearing in *Lloyds Bank Review,* sterling is maintained sound not through any qualities inherent in the system but through the wisdom and ability of those in charge of its management.

Thanks to the relatively moderate extent and gradual character of its depreciation, sterling was able to fulfil satisfactorily its rôle as a standard of value. But owing to the persistence of its internal depreciation, post-War sterling has not been ideal as a standard of deferred payments or as a store of value. Although debtors have benefited by the decline in the real burden of their liabilities their gain has been the loss of creditors, investors in fixed interest-bearing securities, and other recipients of deferred fixed payments such as pensioners.

Sterling's rôle in the price system has been adversely affected by the rising trend of prices and by the artificial

B

dislocations in the relations between controlled and uncontrolled prices. On the whole it fulfilled, however, its technical 'static' functions reasonably well. Its 'dynamic' function as a major factor in the economic trend was that of a stimulus given by rising prices and the expanding volume of money to War-time production, to post-War reconstruction and to the development of the Welfare State. In later post-War years there have been growing signs that Britain's recovery has been over-stimulated by an unduly expanded monetary system, causing excessive consumption, to the detriment of the balance of payments. However, there has been no sign of a runaway inflation. From the end of 1951 efforts were made to reverse the monetary trend and to mop up the part of the monetary circulation which, in the opinion of the authorities, was excessive. To that end the policy of 'cheap money' was brought to a conclusion after an almost uninterrupted run of nearly 20 years. Notwithstanding this, the volume of currency and credit continued to expand, largely owing to expenditure on rearmament.

Much as the British monetary system has altered during the lifetime of our generation, its fundamental changes have been less pronounced than one is inclined to think on the basis of its outward changes. Admittedly, instead of having a gold currency or a currency convertible into gold, we now have an inconvertible paper currency. In spite of this it would be a mistake to assume – as many people do – that sterling is now entirely divorced from gold. At the time of writing its value is pegged almost as rigidly in terms of gold as it was under the gold standard. Nor is the volume of currency and credit altogether independent of the volume of gold. In practice any substantial decline of the gold reserve is liable to induce the Government to raise the Bank Rate and enforce credit restrictions in order to strengthen sterling, while any substantial increase of the gold reserve enables the Government to lower interest rates and relax credit restrictions. The authorities are thus not altogether free in determining the volume of money.

Although Britain abandoned the gold standard in 1931,

it is arguable that in 1939, by rigidly pegging the value of sterling in terms of dollars based on gold, she has returned to a form of gold standard. It is true that the system that has been in force in Britain since 1939 is not the gold standard in the conventional sense of that term. But there is room for more than one definition of 'gold standard'. According to what may be regarded as the common-sense definition, the gold standard, as its name implies, is a system under which gold is the standard of value. The status of sterling conforms to this definition so long as it remains stable in relation to gold – as indeed it has done ever since 1939. Nevertheless, since such an unconventional definition might cause confusion we propose to use the term in its accepted sense.

In spite of the similarity between the fundamental characteristics of the present system and that of the nineteenth century there are considerable differences between the rôle of money in our economic and social system then and now. This is largely because the ends and means of monetary policy have undergone far-reaching changes. The instrument is fundamentally the same, but it is now used for different purposes and in a different way.

CHAPTER THREE

What is Monetary Policy?

THE term 'monetary policy' is of comparatively recent
origin. It did not appear in economic literature, political
debates, and in the Press until the nineteenth century. Yet
monetary policy has been pursued since time immemorial.
Early writers on the subject of money from Aristotle and
Xenophon onward dealt with questions of monetary policy
without referring to them as such. Long before their writings
practical administrators had taken decisions relating to the
monetary system without being aware that they were pursuing monetary policies. They had done so probably with
little or no theoretical background. They may have experi-
mented with money, learning from the lessons of the past,
or through trial and error at the expense of their community. Or they may have followed monetary developments
elsewhere, learning at the expense of other communities.
As a rule, however, there were no easily accessible records
of the results of past monetary experiments, or of those of
contemporary distant communities, so that statesmen and
administrators had to rediscover the same elementary truths
after making the same mistakes again and again.

It would be interesting to speculate how monetary history would have been affected if the ancient Greeks had
devoted as much attention to monetary theory and policy
as they did to philosophy and the arts, or if the best brains
of ancient Rome had brought monetary knowledge to the
same high standard as they brought legal knowledge. Conceivably the Roman Empire, the stability of which became
undermined partly as a result of the confused monetary
situation prevailing during and after the third century A.D.,
might have prolonged its existence by centuries if its rulers
had known more about monetary policy. It is also possible
that the late mediaeval period might have been a period

of progress instead of virtual stagnation if Europe had borrowed the idea of paper money from China in the eleventh century. It might then have been possible to mitigate the handicap of inadequate metallic supplies that held up production and commerce until after the discovery of the gold and silver resources of the New World.

Although in the mediaeval period there were isolated instances of attempts by writers to teach Governments how to run their monetary systems it was not until the beginning of the modern period that we encounter an extensive literature on the subject of monetary policy. It is worth noting that it is always during troubled or unsettled periods that writers on monetary policy become active. During the sixteenth century the inflation caused by the heavy influx of precious metals from the New World gave rise to extensive literature on the subject, especially in Spain and in France. In Britain there was a crop of contributions to problems of monetary policy towards the end of the seventeenth century, inspired by the economic and financial troubles of the nineties. During the same period the difficulties caused by commodity-currencies and paper money in the North American Colonies gave rise to some interesting writings on the subject. In the eighteenth century John Law's experiment with paper money gave a strong stimulus to the study of monetary problems, and so did the inflation that accompanied the American War of Independence and the French Revolution.

It was not until the nineteenth century that questions of monetary policy came to be investigated systematically. They were taken up by theoretical and practical experts in connexion with the financial problems inherited from the Napoleonic Wars, and subsequently in connexion with the periodically recurrent business cycles. By the end of that century the original trickle of literature on monetary policy developed into a vast flood. It continued to grow throughout the twentieth century, and it may be claimed that in our days few specialized subjects have a more extensive literature than monetary policy.

Notwithstanding this, relatively little thought has so far been given to finding a definition for the meaning of monetary policy. Although the term is used with increasing frequency by experts and laymen, it has occurred to very few of those who write or talk about monetary policy to define what precisely they mean by it. Most of them assume that the actual scope of the discussions on the subject implies the definition. While it would be too much to expect those concerned with some current problem of monetary policy to embark on an attempt at defining the scope of the whole subject, clearly it is the duty of the monetary economist dealing with the principles of monetary policy to state precisely what he means by it.

In my *Primitive Money* I define monetary policy as 'the attitude of the political authority towards the monetary system of the community under its control'. A monetary policy may be either active, when it involves decisions to apply measures, or passive, when it involves decisions to abstain from applying measures. A passive attitude towards monetary developments, in order to constitute monetary policy, must be deliberate.

The above definition is admittedly too vague to be of sufficient practical use. Among the authors who have taken the trouble to provide a definition, Geoffrey Crowther in his *Outline of Money* adopts a useful line by defining the object of monetary policy as the effort to reduce to a minimum the disadvantages resulting from the existence and operation of a monetary system. Perhaps it would be more constructive to amend this definition by indicating as the object of monetary policy the increase of the advantages as well as the reduction of disadvantages resulting from the monetary system. Even thus amended the definition only applies to an ideal monetary policy. We might say that in theory the object of monetary policy *should be* as indicated above. In reality throughout monetary history we often encounter instances when the result of monetary policies was an increase of the disadvantages derived from the monetary system rather than their reduction. When politicians or administrators decide to plunge their country into inflation for inadequate economic reasons they abuse the monetary system. Their decision is undoubtedly an act of monetary policy, even though it does not aim at minimizing the disadvantages or increasing the advantages derived from the monetary system.

It is, of course, possible to try to interpret 'advantages' and 'disadvantages' in a sense that would come within the terms of our definition. It is arguable, for instance, that the frequent debasements of the French coinage during the Middle Ages were justified from a national point of view as the only means by which the French kings were able to finance their defensive wars against English invasions. Likewise although the inflation of paper currency that accompanied many major wars from the American War of Independence onwards inflicted grave economic and social hardships on the nations concerned, it may be claimed that it was justified as the means for financing fights for national survival. In this sense it may be argued that the inflationary monetary policies adopted by many Governments during the Napoleonic Wars and the two World Wars had for their object to secure advantages from the working of the monetary system, even though those advantages were outside the monetary, economic, or social sphere. To be able to finance a war with the aid of inflation may be claimed to have political and military advantages. Even inflationary policy pursued to prepare and wage an aggressive Imperialist war – as during Hitler's rearmament of 1933–39 and his war of 1939–45 – may be said to aim at advantages, at any rate if viewed from the one-sided point of view of the regime that pursues it.

There were many other instances in which decisions on monetary policy could not possibly be claimed to have served the public advantage in any sense. The coinage was debased on various occasions for the sake of meeting the excessive requirements of extravagant royal courts. For instance, Charles the Bad, king of Navarre, debased his country's coinage by one-third in 1383, with the declared object of securing funds to celebrate the release of the heir to the throne from French captivity.

In such instances, as in the case of debasements or inflation for the sake of financing aggressive wars, a bad monetary policy did not even have the excuse of trying to serve the advantages of the community as a whole. Both its method and its object were bad, so that the end could not be claimed to have justified the means. In spite of this fact such debasements, and more recently Hitler's inflation, must be regarded as coming within the scope of monetary policy. A bad monetary policy is none the less a monetary policy for being bad.

A different approach may be attempted by defining monetary policy as including all monetary decisions and measures irrespective of whether their aims are monetary or non-monetary, and all non-monetary decisions and measures that aim at affecting the monetary system. Under this definition we could include within the scope of monetary policy not only measures of every kind which are taken for the purpose of influencing the value, volume, etc., of money, but also monetary measures which pursue non-monetary economic, social, or political aims. From this point of view debasement or inflation undertaken for no matter what purpose would come within our definition. Likewise non-monetary measures such as control of prices or wages, physical controls, Budgetary measures, export drives or import cuts, etc., would be included within the scope of monetary policy in so far as their primary aim is to influence the monetary situation. One of the earliest forms of highly developed deliberate monetary policy was Mercantilism which aimed largely at monetary ends partly with the aid of non-monetary means.

In order to circumscribe the scope of monetary policy it is necessary to draw a distinction between monetary policy on the one hand and fiscal policy, banking policy, financial policy, and economic policy on the other. These various policies overlap with monetary policy to a very considerable extent and it is not easy to draw a borderline between them.

Nevertheless, it is necessary, and usually possible, to ascertain whether a measure is aimed at producing mainly monetary or non-monetary results.

Fiscal policy covers the ground of Government finance, that is, revenue, expenditure, borrowing, debt repayment, and other public debt operations. It is almost impossible to envisage any major measure affecting the Budgetary position or any decision concerning the public debt which would not produce some effect in the monetary sphere even if no such effect were intended or desired. Accordingly fiscal measures have come to be regarded in our days as constituting measures of monetary policy. In reality this view is too sweeping. Important measures of taxation may fall outside the scope of monetary policy if they consist in the replacement of one source of revenue by some other source, so long as they are not liable to affect materially the level of prices, the volume of purchasing power, or some other major factor in the monetary situation. Likewise a decision determining the terms of a conversion scheme, as a result of which a maturing Government loan is replaced by another Government loan, does not come within the scope of monetary policy unless its aim is to affect the liquidity of the banking system, that is, the proportion between the banks' holdings of long-term and short-term securities, on which the banks' willingness to grant credits largely depends, as we propose to show in a later chapter. An increase or reduction of various classes of expenditure does not as a rule come within the scope of monetary policy unless the grand total of expenditure is materially affected or unless the change from one type of expenditure to another affects materially some major factor in the monetary situation.

It goes without saying that monetary policy and banking policy are closely inter-related. The volume of credit constitutes the most important element in the monetary situation in a modern community. It is arguable therefore that any banking measure affecting it comes within the scope of monetary policy even if it is not initiated by the authorities but by the banks themselves, provided that they act on what they know or assume to be the official policy. There are, on the other hand, many kinds of decisions and measures within the sphere of banking policy which are outside the scope of monetary policy. The credit policy of the banks, in so far as it affects not the total volume of loans but their distribution among categories of borrowers, may or may not affect the monetary situation according to the nature of the categories affected and the extent of the effect. An expansion of consumer credits, for instance, or of credits for capital investment, is liable to become a factor in the monetary situation. On the other hand an increase in the volume of credits in one branch of industry and a simultaneous and corresponding reduction of credits in some other branches is not likely to produce any monetary effect. Likewise changes in the charges made by banks to their customers – apart from changes made in interest rates – remain within the scope of banking policy unless their nature and extent is such as to influence the monetary situation. This may be the case if banking charges are reduced in order to encourage the banking habit, and thereby to reduce requirements for notes, or if they are increased in order to discourage borrowing.

The policy relating to new public issues of securities, or to limitations on the construction of factories, may pursue monetary ends if it aims at influencing the total volume of capital investment. If it merely aims at discouraging certain types of issues – whether in order to safeguard the investing public or to prevent unwanted expansion in certain industries and encourage expansion in other industries – it does not come within the scope of monetary policy.

Monetary policy is, strictly speaking, part of the broader sphere of economic policy. It is possible and necessary to distinguish between monetary policy and non-monetary aspects of economic policy as they affect industry, commerce, agriculture, labour, etc. Economic policy aiming at expansion or contraction in the volume of production is liable to produce monetary effects even if its aim is not primarily within the monetary sphere. Although the level of wages is a matter of first-rate importance from the point of view of monetary policy, a wages policy may concern itself with matters other than the total of wages. It may aim at encouraging coal mining by means of raising miners' wages above the general level, or at encouraging the training of skilled labour, or at some other non-monetary end. It is often a matter of degree whether some economic policy measure comes within the sphere of monetary policy. Any measure resulting in a more equal or less equal distribution of income concerns the monetary situation if the change is substantial, even though it pursues primarily a social objective.

There is bound to be an immense variety of border-line cases. Whether or not they come within the sphere of monetary policy depends not so much on the nature of the action and its actual result as on the Government's intention. For 'policy' implies deliberate decisions. This does not mean, however, that if a Government embarks on large-scale spending on rearmament or social services, without taking into consideration the inflationary effects of its action, it can disclaim the pursuit of a deliberate inflationary monetary policy.

The scope of monetary policy has widened immensely within the brief span of our lifetime, and even within the last ten years or so. The extent to which Budgetary and other non-monetary measures are adopted largely if not entirely with an eye on the monetary situation has increased. Indeed, as we shall see later, a school of thought has developed among economists and practical experts, especially in the United States, which advocates that monetary measures in the narrower sense of the term should be replaced largely by fiscal measures aiming at monetary ends. In Britain and other countries physical controls are advocated in many quarters as substitutes for conventional measures of monetary policy. In so far as rationing, price controls, import and export controls, etc., affect the monetary situation their deliberate application to serve partly that purpose comes within the scope of monetary policy.

Monetary policy stands somewhere half-way between monetary theory and monetary practice. The former is concerned with broad principles which should form the background to monetary policy and which are liable to affect it. The latter is concerned with practical measures which translate monetary policy decisions into action involving a mass of technical detail. It is difficult to determine the borderline between monetary policy and monetary theory. Many theoretical principles imply or suggest decisions of policy. On frequent occasions policy decisions arise logically from the acceptance of certain theoretical principles, even though those responsible for the actual decision may not necessarily be aware of this. Only too often, however, monetary theories are too far divorced from reality to be of practical use for guidance to monetary policy. They apply to hypothetical conditions elaborated for theoretical purposes. Moreover, the same theory is liable to lend itself for serving as a basis for different policies. Nevertheless, a thorough knowledge of monetary theory and its latest developments is essential as a background to monetary policy decisions.

The actual execution of details of a monetary policy is necessarily in the hands of Government officials or Central Bank officials whose concern lies entirely within the practical sphere, and who are not necessarily required to appreciate the broad principles of the monetary policy they apply, let alone the theoretical principles serving as its background. Those responsible for decisions of monetary policy, on the other hand, may not be sufficiently acquainted with the practical details the knowledge of which is indispensable not only for the execution of their policy but also for its planning. Such details may concern the money market, the foreign exchange market, practical banking, price control, etc. There must obviously be co-operation with practical men to bridge the gap. It is at times impossible to ascertain the point where policy begins and technique ends. There are, however, subjects which quite evidently come within the definition of technical details. For instance, official tactics in the foreign exchange market or money market are clearly distinguishable from strategy in those spheres. At the same time the systematic application of certain tactics is often a matter for policy decision.

Within the broad category of monetary policy it is possible to distinguish sub-divisions such as currency policy, credit policy, discount rate or interest rate policy, open market policy, reserve policy, foreign exchange policy, gold policy, price policy, etc. All these policies are sub-divisions of monetary policy just as monetary policy itself is a sub-division of economic policy, and economic policy may be said to be a sub-division of public administration or social policy. Nevertheless, some of the policies enumerated above have aspects which fall outside the sphere of monetary policy. For instance, price policy may pursue the end of changing the level of certain groups of prices in relation to each other with some non-monetary object in view. Generally speaking, it is only if price policy aims at affecting the average price level, or those elements in the price level which determine the cost of living of the wage-earning classes, that it may come within the sphere of monetary policy.

According to a fairly widespread conception, decisions concerning fundamental changes in the monetary system are beyond the scope of monetary policy, which is supposed to be confined to the working of the system of the day. Under that conception a change in the Bank Rate or of the exchange parity of the currency is an act of monetary policy, but the adoption or abandonment of the gold standard or the adoption of exchange control is a change of the whole system and amounts therefore to a measure of monetary reform. There seems to be no justification for such discrimination. Often a fundamental change of the monetary system is brought about by decisions which at the time they are made are considered merely tactical decisions. Moreover, fundamental changes are usually undertaken with the object of influencing the immediate monetary situation. For instance, the gold standard may be abandoned in order to be able to expand credit more freely, or to allow exchange rates to fluctuate. In any event it is difficult to see into what category other than that of monetary policy decisions relating to changes in the system could be classed.

There is also some tendency in many quarters to discriminate between short-term and long-term monetary measures. But, as Crowther rightly points out in his *Outline of Money*, any long-term tendency is made up of short-term fluctuations, and usually long-term trends can only be influenced through the medium of short-term fluctuations. It is only when official action is directed against some purely technical aspect of the monetary situation that the scope of this action can be claimed to be too narrow to come within our definition of monetary policy.

The monetary situation is liable to be influenced by private as well as by official action. An outstanding example of the former was the effort made by McKenna, Chairman of the Midland Bank, during the twenties to bring about an expansion of credit by importing gold when such transactions could hardly be profitable. Banks in the United Kingdom are in a position to influence monetary policy by deciding to alter their conventional cash or liquidity ratios. The Trade Unions may influence the monetary trend materially by deciding for or against upholding an official policy aiming at wages restraint.

Although these and similar decisions unquestionably affect the monetary situation they cannot be considered to come within the scope of monetary policy – which to our mind implies official decision or action – unless they are inspired by official policy. If we were to accept the principle that private decision or action may also constitute monetary policy it would be impossible to draw a borderline. After all, the attitude of each firm or individual in deciding whether to spend or save, whether to borrow or lend, whether to cut prices or hold out for higher prices, whether or not to resist paying high prices or wages, etc., is liable to affect the monetary situation. Decisions taken by large firms or wealthy individuals are, of course, liable to produce a more pronounced effect than those of the average business man, consumer or wage-earner. The effect of the decisions of any one of us may be infinitesimal, but the combined effect of action by millions of individuals or thousands of firms, or the attitude of certain categories of producers or consumers, may well be so strong as to defeat the object of the official policy, or, alternatively, to support it effectively. Nevertheless, it would be absurd to regard an individual's decision whether to buy Savings Certificates or a television set as a decision of monetary policy.

We are apt to think of monetary policy as something essentially national. It is possible, however, to envisage an international monetary policy. In fact to some extent at any rate that is not a Utopian dream but is already practical reality. Within limits a large number of Governments have relinquished part of their power in the sphere of monetary policy, either through agreements with other Governments limiting that power, or by submitting to the authority of some international body. About this more will be said in Chapter 35. The aim which is regarded by many people as ideal is to give some international authority full powers to determine the world's monetary policy. It seems inconceivable, however, that such an ambitious object could be attained unless and until the nations are prepared to relinquish their sovereignty and submit to the will of some international Parliament and Government. As things are at present and as they are likely to remain for a long time, monetary policy is essentially national. Even to the extent to which major decisions are at present subject to international consultations, negotiations, or approval, the Governments have reserved the right to terminate any arrangements to that effect. This means that their willingness to abstain from exercising freely their right to take monetary decisions may be treated as part of their national monetary policy.

PART TWO

The Ends of Monetary Policy

*

CHAPTER FOUR

Alternative Ends

In Chapter 3 monetary policy was defined as the official effort to increase the advantages of the monetary system or to reduce its disadvantages. It is simpler, however, to lay down such a broad rule than to determine the meaning of 'advantages' and 'disadvantages'. What may be regarded as an advantage or disadvantage is largely a matter of opinion. It often depends on our point of view or on our interests. Admittedly certain developments are on balance inherently advantageous or disadvantageous. Even so there remains the question of their order of priority. As we shall see in subsequent chapters monetary policy can pursue many different ends. It can aim at achieving various advantages or preventing various disadvantages.

Very often the monetary authorities are confronted with the choice between alternative ends. No dilemma arises when several ends can be achieved by the same means. For instance, an expansion of credit can serve the end of stimulating trade, raising prices or preventing them from falling, and lowering interest rates. Assuming that those in charge of monetary policy are in favour of all these ends, or at any rate are not against any of them, their task is simple. Their difficulties begin when they are in favour of some ends and opposed to others. They may be in favour of stimulating trade and of lowering interest rates, but they may be opposed to a rise in prices. In such a situation they have to decide whether it is more important to forgo the advantages of a trade expansion and cheap money for the sake of avoiding a rise in prices or whether they are prepared to sacrifice stability of prices for the sake of stimulating trade and lowering interest rates.

The question of priorities among the ends of monetary policy assumes considerable importance when the alternative ends to be pursued are incompatible with each other or conflict with each other. As we saw from the above example certain ends can be pursued only at the expense of other ends. Very often certain advantages can be achieved by monetary policy only at the cost of sacrificing other advantages or submitting to disadvantages in some other direction.

The first step for those responsible for the shaping of monetary policy, and for those who wish to take an intelligent interest in it, is to form a clear idea about the range of choice between its various ends. It is impossible for anyone who has not studied the subject systematically to realize the wide variety of uses to which monetary policy can be put. Even amongst those who have spent their lives in the theoretical study of monetary policy or in its practical application there may be many who have never deemed it necessary to elaborate a comprehensive list of its possible ends. They are not, of course, unaware of the manifold uses of monetary policy. But they do not consciously weigh the arguments for and against any monetary decision according to the way in which it is liable to affect all the diverse ends. Only too often they are only concerned with the particular end that is supreme in their minds. Yet it is of the utmost importance that the effects of their monetary policy from the point of view of all the alternative ends should be borne in mind.

Very often the monetary authorities are in a position to kill several birds with the same stone. If this cannot be done it is necessary for the monetary authorities either to make up their mind which ends to pursue, or to strike some compromise between the rival claims of the various ends, or to take additional action to minimize the unfavourable effect their policy is liable to have from the point of view of the ends which they feel impelled to sacrifice.

There is no universally accepted or acceptable set of rules about the point of view from which the conflicting requirements of various ends of monetary policy should be weighed against each other. Economists may well lay down the law about the ideal solution in what they regard as an ideal world. Statesmen and administrators, however, make allowances for practical considerations, having regard to the changing and often conflicting needs of our imperfect world. Their emphasis has to shift between various monetary, fiscal, economic, social, political, and other objectives. Monetary 'purists' may attach the utmost importance to the maintenance of the stable value of money irrespective of the disadvantages such a policy entails in the economic, social, or political sphere. Monetary policy, however, does not exist in a vacuum, but forms part of the much broader system of public administration. Those in charge of monetary policy are not theoretical purists but practical men. While they may listen to economists about the ideal ends that their monetary policy should pursue, they usually allow their decisions to be influenced, rightly or wrongly, by considerations of practical expediency.

Only too frequently the choice does not even rest with the monetary authorities that is, Central Banks and Treasuries. Their hand is forced by policy decisions on the highest level, to sacrifice the end of monetary stability for the sake of meeting the requirements of national defence or for some other consideration that rightly or wrongly takes precedence over monetary considerations. In time of war military ends must prevail over any others, though even then the Government must bear in mind economic, social, and political considerations in shaping its monetary policy. Failure to do so is liable to react unfavourably on the military situation, by causing a fall in the output or by generating widespread discontent.

Emphasis on the alternative ends of monetary policy is liable to change in the course of time. The priority of certain ends may give way to the priority of other ends as a result of the development of the economy or of the development of economic science. The emphasis may be shifted through a change in the social concept or in the political balance of power. Monetary policy is subject to the influence of passing fashions as well as to fundamental trends, not only in the choice of its means but also in the pursuit of its ends.

There can be no rigid line of distinction between the ends of monetary policy and its means. For one thing, whether or not the achievement of certain ends in certain circumstances is practicable depends on the means the monetary authorities are able and willing to employ to achieve those ends. There is bound to be a great deal of overlapping between ends and means. Many ends are at the same time means towards other ends. In a way, all monetary, economic, social, or political ends are, or ought to be, merely means towards the supreme end of human happiness. Nevertheless, it is possible to avoid confusion between ends and means by distinguishing between them according to the main emphasis in the minds of those in charge of monetary policy. A reduction in the price level may be aimed at for its own sake or it may be aimed at for the sake of increasing exports. In given circumstances it may seem reasonable to class it among the ends rather than the means of monetary policy. Such classification may be arbitrary, but this need not give any cause for difficulties provided that we adhere to it consistently.

It is tempting to compare the distinction between the ends and the means of monetary policy with the distinction between military strategy and tactics. Even in the military sphere the borderline between the two is most indistinct. If we were to attempt to adapt the terms 'strategy' and 'tactics' to the sphere of monetary policy we should inevitably encounter difficulties. We could not use 'strategy' as being synonymous with the pursuit of ends and 'tactics' as being synonymous with the application of means. The choice of the means for the execution of monetary policy would very often come under the heading of strategy. Only the technical details of its application would always come within the meaning of tactics. Thus a decision to expand credit would be regarded as a decision of strategy. It is the decision whether it should be expanded by means of lowering interest rates or through Treasury operations that could be regarded as a matter of tactics. Indeed it is open to question whether many technical details which would come under tactics could be regarded as belonging to the sphere of monetary policy at all.

The best way of determining the range of the ends of monetary policy is to enumerate and describe the types of policy that may be regarded as concerning wholly or mainly ends and not means. We propose to do this in the ensuing chapters.

CHAPTER FIVE

Adoption of Money

THE adoption of a monetary system by the tribal or State authority, or the recognition – expressly or by implication – of one that had developed spontaneously on private initiative, constituted the earliest end of monetary policy. All acts of active monetary policy originated from this end. The provision of a technical device which greatly facilitated all economic activities and which became a necessity after a community had reached a certain stage in its progress constituted an act of incalculable importance. Very often the primitive State authority confined itself to allowing money to develop for some time unaided by official action. Even in such instances sooner or later a stage was bound to be reached at which the State authority had to come to a decision whether to allow the monetary system to develop, and, if so, whether it should intervene to confirm, regulate, safeguard, or adjust the system.

To appreciate the significance of this decision we must cast our minds back to distant periods of pre-history or early history before the development of a monetary system. It has often been suggested – not only by economists and economic historians but even by some anthropologists who ought to know better – that communities without some rudimentary form of money have never yet been found. This assertion is in striking conflict with factual evidence about the early periods of some historical races, and even more with what we know about primitive communities in recent periods. There are, in fact, many known instances of communities in which it has so far been impossible to find any evidence of the use of any kind of money up to a certain stage in their evolution. Admittedly this does not conclusively prove that they did not possess a monetary system. Possibly a more thorough investigation might produce evidence indicating the existence of some primitive form of money that has so far escaped our attention. But on the basis of evidence at present available those communities must be regarded as having been at one time moneyless. Those who deny that there have ever been moneyless communities are entitled to insist that final judgement should be reserved pending closer investigation. They are not justified, however, in stating categorically that moneyless communities have never been found. The onus of proving the existence of money in communities which are at present claimed to have been moneyless rests on them.

Everything depends, of course, on what we mean by money. If we apply a narrow and rigid definition it is, of course, possible to quote a very large number of historical and ethnological instances of moneyless communities. Many authors are inclined to define money in accordance with modern usage. On the basis of such a definition it inevitably follows that many primitive communities in recent times, and civilized communities during early historical periods, should be described as moneyless. They had no money in the modern sense of the term any more than they had government, or religion, or legislation, in the modern sense of these terms. The other extreme is represented by the school of thought which applies an unduly elastic and loose definition of money, as a result of which any object which is used in barter transactions more frequently than other objects is claimed to be the currency of the community concerned. On such a basis there is bound to be found a 'currency' in practically every community in the same way as there is bound to be an oldest inhabitant in every village. However, in some instances at any rate the absence of money has been sufficiently firmly established to satisfy all but the most extreme school favouring an elastic definition.

For the purpose of this book money may be defined as an object or unit conforming in a reasonable degree to some standard of uniformity, used for reckoning and making payments and accepted with the ultimate intention of using it for making payments. Many readers would probably prefer different definitions, but it does not really matter so long as they know that the term is employed in the above sense in this book. A moneyless community, for our purposes, is one where there is no money in this sense of the term.

The absence of money in a community may be due to a wide variety of reasons. The following are some of these: (1) Low standard of intelligence. (2) Absence of an adequate sense of values. (3) Low stage of economic development. (4) Absence of a system of private property. (5) Existence of a more or less totalitarian planned economy. (6) Religious objection to the use of money. (7) Existence of a closed self-sufficient economic unit. (8) Extreme distrust in the monetary system.

We need not concern ourselves with instances in which the absence of money is due to the prevalence of a low standard of intelligence or low stage of development. There are, however, a number of instances in which the communities concerned were sufficiently developed for the use of money but abstained from using it as a matter of deliberate policy. The earliest known instance of this kind is that of ancient Egypt. Until a comparatively recent phase of its history it was moneyless in the sense that it possessed no medium of exchange, even though it had an abstract unit of account on the basis of which barter was transacted. The value of goods and services exchanged against each other was reckoned on the basis of a unit of weight of copper. But copper was merely an abstract standard of value and was not used regularly in payment for goods and services. Ancient Egypt had reached a very advanced stage of civilization and of statecraft. It seems reasonable to assume, therefore, that the absence of a monetary system was due not to ignorance, or to any indifference of the State authority towards the existence or non-existence of money, but to deliberate policy preventing its adoption. Indeed the Egyptian State authority was firmly opposed to the introduction of coinage for a long time after its adoption by other Mediterranean countries.

Its attitude comes within our definition of a passive mor̄etary policy.

A more recent and more circumstantial historical instance of deliberate exclusion of money from the economic system is provided by the evidence concerning the Inca Empire before the Spanish conquest of Peru. Prior to the arrival of Pizarro's army, no money had been in use in the country. Although it possessed exceptionally rich gold and silver resources, those metals were not used for monetary purposes. The Inca Empire was a perfect example of a collectivist totalitarian State where every phase of the economic activities of the population was strictly regulated by the State authority. The central administration at Cuzco determined in minute detail what everybody had to produce and how the output should be allocated. There was no need for money in connexion with the production or distribution of goods. Producers of goods had to surrender a fixed proportion of their output to the authorities and the latter provided for the requirements of those who did not take a direct part in production or those engaged in public works which were executed with conscript labour. There was no profit motive and no individual initiative. Wages and salaries as such were unknown. Accumulated possessions were redistributed from time to time. In the circumstances there could be no scope for the use of a medium of exchange or a standardized store of value. There was a limited amount of barter, but there was no evidence of the use of any unit of account, let alone means of payment. The country's large supply of precious metals was used solely for ornamental or industrial purposes. The whole economic system was planned on the basis of elaborate statistics collected by the central administration. Even more than in the case of Ancient Egypt the absence of money was due to deliberate policy.

Another instance in which the State authority deliberately abstained from adopting money was the Jesuit Republic of Paraguay during the sixteenth and seventeenth centuries. The Jesuits established a benevolent dictatorship in Paraguay in order to safeguard the population against the cruelty and rapacity of the conquistadores and of the adventurers who usually followed in their wake. They transacted a certain amount of foreign trade with the aid of money but organized the internal economy of the country on a planned moneyless basis. The system continued to a large degree even after the Jesuits had lost their administrative authority. Barter continued to prevail right to the end of the eighteenth century, and all salaries and taxes were payable in kind. There was not even a unit of account to facilitate barter, which was based on fixed lists of the exchange values of goods in terms of other goods.

The system of the Jesuit Republic of Paraguay under which money was used for foreign trade but not for domestic requirements had many precedents in mediaeval Europe. The history of that period abounded in instances of closed economies which were for all internal purposes moneyless. Many large monasteries and baronial estates were such economic units. They were practically self-sufficient and under an authoritarian regime their production and distribution was planned without the use of money. Everybody had definite functions to perform, not in return for payment in money but as a duty to the community, which in return provided them with what they needed. There were similar closed economies in more recent periods in Latin America where certain large estates – the *pueblo* and the *hacienda* – achieved almost complete self-sufficiency and no money was used in their internal economies.

More recently certain religious communities, especially in the United States, operated moneyless systems. Some such communities are still in existence. They are closed economies the members of which regard themselves and each other as members of a large family within which everyone contributes his share of the work and everyone gets his share of the result.

After the Communist Revolution of 1917 in Russia it was expected for some time that the Soviet regime would adopt a moneyless economy. This at any rate was inferred from the way in which the existing monetary system was reduced to absurdity through extreme inflation. That was done, however, out of sheer necessity, rather than out of deliberate policy, owing to the impossibility of balancing the Budget amidst the prevailing chaotic conditions. During the period when paper money became utterly depreciated and discredited Russia was practically moneyless, though in various localities some limited primitive media of exchange or standards of value came to be adopted spontaneously without State approval. After the end of the Civil War, and with the consolidation of political and economic conditions, a monetary system was established which, in outward form at any rate, conformed to a high degree to the systems in operation in capitalist countries. The extreme depreciation of the currency after the Second World War under the Communist-controlled regime in Hungary is said to have been a matter of deliberate policy the object of which was to wipe out all 'bourgeois' wealth and incomes. The aim of the alleged official policy could not have been, however, the elimination of the monetary system as such, but merely the elimination of the existing currency and its replacement by a newly created currency. It must also be remembered that inflation in anti-Communist Greece or Nationalist China was not much more restrained than in Communist Hungary.

While some Socialist writers flirt from time to time with the idea of a moneyless community the achievement of that aim cannot be regarded as forming an integral part of Socialist or Communist policy. Karl Marx himself regarded the idea as Utopian. Indeed it has always been one of the favourite ideas of those who have elaborated Utopian systems. Sir Thomas More himself envisaged his Utopia as a moneyless community. In order to discredit gold and make it unsuitable for monetary use he suggested that it should be used as a material for the production of degrading objects such as fetters or certain humble household utensils. On the other hand Robert Owen's system, which was put into operation to a very limited extent during the early part of the nineteenth century, cannot be classed among the planned moneyless economies, since it merely aimed at the substitution of labour tickets for the conventional form of money.

For all practical purposes these labour tickets were money under a different name.

Decisions of the authorities in any of the moneyless communities to adopt money or to abstain from opposing its spontaneous development constituted an act of monetary policy. As we said above, sooner or later in the course of economic evolution the State authority of each community must have taken some such decision. This does not necessarily mean that in each instance the chief of the tribe, or the king and his advisers, decided after careful deliberation in favour of adopting money or allowing it to develop. Such a conception would be as unrealistic as that of Rousseau's *Contrat Social*, which assumed that early communities decided by general agreement the form of their respective social systems. Things did not happen that way either in the social or in the monetary sphere. The evolution was to a large extent a gradual and unconscious process the significance of which was probably not grasped for a long time by those participating in it.

It seems reasonable to assume that in the overwhelming majority of instances there was originally no deliberate decision by the State authority to establish a monetary system or to sanction in so many words a monetary system that had developed on private initiative. What must have happened in the very large majority of instances was that at a given stage the State authority came to assist in the adoption or development of a monetary unit by decreeing that certain payments, such as taxation, tribute, fines, blood money, etc. must be made in the form of standardized objects, or that, if made in other forms, they should be reckoned on the basis of some standardized unit of account. Presumably long before the authorities deliberately adopted such media of payment or units of account, the objects or units in question had already been in widespread use on private initiative for the purpose of religious sacrifices or tribute, blood money, the payment of bride price, or in other non-commercial transactions.

According to the classical conception of economic history

money is supposed to have developed through the progress of division of labour and the resulting complexity of trade, which made barter increasingly cumbersome and inconvenient. In my *Primitive Money* I sought to refute this theory on the ground that during early phases of economic evolution non-commercial payments such as those mentioned above were incomparably more important than the limited amount of barter that was transacted. I took the view that long before the progress of commerce and specialization in production through advanced division of labour had reduced barter to absurdity some standardized monetary objects or units must have been in use for non-commercial payments, and that owing to the regular demand for such objects for those purposes they had become eminently suitable for eventual adoption as a medium of exchange.

It seems probable that in many instances long before that stage was reached the tribal or State authority deemed it necessary to intervene in some form. In all probability there was no question of deliberately decreeing that the objects in question should be used as money. They were presumably recognized officially as such by implication, through some measure under which it was made compulsory for members of the community to make or accept certain payments in the form of those objects, or to reckon them in terms of the units employed in transactions with the State authority or with one another. It was probably only at a relatively advanced stage that legislation was enacted giving the means of payment in question a formal status as money. The monetary use of barley and silver in Babylonia, for instance, was regulated legally by the Code of Hammurabi towards the turn of the twenty-first century B.C., but there is documentary evidence of their much earlier joint monetary use under the Dynasty of Akkad towards the beginning of the twenty-eighth century B.C.

It seems reasonable to assume that in most instances when we encounter evidence in the form of legislation regulating the use of money, whether in Babylonia, the Hittite Empire, or ancient China, the laws adopted did not actually establish the monetary system but merely confirmed substantially an existing state of affairs. They regulated and legalized some actual practices which must have been in force for a considerable time before the State authority came to consider it necessary to intervene. Its intervention constituted, nevertheless, a most important act of monetary policy, a landmark in the monetary history of the country concerned. Indeed it is possible to argue – as many authors do – that it was not until this stage had been reached that money came into existence. It is in this question-begging sense that Knapp's *State Theory of Money* is entitled to claim that 'money is the creature of law'.

The adoption of coinage in Lydia by King Gyges in the early part of the seventh century B.C. was by far the most important act of monetary policy in the ancient period, and indeed one of the most important events in the history of monetary policy. There had probably been some primitive forms of money in existence in Lydia before that decision. Nor were the sealed electrum dumps of Gyges the first instances of the monetary use of sealed ingots. The sealing of ingots to guarantee their weight or fineness is believed to have originated in Cappadocia, a dependency of Assyria, towards the end of the third millennium B.C. Such ingots, bearing the seal of a magistrate, were regularly employed in commercial transactions. There were also sealed ingots circulating in Babylonia during the same period, but there is no evidence that the guarantee implied by the seals was that of the Central Government. It seems more probable that it was given by cities, temples, or merchants of standing.

Notwithstanding these precedents the adoption of coinage in Lydia, and its almost simultaneous adoption in the Greek city state of Argos and also in ancient China, constitutes a most important landmark in the evolution of monetary policy. It is the first clear instance of a policy which has remained in force right up to our day, under which the State authority does not confine itself to the approval of some existing currency or even to decreeing its creation, but takes it on itself actually to provide the community with a standardized medium of exchange. Henceforth this came to be considered as forming part of the functions of the State, although in many communities during the mediaeval period this function was relinquished on frequent occasions in favour of private interests, and during the modern period it was ceded to banks of issue.

It must be borne in mind, however, that the power of the State to adopt a monetary system or to maintain it is not unlimited. It is impossible to force a monetary system on a community which is not ready for its adoption or which does not trust the money chosen by the State authority. In many instances throughout history communities relapsed into natural economy as a result of an extreme depreciation of the currency, notwithstanding the effort of the State authority to maintain it in monetary use. This is but one of the innumerable instances to show that monetary policy is far from being all-powerful.

Modern colonizing Powers which tried to force primitive communities to adopt a monetary system encountered at times considerable difficulties. It was not until the economic and cultural development of these communities had reached a relatively advanced stage that they began to respond to these efforts. The monetary system, in order to be acceptable and in order that it should work satisfactorily, must bear some relation to the economic and cultural background, and this must be borne in mind by the State authority in its decision to adopt a monetary system.

In itself a decision by the State authority to adopt a monetary system was not necessarily sufficient to ensure the achievement of that end. It was necessary to enact some form of law and to enforce it. The practical use of the monetary object by the State authority for making and accepting payments in itself went a long way towards ensuring the adoption of money. Various ways in which money was made more suitable to fulfil its functions – the adoption of coinage was one of these ways – also reinforced the decision to adopt money. Nor was it enough to ensure the adoption of money. On many occasions throughout history the Governments

C

had to pursue a policy to ensure that the money of their choice remained in monetary use, in face of a strong inclination on the part of the community to reject it and either to revert to natural economy or to adopt spontaneously some unauthorized form of money. Measures to force the community to retain the legal money in monetary use, or decisions to replace the discredited money by some new money, were adopted on many occasions by the State authorities in pursuing the end of imposing on the community a money of their choice.

CHAPTER SIX

Choice of Monetary System

THE choice of a monetary system is a monetary policy decision of the utmost importance. To a very large extent it pre-determines the ends of the monetary policy which have to be pursued once the system chosen by the State authority has become operative. The decision whether to choose a scarce or a plentiful object to serve as currency is bound to influence the basic monetary trend. In primitive communities the monetary object chosen was in a large number of instances something which could not be produced within the community and which was bound to have therefore a scarcity value. For instance in many African communities salt was for a long time the favourite medium of exchange because the demand for it usually exceeded the available supply. In various Pacific islands the shell currency in monetary use consisted of shells which had to be imported from some remote island in preference to those which could be picked up on the local beaches.

It would be a mistake, however, to conclude from such instances that primitive monetary policy always aimed at choosing a monetary system that tended to keep money scarce – that, in the jargon of economists, it was necessarily 'deflationary'. For in a very large number of instances monetary policy pursued exactly the opposite end. It was the staple product of the country which was selected for monetary use. By such means an adequate and even plentiful supply of the monetary object was ensured, and also a steady and substantial additional demand for the staple product of the community.

In many ethnological and historical instances the same communities adopted systems that combined the use of some relatively scarce object with that of some relatively plentiful one. Thus in the monetary system of Babylonia

the inadequate monetary supply of silver was supplemented
by the monetary use of barley, which was the staple product
of the fertile plains between the Tigris and the Euphrates.
One of the reasons why during most of the course of history
more than one object was used for monetary purposes was
precisely the inadequacy of the quantity of the object which
was considered the most suitable for that purpose.

In my *Primitive Money* I give a detailed account of the
very large number of objects or units chosen for monetary
use. The use of more than one object in the same community
resulted in an almost infinite variety of combinations. In
addition the use of the same object or unit gave rise to several
different systems according to the way it was applied for
monetary purposes. In a large number of instances the
choice was made spontaneously and largely unconsciously
by the community itself. Nevertheless, as we saw in the last
chapter, the tribal or State authority sooner or later played
a decisive rôle, if not in choosing the system at any rate in
officially recognizing, confirming, and regulating it. At a
more advanced phase the choice and the change of the
monetary system had become increasingly a matter of monetary policy decision, although in many instances the hands
of the State authority were forced by spontaneous monetary
developments that preceded its decision.

Generally speaking it is true to say that by the time the
stage was reached at which metals came to be used as
money the State authority had come to play a decisive rôle
in the choice of the monetary system. Monetary policy in the
countries of the ancient Mediterranean civilization aimed,
whenever possible, at the monetary use of a metal which
happened to be produced in the country concerned. It was
not by accident that lead was the original currency of
Assyria. The reason why silver was preferred to gold by the
Semitic races in Western Asia – to such an extent that in
Semitic languages the same word was used for 'money' as
for 'silver' – was that these countries did not possess any
gold resources. The coinage adopted in Lydia during the
first half of the seventh century B.C. consisted of punch-

marked dumps of electrum because in Lydia the gold ore had a silver content and metallurgy did not until later reach a sufficiently advanced stage to separate the two metals. On the other hand silver was adopted as the principal currency of Athens because of the rich silver deposits at Laurion. Both Persia and Macedonia chose gold for their coinage because they happened to be rich in that metal.

There is at least a possibility that the reason why Sparta selected iron for her clumsy currency was not really the pursuit of a deliberate policy of austerity but the fact that the Peloponnesus contained the most important iron mines in ancient Greece. The choice of copper in Sicily and in early Rome was again connected with the nature of the metal resources available locally. Nor would the ancient Britons have used sword-shaped iron bars as their currency at the time of Julius Caesar if they had had to import the metal for that purpose.

At a later stage of monetary history gold and silver became universally adopted as monetary metals in most civilized countries, irrespective of whether they were able to mine the metals at home or whether they had to depend on imports for their monetary supplies. Both gold and silver were used simultaneously for monetary purposes in many countries from the seventh century B.C. to the nineteenth century A.D. There remained, however, wide scope for monetary policy decisions to determine which of the two metals should be the main currency and which should act as a secondary currency. This did not always depend on the authorities, but in theory at any rate they had the initiative in influencing the relative monetary rôles of the two metals according to the figure at which they fixed the gold-silver ratio. Decisions to alter that ratio, to debase the coinage, or to fix the terms of recoinage went beyond mere changes in the monetary units. They very often resulted in fundamental if temporary changes of the monetary system, because silver was replaced by gold as the main monetary metal or *vice versa*. The highly involved bimetallist system provided a wide scope for such fundamental changes.

The advent of paper money introduced yet another element of complication and further widened the scope of monetary policy in respect of the choice of the system. During the course of the eighteenth century most Governments decided to adopt paper money to supplement their coinage. The question whether it should be issued by the Government or by privileged banks, which was an important policy decision, had to be settled, just as in earlier centuries the State authority had to decide whether coinage should remain in its own hands or whether this right should be ceded to private interests.

The authorities had also to choose between the systems of convertible and inconvertible paper money. Originally most note issues were intended to be convertible, and their purpose was to serve not as a non-interest-bearing Government loan but merely as a convenient device to facilitate monetary circulation. In most instances, from the mediaeval experiences of China onward, suspension of convertibility was not the result of any preconceived deliberate policy. There were instances, however, in which the suspension of specie payments was decided upon as a matter of expediency in preference to other measures which might have arrested the decline of the metallic reserve. In particular Russia and the Austro-Hungarian Monarchy in the nineteenth century provided instances of such policy decisions as a result of which the system of convertible paper money was replaced by one of inconvertible paper money. Restoration of convertibility is yet another policy decision changing the whole monetary system in operation in the community concerned.

Decisions to abandon the bimetallic standard, under which both gold and silver served as a basis for the currencies with a fixed ratio between them, and to replace it by the gold standard, were made by most Governments of the Western civilization during the latter part of the nineteenth century. This was an important policy decision and was accompanied in many countries by bitter political controversy. In the United States a Presidential election was fought over it in the nineties, and the slogan of Bryan, the candidate favouring bimetallism: 'You shall not crucify mankind upon a cross of gold' will long be remembered.

Many important countries had adopted some form of gold standard by the end of the nineteenth century, though relatively few countries had a fully effective gold standard in actual operation, in the sense in which the system was defined before 1914. In many instances before the First World War a system was chosen under which the notes remained inconvertible but the exchange value of the currency was maintained stable in relation to gold. This system is sometimes called the gold exchange standard, though properly speaking that term should be reserved for the system in which the monetary authorities are under legal obligation to convert their currency into another currency which itself is on the gold standard. The Indian rupee before 1914 provided the classical example of that system. Many countries were on a gold exchange standard in fact if not in law, because, although their Central Bank was under no legal obligation to convert its notes into some currency that was convertible into gold, in practice it intervened in the foreign exchange market whenever this was necessary in order to maintain the national exchange stable in relation to the convertible currencies. In a number of countries before 1914 a 'limping standard' was in force under which silver was allowed to retain a certain limited rôle. For instance in France the Central Bank reserved the right to pay out silver instead of gold in certain circumstances when the French authorities were anxious to moderate the drain on the Bank of France's gold reserve. The choice of one or other type of the gold standard and its effective adoption constituted one of the major ends of monetary policy.

After the First World War various types of gold standard were adopted in various countries. Indeed, when in the early thirties the League of Nations published a volume containing the details of the gold legislation of all member countries, it was found that there were very few in which the rules were absolutely identical. The reconstruction of the currencies in a number of countries under the auspices of the League's Finance Committee introduced a certain degree of uniformity, because the adoption of certain rules regarding the form of gold standard to be applied was made one of the conditions for the grant of financial assistance by the League. Even so there were minor discrepancies.

Britain decided in 1925 to adopt the 'gold bullion standard' as distinct from the full gold standard with gold coins circulating freely as before 1914. This meant that the notes were not convertible into coins, but foreign holders of sterling were entitled to buy ingots from the Bank of England at its official selling price, for shipment overseas, or for keeping on deposit with the Bank. A number of countries adopted either the same system or the gold exchange standard. The Central Banks of the latter, instead of aiming at building up large gold reserves of their own, endeavoured to accumulate large foreign exchange reserves consisting mainly of currencies on a gold basis such as sterling and dollars. The Central Banks were buyers of dollars or sterling whenever an excessive supply tended to cause an unwanted appreciation of the national currency, and sellers whenever an excessive demand threatened to cause a depreciation.

The adoption of some form of gold standard by most countries constituted an important policy decision, replacing as it did inconvertible and fluctuating paper currencies by more or less convertible and stable currencies. Decisions in the opposite sense were taken during the thirties when, following on the suspension of the gold standard by Great Britain in 1931, most countries adopted fluctuating paper currencies during subsequent years. Many currencies were made inconvertible in the full sense of the term. Not only did the monetary authorities cease to convert them into gold or foreign exchanges either at the fixed or at the fluctuating rate, but residents of the countries and foreign holders of their currencies were forbidden by law to acquire foreign currencies in the open market.

This brings us to another important set of monetary policy decisions aiming at a fundamental change in the monetary system in force, namely, the adoption and removal of exchange restrictions interfering with the freedom to transfer money abroad. There is nothing new in that system, which had operated in various instances already during the ancient period and the Middle Ages, when on many occasions restrictions were imposed on international movements of gold or silver and on exchange operations between national and foreign coins. Later these rules came to be supplemented by restrictions on transactions in foreign bills.

During the first World War and the period of inflation that followed it, many Governments adopted exchange restrictions. It was not until the thirties, however, that the system reached its full development. In this respect the choice of the Governments between the various systems of restricted currencies was even wider than in respect of their choice of the exact type of gold standard. Having decided in favour of the principle of exchange restrictions the Governments had to decide on the nature and extent of those restrictions. They had to decide whether to forbid capital movements only or whether to place under official control also exchange transactions arising from current foreign commerce. They had to decide if and to what extent free dealing in the open market in foreign exchange should be allowed to continue.

Again the authorities in many countries had to decide whether, having suspended free dealing in foreign exchanges, they should allocate the foreign exchanges required by importers and others for approved purposes, or whether they should adopt the 'exchange clearing' system invented in 1931. During the thirties a very large number of Governments in Central and Eastern Europe and also some Governments in Western Europe concluded such clearing agreements, the nature and operation of which will be explained briefly in Chapter 32. There was an endless variety in the terms of such agreements. The international aspects of the monetary system of some countries came to be based almost entirely on them. They were not always confined to relations between two countries. In addition to bilateral clearing systems some countries adopted triangular and multilateral systems under which three or more countries participated in the arrangement.

The thirties witnessed the development of currency areas under which a number of countries established closer monetary relations with each other than they had with the rest of the world. This system was not altogether new. It had existed before the first World War in the form of arrangements such as the Latin Monetary Union, the Scandinavian Monetary Union, etc. Those arrangements, however, amounted to no more than the adoption of identical official gold parities and in some cases identical names for the monetary units.

In 1932 the foundations were laid for the Sterling Area, which was quite a different system of currency union. In fact the system actually came into operation in September 1931, when, following on the suspension of the gold standard in Britain, practically all countries of the British Commonwealth decided to allow their currencies to fluctuate in terms of gold in sympathy with sterling in order to maintain rigidly stable relations with sterling. The Ottawa Conference of 1932 led to the formal establishment of the Sterling Area. In addition to stability in relation to sterling it created a certain uniformity of monetary policy in other respects. Subsequently, when after the outbreak of the Second World War Britain and other countries adopted exchange restrictions, the freedom of the exchange operations within countries of the Sterling Area was maintained and assumed considerable significance. Decisions to form such international monetary unions, to join existing unions, or to relinquish membership of them constitute very important monetary policy decisions affecting the monetary system.

Another way in which the Government has to take monetary policy decisions is in respect to the extent to which actually operating systems are provided with legal foundations. Writers in the 'thirties learnt to discriminate between *de jure* stabilization and *de facto* stabilization, according to whether the exchange rate of the national currency is maintained stable by the Government with or without legal obligation to do so. Changes in the extent to which various types of currency are legal tender are also decisions resulting in changes in the monetary system. Decisions admitting or preventing the monetary use of foreign coins or notes formed yet another category of monetary policy decisions affecting the monetary system. For instance after the Second World War sovereigns became a most important currency in Greece through the initiative of the public, but their monetary use was officially confirmed and regulated to a large degree by the Greek monetary authorities.

There are innumerable changes of detail decided upon by the monetary authorities which are liable to modify the monetary system to some degree. These will be dealt with in later chapters covering the various aspects of monetary policy.

To what extent is the selection of a particular monetary system an end in itself and to what extent is it a means with the aid of which the Government intends to pursue its monetary policy? Beyond doubt, certain systems are often selected because they are liable to make the pursuit of certain policies possible or even necessary. Nevertheless, the importance of choosing a system which, in the Government's opinion, is best suited to the requirements of the country in prevailing circumstances is so overwhelming that the decision may rightly be claimed to pursue primarily that end, even if the adoption of the new system is liable to predetermine the subsequent pursuit of certain other ends. The restoration of the gold standard in Britain in 1925 was an end of the monetary policy pursued ever since 1918. It compelled the Governments holding office between 1925 and 1931 to follow restrictionist monetary policies in order to be able to maintain the gold standard. These policies were the means to the end of maintaining the gold standard. On the other hand it is conceivable that in other instances the gold standard was adopted as a means to the end of making the pursuance of a deflationary or anti-inflationary policy inevitable.

CHAPTER SEVEN

Determining the Value of Money

THE determination of the value of the monetary unit has always been regarded by most people as one of the most important – if not *the* most important – ends of monetary policy. Beyond doubt the State authorities have considerable power in this sphere, though not nearly as much as was attributed to them by a school of thought that gained prominence during the early part of this century. The conception that the State is in a position to determine the value of money is not new. It appears in the writings of mediaeval authors who regarded the Prince as all-powerful in this respect, as in so many others. In its modern form it originated in G. F. Knapp's famous work *The State Theory of Money*. This much-quoted work emphasizes the powers which the State possesses of ensuring the monetary use of the object of its choice and of determining the nominal value of the monetary unit irrespective of its intrinsic value. In all fairness to Knapp it must be admitted that it was not he but the interpreters of this theory who put forward the view that the State is in a position to determine not merely the choice of money and its nominal value, but also its purchasing power. This view misrepresented Knapp's basic theory, which does not go beyond claiming that the State was in a position to ensure the *validity* of some object chosen for monetary use. To claim this is something quite different from suggesting that the State has unlimited powers in determining the *value* of money.

Opponents of Knapp's theory, provoked by its exaggerated interpretation by its supporters, are inclined to fall into the opposite extreme. They flatly deny that the State has any powers at all to impose its will in face of economic trends which alone determine the value of money. They hold the State theory responsible for the German inflation during and after the First World War. According to them it was the belief in the omnipotence of the State in the monetary sphere, generated by Knapp's theory, that encouraged the German Government to embark upon an unlimited issue of paper money on the assumption that it would be in a position to maintain the value of the mark notes notwithstanding the increase in their quantity.

Critics of Knapp triumphantly pointed out that the disastrous collapse of the mark after the First World War conclusively proved the worthlessness of the State theory by showing how utterly helpless the State was in the face of major economic forces.

The truth lies between the two extreme views. Even though the capacity of the State to determine the value of money is far from absolute, it is in given circumstances very considerable. Its powers are not confined to choosing the money and ensuring that it is accepted in payment. The State is in a position to determine or influence the value of money to a large extent in more than one sense.

(1) *Choice of monetary unit.* The power to choose the currency gives the State a considerable power to determine the value of money. The State authority is in a position to decide whether objects or units of high or low value should serve as money. By this decision alone it can decide whether prices should be high or low in terms of the monetary unit. On the face of it this is merely a matter of simple arithmetic. Whether the unit is, say, an ounce of silver or a pound of silver does not really affect the value of silver, even though prices in the former case are sixteen times as high as in the latter. In reality, the magnitude of the unit does tend to affect the cost of living to some extent. This fact was discovered in West Africa when coins took the place of cowries as currency. Even the smallest coin was equivalent to a very large number of cowries, and prices of the cheapest goods and services rose to the minimum level which could be expressed in the lowest denomination

of the new unit and which could be paid in the smallest coin in circulation.

The State is, of course, in a position to fix a number of units and sub-divisions of multiples of units for various requirements. During the Ancient period the most generally known unit was the talent, which was, however, a very large unit, so that only princes and the wealthiest members of the community were in a position to transact business in it. For the requirements of the less wealthy classes the State authority in various Eastern countries fixed the unit of the mina, and smaller units such as the drachma and the obol in Greece.

The need for the State authority to choose currencies of various values to circulate concurrently was realized at an early stage. In primitive communities we encounter many instances of the use of different moneys by different classes. In some of these instances there was practically no connecting link between these currencies, and price levels expressed in them were largely independent of one another. Certain goods could only be purchased against one or the other of the currencies. In other instances, however, the State authority determined the ratios between the various officially chosen or officially recognized currencies, and these ratios were often largely artificial and independent of economic considerations.

Indeed such is the power of State authority in determining the value of monetary units that at times it can defy not only economic laws but even the laws of simple arithmetic. The Chinese Emperor Wang Mang, who ruled from A.D. 8 to 23, introduced a new copper coinage in which the smallest unit contained proportionately the largest amount of metal and each higher denomination contained proportionately less metal. The largest coin contained only one quarter per cent as much metal per unit as the smallest coin. Such abnormal ratios could, of course, only be maintained with the aid of drastic penalties against those who refused to comply with the law. Even so, the system did not work very smoothly, and in A.D. 14 a new system was introduced in which the disproportion was considerably less pronounced, though the laws of arithmetic continued to be defied.

A more recent instance of the power of State authority to interfere with the arithmetic of the monetary system was found in the French Sudan by the German traveller Lenz during the 1880s. In Timbuktu eight times ten cowries had to be reckoned as 100, ten times eighty (nominally 100) was reckoned as 1,000, and so forth, so that what was called 100,000 was really only 64,000.

(2) *Choice of monetary material.* The power of the State authority to choose the monetary material and to determine the extent of its monetary use is bound to influence considerably the value of the material chosen. The monetary use of any object necessarily creates a very considerable additional demand for it. Unless it is accompanied by a corresponding increase in the output of the monetary object its value in terms of goods and services is bound to rise considerably. What usually happens is that its monetary use tends to increase its value and its increase in value in turn tends to stimulate an increase in its production whenever that is possible. When the supply of the monetary material is limited, however, as in the case of the precious metals, the increase of its monetary use through State decisions necessarily entails an increase in its value. It is not generally realized that, although gold has a by no means inconsiderable value as a metal for industrial or ornamental purposes, it owes a very large part of its value to its widespread monetary use. But for the withdrawal of very large quantities of gold from the market for monetary requirements, its price would be considerably under its present level, in spite of the unquestionably high intrinsic value of the metal.

The claim is justified, therefore, that even gold owes a very large proportion of its value to monetary policy decisions by a large number of Governments. This fact was brought home very clearly by the heavy slump in the value of silver during the lifetime of the present generation. The slump was brought about during the inter-War period by monetary policy decisions in China and elsewhere to discontinue the use of silver as money. The extent to which its demonetization during the late nineteenth and early twentieth centuries affected its value may be appreciated from the fact that while the proportion of the value of gold to that of silver from the ancient period to the late nineteenth century varied within the approximate range from 1 to 8 to 1 to 15 its present proportion is 1 to 56. Although the slump was due in part to the increase in the output of silver through recent mining and metallurgical developments lowering its cost and increasing its quantity, to a large extent it was the consequence of monetary policy decisions. There can be no doubt that gold would suffer a slump of a comparable extent in the unlikely event of monetary policy decisions curtailing its present limited monetary use as reserves for international payments.

(3) *Maintenance of the value of the monetary unit.* Monetary policy plays a highly important part in defending the value of the monetary unit against adverse pressure. It is one of the principal duties of the State authority to try to safeguard the value of the national currency. The earliest steps taken to that end were measures against counterfeiting currency. Indeed the main object of the adoption of coinage through affixing an official seal to pieces of monetary metal was to make debasement of that metal more difficult. It was not as if the State itself had insurmountable objections to debasement. That practice soon came to be regarded, however, as a profitable State monopoly. Polycrates of Samos brought it to a fine art in the sixth century B.C., and his example was followed by innumerable rulers during the ancient and mediaeval periods and even in more recent centuries. Nevertheless, the State authority employed all its might to prevent debasement by private enterprise. It continued to do so after the adoption of paper money, the counterfeiting of which it has sought to prevent by international conventions ensuring co-operation between States. Nevertheless some Governments themselves are not averse

to printing large quantities of paper money as an easy way of covering their budgetary deficits.

Some State authorities also endeavoured to uphold the value of their coinage by a relatively frequent replacement of worn coins and coins debased as a result of deliberate clipping. In many instances, however, it was considered profitable or expedient to lower the value of the new coins to the depreciated value of the coins in circulation. In other instances the State authorities decided in favour of restoring the old value of the coinage either by bearing the loss on the exchange of good coin for bad or by inflicting a corresponding loss on the public by accepting the worn or clipped coins at a reduced value in exchange for the new coins.

Monetary policy plays a very important part in defending the exchange value and the internal purchasing power of the national currency by a wide variety of means which will be discussed in detail in later chapters. Policy decisions to that end cover measures aiming at preventing an undue increase in the quantity of money and purchasing power, moderating the effect of any increase on prices, safeguarding the exchange rates at an approved level, etc. To the extent to which these devices are practised successfully the State authority does indeed influence the value of money considerably, in spite of what Knapp's opponents think. The State has means at its disposal for defying, at least in part and temporarily, the economic forces making for a currency depreciation. Such measures include Bank rate change, fiscal devices, price control, rationing, exchange control, subsidies, official operations on the money markets, foreign exchange markets and commodity markets, etc.

As for the power of the State to bring about a deliberate depreciation in the value of the national currency, or to prevent an appreciation which would take place if natural tendencies were allowed to produce their effects, it is almost unlimited. There have been many instances in monetary history of debasements and devaluations, undertaken by the State authority not under irresistible pressure of economic

forces nor as a legal confirmation of actual depreciations
which had already taken place, but as a matter of deliberate
monetary policy for the sake of financial or other advantages. In many other instances the official monetary policy
successfully resisted tendencies which, if allowed to take
their course, would have raised the purchasing power or the
exchange rates of the national currency above the level
approved by the authorities.

(4) *Changes in the value of monetary units.* One of the unques-
tionable merits of Knapp's theory is that it draws attention
to the power of the State to fix the ratio between a new
monetary unit and the monetary unit it replaces. If Britain,
for instance, were to decide to reckon in future in terms of
crowns instead of pounds the State is in a position to enact
legislation fixing all outstanding liabilities at four crowns
for each pound. The price level would be determined immediately after the change by the ratio between the old
and the new units. The nominal amounts in which prices
are expressed would be in the above instance four times
higher than they had been immediately before the change.
Needless to say the State authority could not prevent an
immediate rise or fall in prices following on the change if,
as a result of the operation of economic forces, such rise or
fall would have taken place in the absence of a change of
the monetary unit. Indeed the change in the unit itself
might conceivably set into motion additional trends which
would affect the value of the new unit after the change.
All the Government can do is to define the new unit in
terms of the old unit at the moment of the change, and to
ensure that the payment of old liabilities contracted in
terms of the old unit should become dischargeable in terms
of the new unit on the basis of the official ratio. If four
new units were made equal to one old unit, then a liability
of 100 old units would become a liability of 400 new units –
unless the State chose to decree otherwise.

During the period of metallic currencies the State authority was in a position to change the value of the monetary
unit by means of debasement. This could assume various

forms. The Government was in a position to issue coins with
the same nominal value but containing less metal. This was
done repeatedly in Rome during the Punic Wars. Or it
could maintain the metallic content of the coins unchanged
while decreeing that they be acceptable in debt settlement
for larger amounts than before. The first known instance
of such a measure was that of Solon in Athens in the sixth
century B.C. Yet another method of changing the value of
money through State action is the changing of the price
at which the Mint accepts metals for coinage. Increasing
the seigneurage – that is, the profit charged by the Mint for
the coinage of the metals – was a favourite device throughout the Middle Ages and the two centuries that followed.
England was one of the first countries to do away with
seigneurage and pay the full value of the monetary metals
to those who delivered them to the Mint.

Changes in the value of the monetary units could be
brought about by changing the gold–silver parity (the value
of gold expressed in silver, or *vice versa*) in countries where
both metals played a monetary rôle. The possibility of
influencing the flow of bullion by changing the gold–silver
ratio provided ample scope for monetary policy. If an ounce
of gold in the Low Countries was equivalent to, say, thir-
teen ounces of silver, and the English authorities wanted
to attract more gold, all they had to do was to raise the
gold–silver ratio in England to, say, fourteen, to make it
profitable to ship gold from Antwerp for sale to the Royal
Mint in London. Such changes were of very frequent occurrence.

Although history produced many instances of drastic debasements of coinage their extent was insignificant compared with the extent of devaluations of paper currencies.
Paper money was first invented in China in the eleventh
century. Its history is the history of a long succession of
devaluations. Each one of them is evidence to show the
power of the State to determine the value of money by
changes in a downward direction.

John Law's experiment in France between 1718 and 1720

provided an unusual instance of changing the value of currency as a matter of monetary policy. His idea was to strengthen confidence in his paper money by trying to discredit gold and silver coins. He sought to achieve this end by frequent changes in the value of the coins in terms of paper money, as a contrast with the 'stability' of the nominal value of his notes. Between September 1719 and December 1720 he changed the value of gold coins on twenty-eight occasions and that of silver coins on thirty-five occasions in an effort to induce holders to rid themselves of such 'unstable' currency and seek safety in converting their coins into 'stable' notes. The disastrous failure of the experiment shows that monetary policy is helpless in face of economic forces brought about by large-scale inflation.

One of the most interesting instances of devaluation was provided by Austria during and after the Napoleonic Wars. In 1811 the florin notes were devalued to one-fifth of their original value, and in 1817 they were further devalued to two-fifths of their reduced value, so that twenty-five florins became reduced to two florins. Simultaneously with this devaluation a detailed schedule was issued indicating the rates at which debts contracted in the old currency at various times during the period of depreciation were to be repaid in the new currency. Allowance was made in this schedule for the degree of the actual depreciation of the florin at the time when the debt was contracted. The object of this measure was to safeguard creditors against being victimized through the repayment of their claims in devalued currency. It tried to achieve a kind of rough justice – which is more than could be said about most other devaluations in monetary history.

The periods that followed both World Wars provided a large number of instances of the fixing of the value of currencies as a matter of policy. In Czechoslavakia, Yugoslavia, Rumania and Poland, several different currencies were in circulation in the various territories taken over after the Armistice of 1918. It was one of the tasks of the monetary policies of the Governments concerned to unify the monetary system and to that end to fix a ratio between the various currencies. As a general rule that ratio was fixed not on the basis of the prevailing market exchange rates but in such a way as to secure an advantage to the peoples of the territories taken over by the countries concerned, by exchanging their notes at rates higher than the prevailing market rates. This is another instance of the power of the State authority to determine the value of a currency independently of the natural economic forces.

Changes decreed by Governments in the value of their national currencies have not always been in a downward direction. There are many instances in monetary history of upward revaluations in connexion with coinage reforms following a bad period of debasement. In more recent times both Sweden and Canada revalued their currencies after the Second World War. Instances of revaluations are, however, incomparably less frequent than those of devaluations, and the secular trend of the value of money over a period of centuries is distinctly downward. This is recognized and accepted by most Governments. They are, on the whole, inclined to abandon resistance to any persistent downward trend, and do not attempt to reverse it. One of the abortive attempts at swimming against the tide was that of Great Britain after the First World War, when the official monetary policy aimed at raising the value of sterling to its pre-War level of $4.86. This end was achieved in 1925, but within six years the Government felt impelled to abandon its efforts to maintain sterling at its pre-War level, and allowed it to depreciate in 1931.

Instances of monetary policy decisions resulting in changes in the value of currency could be multiplied almost indefinitely. Admittedly in a large proportion of such instances the hands of the authorities were forced by powerful trends. Their action in devaluing or revaluing was the consequence of fundamental changes which could not be prevented or reversed without efforts involving major sacrifices. Even so there are a sufficient number of instances to show that to a very large extent Governments are the masters of the monetary destinies of their countries. Their decisions to change the value of their currencies often became inevitable as a result of the deliberate pursuit of economic, social, or political policies, the importance of which, in their opinion, overshadowed purely monetary considerations. In the majority of instances, however, a stage must have been reached some time or another, when the Governments were confronted with the dilemma whether to pursue their various policies at the cost of monetary stability or to abandon them in order to save their currency. For this reason it seems justifiable to take the view that even though subsequently their hands may have been forced by trends which they could not foresee in good time, the depreciation or appreciation of their currencies was strictly speaking the outcome of monetary policy decisions taken at some stage.

The realization of this should go a long way towards disposing of much one-sided criticism of Knapp's theory concerning the power of the State to determine the value of money. What the critics really mean is that the State has no power to eat its cake and keep it. Given the adoption of various inflationary economic, social, and political policies the Government is, of course, powerless in the long run to prevent these policies from producing their natural, logical and inevitable effects on the value of money. That effect may be delayed with the aid of various measures of control and intervention, but in the long run it cannot be prevented except through a timely reversal or abandonment of the policies responsible for the trend they generate. To do so may be considered politically inexpedient or economically costly. What matters from the point of view with which we are concerned in this chapter is that the decision rests with Governments and their Parliamentary majorities.

We are, therefore, entitled to claim that the State authority has immense power in determining the value of money. It has not the power, however, in the sense in which supporters of Knapp claim it to have. They are right in claiming that the State has the power to bring about changes in the value of money by a stroke of the pen. They are wrong in assuming that the passing of laws is in itself sufficient to ensure the maintenance of that value. A great deal more is required to achieve that end, in the form of monetary policy decisions and their application. Even those decisions are far from being able to produce the full effect aimed at. Nevertheless, as we shall see in the following chapters, they are apt to produce far-reaching effects. And if Governments are prepared, rightly or wrongly, to sacrifice every other consideration for the sake of a policy aiming at maintaining the value of money, that policy is often able to achieve its end.

CHAPTER EIGHT

The Pursuit of Internal and External Stability

THE last chapter dealt with the power of the State to determine the value of its money. In the present and the two following chapters we shall examine the ends for which that power can be used. From this point of view there are, broadly speaking, two schools of thought, according to whether money is regarded as a technical device or as a major instrument of economic policy. The first conception is a static one, and favours a monetary policy aiming at stability. The second conception is essentially dynamic and favours a policy aiming at changes, whether in the direction of a rise or a fall in the value of money. Those who regard money as a mere technical device, the object of which is to facilitate the smooth functioning of the economy, do not expect monetary policy to influence fundamental economic trends. They expect money to remain 'neutral', which means that it is not supposed to cause a general rise or fall in prices, nor to stimulate or handicap production, distribution, or consumption. Under this conception the main task of monetary policy should be to prevent any departure of money from 'neutrality'. A well-behaved money is one which does not cause any movements of the general price level. This was the predominant view during the first three decades of the twentieth century. The monetary system and monetary policies responsible for its management were subject to much criticism during that period, mainly on the ground of the instability of the value of money.

On the other hand, those who consider money a major dynamic factor, and a major instrument of economic and social policy, take the view that monetary policy must aim at intervening actively to influence economic trends. An important school of thought – which achieved the zenith of its power during the twenty years between 1931 and 1951

– advocates the use of money as a means of stimulating production with the aid of an expansionary monetary policy. It favours an increase in the quantity of money in order to finance the production of more goods and to enable consumers to buy more. A rising trend of prices usually accompanies the successful application of an expansionary monetary policy. In the view of some of the supporters of such an 'inflationary' policy this is a necessary evil, but it is worth while for the community to put up with it for the sake of the beneficial effects of monetary expansion.

The opposite extreme is represented by the school which holds the view that monetary policy must aim at ensuring a steady fall of prices in accordance with the downward trend in the cost of production, or in order to be on the safe side against the ever-present forces of evil that would be making for inflation in the absence of such safeguards. According to this 'deflationary' school money must always be kept in short supply.

Although it is easy to quote early instances of inflationary and deflationary monetary policies, it seems probable that in the majority of instances throughout history the aim of monetary policy was the achievement of stability. When other aims were pursued it was not because a rise or a fall in the price level was preferred to stability. Inflationary policies were usually adopted during periods of war, though occasionally the extravagance of princes – or, for that matter, of Parliamentary Governments – forced their countries into inflation in time of peace. In so far as deflation was a result of deliberate policy and not of circumstances over which the authorities had no control, it occurred on many occasions as a result of excessive measures taken to ensure that money remained sufficiently scarce to ensure its stability.

The adoption of precious metals for monetary purposes was in itself, consciously or otherwise, an act in accordance with the requirements of monetary stability, owing to the relative scarcity of these metals. It is true, from a very early stage metallic moneys were frequently debased; their quantity was thus increased and their value reduced. Many rulers, though trying hard to avoid this, were unable to resist the temptation to debase their coinage. Others, however, went out of their way to restore monetary stability through re-coinage operations by which the excessive quantity of debased coins was replaced by a smaller quantity of full-valued coins.

The adoption of paper currency provided additional temptation and opportunity for departures from the policy of stability on a hitherto unknown scale. The early history of paper money abounds in such instances. After the Napoleonic Wars, however, most European Governments endeavoured to maintain the stability of their currency by maintaining a metallic standard, and thereby putting an automatic brake on monetary expansion. Viewed from the perspective of history the century that followed the Battle of Waterloo may appear to us a very stable century. In reality even during that period monetary trends showed noteworthy ups and downs which, moderate as they may seem to us after the experience of the First and Second World Wars and their aftermaths, were considered very unsettling in their days. To a large degree they were connected with changes in the output of monetary gold in relation to expanding commercial requirements, and with the abandonment of the monetary use of silver.

The discovery of the Californian and Australian gold fields towards the middle of the nineteenth century, and again the South African and Alaskan gold rush towards the end of that century, resulted in rising trends in the volume of money and in prices, not as a matter of monetary policy but through the automatic working of the gold standard, under which system an increase of the gold reserves meant a monetary expansion. In between those two gold rushes the additions of new gold to the world's monetary gold supplies failed to keep pace with the needs of expanding trade. There were in consequence shortages of money, all the more so as expansion of population, technical progress, and the rising standard of living made for larger monetary requirements. The result was a deflationary trend accentuated by the de-monetization of silver in many countries.

It is, therefore, incorrect to claim that during the nineteenth century stabilizationist monetary policy fully achieved its end. The intention had been, however, to maintain relative stability by adhering to a system which ensured relative scarcity. The maintenance of a metallic standard set a limit to the increase in the quantity of notes, and also in the volume of credit which came to play an increasingly important part in the monetary system. The view was held widely if not generally that the working of the automatic gold standard with the minimum of official interference was the best – indeed the only – way of ensuring relative monetary stability in the long run.

It was not until the period between the two World Wars that an alternative means to the same end began to emerge in the form of scientific monetary management. From the late twenties onward the view was gaining ground that monetary trends should not be left to the caprices of nature but should be made independent of the ebb and flow of newly mined gold supplies. The idea originated with the opponents of monetary stability who had hoped that through an abandonment of the gold standard it would be possible to embark on a degree of monetary expansion which had been impossible so long as the restraining influence of the gold standard had continued to prevail. It was taken up, however, also by many monetary economists and monetary authorities who favoured the maintenance of the gold standard but realized the need for its more elastic application.

The 'managed' gold standard which developed during the twenties aimed at maintaining monetary stability by neutralizing the effects on price levels of an unwanted increase or decrease of the gold reserves. This was done primarily not on account of any disturbing effects of fluctuations in the gold output but in order to minimize the inconvenience caused by fluctuations in the gold reserves of individual countries. During the late twenties when Britain lost gold the decline of her gold reserve was not allowed to produce its full effect on the volume of credit. On other occasions a credit expansion through an unwanted gold influx was prevented by official action in the opposite sense. This policy of 'neutralization' was practised more systematically in the United States.

One of the reasons why even some highly orthodox quarters were inclined to favour the replacement of the automatic gold standard by the managed gold standard was the realization that the world's supply of monetary gold was no longer sufficient to ensure the smooth working of the automatic system which made for a decline of prices through monetary scarcity. This was partly because of the maldistribution of gold that developed during and after the First World War. A disproportionately large percentage of the monetary gold supplies found its way to the United States, and, owing to the persistently favourable American balance of payments, there was no possibility of securing a more even distribution. The rest of the world had to be content with an inadequate stock of the monetary metal. Its inadequacy became accentuated because, while the price of gold remained at its pre-1914 figure, the prices of practically all goods and services remained well above their pre-War level. A smaller amount of gold in the world outside the United States had to finance a much higher turnover of trade. And since the current output of newly mined gold was not sufficient to make up for the deficiency, monetary policy experts all over the world elaborated devices for economizing in the use of gold. These devices – which will be examined in the chapters dealing with the means of monetary policy – aimed at maintaining the stability of the value of money. It was rightly feared that a world-wide scarcity of gold might result in a heavy decline in prices. This was in fact what happened eventually in spite of efforts to economize in the use of gold. Stabilizationist policy was no more successful during this period than it had been in the nineteenth century. But it seems reasonable to suggest that in the absence of that policy the fall in prices would have been even sharper, or that it would have culminated long before 1931 in a slump of prices and the abandonment of the gold standard.

The managed gold standard during the twenties provided a useful transition from stabilization policy under the gold standard to the stabilization policy under inconvertible paper currency. During the thirties the gold standard came to be suspended everywhere, but the methods of managing the gold standard in the interests of stability were largely retained and adapted to the requirements of managing inconvertible currencies to the same end.

At the same time, however, while the technique for maintaining stability has improved, the objective of a stable monetary system to be pursued by monetary policy was largely replaced by one of monetary expansion. This was because the downward trend in world prices during the early thirties caused grave disturbances in world economy. The idea that it is the object of monetary policy to arrest and reverse this process and to prevent its recurrence at all costs, even at the cost of producing some inflation (or, as it came to be called, 'reflation'), became increasingly popular.

By 1937, however, the United States Government adopted the view that the rise in prices had gone far enough. Once more the monetary authorities in Washington reverted to the pursuit of stability. In Britain by the late thirties the problem which the Government had to face was not one of choosing between deflation and reflation but one of preventing rearmament from producing an inflationary effect. Even though the extent of rearmament was negligible until the outbreak of the Second World War, from 1937 onwards the Government was preoccupied with fiscal and other measures aiming at preventing a rise in prices.

With the outbreak of the War in 1939 monetary policy in all well-organized countries came to concentrate on an effort to keep wartime inflation under control. On the basis of the experience of the First World War, and also on the basis of the experience of Nazi Germany during the rearmament drive of the late thirties, various devices were adopted to neutralize inflation or to suppress its effect on prices. As the War was proceeding these devices became increasingly effective. Every belligerent Government realized that in wartime conditions it would be useless to try to prevent inflation altogether. Indeed they went so far as to admit to themselves the need for a certain degree of inflation to stimulate the economic war effort. Their monetary policies aimed at keeping down the extent of inflation as far as possible, and in so far as inflation had to take place they aimed at preventing it from producing its full effect on prices. In face of the practical arguments in favour of minimizing the inevitable rise in prices for the duration of the emergency, theoretical arguments against price controls and against physical controls pursuing the same end were brushed aside. Never before in modern history had the pursuit of stability assumed the form of such far-reaching and effective Government action interfering with economic trends. Considering the extent of war-time inflation, the extent of the rise in prices was in most countries remarkably moderate.

The comparative success of the stabilizationist policies pursued during the War encouraged their continuation after the War, at first in the interest of reconstruction and then in that of raising the standard of living. As during the War, the object of monetary policy was to combine the advantages of an expanding monetary system with those of an outward stability. In most countries the Governments aimed not at the elimination of inflation but at the suppression or mitigation of its effects on prices. The difference between monetary policies in the thirties and those in the late forties and early fifties was that for some years before the War a rise in prices was the declared object of the authorities, while after the War they sought to disclaim responsibility for it. The pursuit of stability was not openly discarded as the end of monetary policy. The Government paid lip service to it, but was not prepared to adopt measures which would have checked the rise in prices, because it would have checked or at any rate materially mitigated and also delayed the rise in the standard of living. That rise was achieved largely through monetary expansion at the cost of a gradual depreciation of the purchasing power of money. Indeed it may be said that the post-War Governments were in favour of stability, but only in so far as its achievement did not call for measures that would have been detrimental to social security, expansion of productive capacity, or rearmament.

Hitherto we have been dealing with the pursuit of stability without trying to discriminate between internal and international stability of currencies. Under the classical conception the same policies are calculated to further both the end of a stable domestic price level and that of stable exchange rates. This view was powerfully reinforced during and after the First World War by Cassel's Purchasing Power Parity Theory, according to which exchange rates were determined by the relative changes in the domestic price levels of the countries concerned, and a rise in prices at home is accompanied by a depreciating trend of the exchange rate. On this assumption the only effective defence against exchange depreciation in the long run would be a prevention of inflation at home.

Other economists of the same period argued in the opposite sense, claiming that the domestic price levels of countries with inconvertible paper currencies were determined by the movements of their exchange rates. Beyond doubt a sharp depreciation of an exchange through speculative causes tends to bring about a sharp rise in the domestic price level of the country concerned, unless the movement is reversed before it has produced its effect. For this reason it was urged that internal monetary policies could not be pursued effectively unless and until the disturbing influences affecting exchange rates – adverse trade balance, speculation, international movements of funds, etc. – are eliminated. Both theories contain a great deal of truth. Instead of being rival theories, in reality they complete each other. What matters from our point of view is that under their joint influence the concept that the interests of internal and external stability are identical became firmly established in the twenties. This in spite of Irving Fisher's proposal that domestic prices in the United States should be kept stable by means of adjustments of the gold value of the dollar, which would of course mean fluctuating exchange rates.

During the thirties the possibility of a conflict between the requirements of internal stability and those of external stability came to be widely realized. Deflation was proceeding rapidly all over the world, though in some countries faster than in others. This meant that, given stability of exchanges, the price levels in some countries became higher than in others even in the absence of any inflationary policy that would tend to produce that result. The country which was unable or unwilling to swim with the deflationary tide fast enough had to suffer grave disadvantages because its prices were relatively high and non-competitive. It was losing markets abroad and even at home. Confronted with such situations the monetary authorities had to decide whether to restore equilibrium by enforcing a sufficiently drastic deflationary policy or whether to take the line of least resistance by reducing the external value of their currency. By means of a devaluation or depreciation it was possible to restore equilibrium between the higher domestic price level and the lower world price level with a stroke of the pen.

Concern about the stability of the external value of money is presumably as old as the monetary system itself. It is only in modern times, however, that the close association between monetary policies and domestic prices has come to be fully realized. This is partly because the statistical measurement of changes in the average price level is a comparatively recent invention, and partly because until recent centuries the response of price levels to monetary changes was relatively slow and incomplete. On the other hand changes in the international value of money had always been evident – at any rate to those directly concerned with commercial and financial transactions between countries. Opposition to debasements during the Middle Ages was mainly due to their effect on the value of the national coins abroad, and probably to a much less extent to fears of a rise in the domestic price level.

A century of uninterrupted stability in the exchange value of sterling was accompanied by fairly wide fluctuations in its domestic purchasing power. Nevertheless, when in 1931 the gold standard was suspended the depreciation of the international value of sterling was viewed with indifference by the British public. 'A pound is a pound, no matter at what rate it is quoted in the foreign exchange markets,' sums up the reaction of the man in the street. In many other countries, with experience in more advanced inflation, the general public became much more exchange-rate conscious. Indeed a stage was reached in some countries when domestic prices came to be adjusted daily, and even hourly, to the changes in the quotations of foreign exchanges. In such countries internal stability was of course inconceivable without external stability. On the other hand in countries such as Britain it was possible for monetary policies aiming respectively at internal and external stability to come into conflict with each other.

One of the reasons why in Britain there is a possibility of internal stability even in the absence of external stability is that she is part of the Sterling Area which supplies a large proportion of her food and raw material requirements. Since currencies of the Sterling Area usually appreciate or depreciate in sympathy with the pound, the sterling price of imports from the Sterling Area is not affected directly and immediately by a change in the external value of sterling. This circumstance tends to reduce the extent to which the domestic price level is liable to be affected by exchange fluctuations. Hence the policy of sacrificing external stability for the sake of maintaining internal stability stands a better chance of succeeding than it would in some isolated country.

The alternative policy aims at upholding external stability at the cost of submitting to unwanted changes in the domestic price level. Such changes may come about as a result of changes in world prices or as a result of monetary measures taken in defence of the external stability of the exchange.

D

For instance, in 1931 Britain might have saved the external stability of sterling if the Government had taken timely and drastic deflationary measures leading to a sharp fall in the domestic price level. Instead, sterling exchange was allowed to depreciate in order to avoid the need for bringing about such a fall, even though deflationary measures were taken eventually to minimize the depreciation of sterling.

Between 1931 and the outbreak of the Second World War British monetary policy aimed at the internal stability of sterling at the cost of external instability. From time to time the sterling exchange was allowed to depreciate in order to avoid an internal deflation. It was allowed to appreciate when exchange stability would have meant a rise in the domestic price level. In 1933 the United States adopted a similar policy. One of the aims of the deliberate depreciation of the dollar was to check and reverse the deflationary trend that was causing immense economic and social hardship. There was for some time during the thirties a period of competitive currency depreciation during which the Governments aimed at safeguarding themselves against internal deflation by outbidding each other in the depreciation of their exchanges. This policy came to a standstill as a result of the Tripartite Currency Agreement of 1936, between the United States, Great Britain, and France.

The main object of the Bretton Woods Agreement was to prevent the resumption of competitive currency depreciation after the war. Nevertheless, the Bretton Woods system admitted the principle that if the price level of a country finds itself to be out of equilibrium with the world price level, that country is entitled to restore equilibrium through a devaluation or a revaluation of its exchange, in order to obviate the necessity for lowering or raising its domestic price level. The fact that some countries were actually authorized by the International Monetary Fund, which controls the application of the principle, to alter their exchange parities, has proved that the principle established at Bretton Woods can operate in practice. Neither the International Monetary Fund nor indeed the Governments of the member countries were keen on resorting too frequently to such adjustments. They were prepared to put up with considerable inconvenience to avoid a change in their exchange parities. For instance, although it became increasingly obvious in the early fifties that prices in France were too high, the French Governments which followed each other in office in close succession were unwilling to adjust the situation by means of another devaluation of the franc. They were prepared to put up with grave economic and political difficulties in pursuing the end of the international stability of the franc. In this respect they merely reverted to the policy pursued during the thirties when France kept aloof for a long time from the policy of competitive currency depreciation and preferred to put up with an endless succession of crises rather than devalue the franc. The same policy was followed during the early thirties by Mussolini, who declared in 1926 that he would defend the lira with the last drop of his blood. It was pursued by Germany after the depreciation of sterling, and the resulting internal difficulties were largely responsible for the advent of Hitler in 1933.

In reality the conflict between the requirements of internal stability and those of international stability is in many instances not so sharp as it might appear from the foregoing. The reason why the French Governments in the fifties were unwilling to devalue the franc was not that they attached undue importance to its external stability but that they realized that another devaluation would only set into motion a fresh vicious spiral leading to a further rise in the domestic price level. This was the experience of France throughout the post-War period. Each successive devaluation secured only a temporary respite; prices soon caught up with the depreciation of the international value of the franc, and even went beyond it, so that after a year or two the price level in France was once more too high compared with the world level. In the case of France the pursuit of stability called for internal disinflationary measures which, if effective, would have safeguarded the external as well as the internal stability of the franc.

A stabilizationist monetary policy is concerned only with the stability of the average price level. There may be wide movements in individual prices or groups of prices without calling for official action to safeguard stability so long as the changes in the prices more or less offset each other. According to one school of thought, the function of a monetary policy should confine itself to neutralizing any *monetary* trends that threaten to upset stability. If price movements are caused by *non-monetary* factors such as, for instance, failure or super-abundance of a crop, there is no cause for official intervention. This view is not held generally, however. It has been gradually realized that a movement of prices initiated by non-monetary causes might easily assume a monetary character by setting into motion a vicious spiral. For this reason among others, Hawtrey and other monetary economists believe that a stabilizationist monetary policy must endeavour to prevent or correct any price movements even if they are due to non-monetary causes.

The difficulty is that the application of this principle may entail inflationary or deflationary action by the authorities even if the monetary situation itself does not call for such action. For instance, should the failure of crops cause a rise in the prices of land products, in the absence of official action this tends to bring about a rise in the average price level. To counteract this the authorities would have to adopt deflationary measures, or at any rate they would have to prevent the rise in prices from bringing about a credit expansion due to larger monetary requirements. Conversely, an exceptionally large crop may cause a fall in the average price level through the fall in prices of land products. The remedy suggested by Hawtrey is expansionary devices which tend to raise the average level of prices.

It is not always easy to discriminate between monetary and non-monetary causes of a change in the price level. The authorities confronted with a rise or a fall are inclined to take action on the assumption that whether or not the evil is due to monetary causes it can be remedied by monetary action.

CHAPTER NINE

The Policy of Raising Prices

As in the previous chapter, so in the present one we are concerned solely with price tendencies bought about as a matter of deliberate policy. We are not concerned here with price increases that occur spontaneously, or with those that come about as a result of the failure of official efforts to prevent them, or as incidental and unwanted results of monetary policies pursuing some other purpose. We are concerned, however, with price increases that take place not as a consequence of deliberate official action, but as a result of decisions to abstain from taking action to prevent it.

Official policy favouring a rise in the price level may be decided upon for the following reasons –

(1) Pursuit of a stabilization policy with an inflationary bias. In an effort to safeguard against the risk of deflation the authorities may take deliberately excessive anti-deflationary measures, thereby causing a rise in prices.

(2) Reflationary efforts aiming at a restoration of prices to their previous higher level.

(3) Deliberate reduction of the burden of public or private indebtedness through raising the price level.

(4) Efforts to improve the 'terms of trade' by raising the prices of exports so that their proceeds should buy a larger quantity of imports.

(5) A policy of stimulating production by means of a deliberate increase of prices in order to achieve a high degree of employment, or in order to make fuller use of the community's productive capacity.

(6) A policy of stimulating consumption by inducing consumers to make their purchases in anticipation of further rises in prices.

Since the dawn of history the progress of mankind in the monetary sphere has been accompanied, temporary intervals apart, by a rising trend in prices. Throughout the centuries prices have been rising to new high levels. Admittedly the progress has not been uninterrupted. In the long run, however, after each period of decline, the price level reached new high records.

To what extent has the depreciation of money during the last five thousand years been due to deliberate inflationary policy? Although there are many instances of such a policy, generally speaking it is correct to say that more often than not currency depreciations throughout the ages were largely due to circumstances over which the monetary authorities had no control. As a result of the improvement of mining and metallurgical methods and of the discoveries of unexplored mineral desposits, there has been a natural increase in the volume of precious metals. From time to time this increase has caused a spontaneous rise in prices. Further, even in the absence of an increase in the volume of monetary metals, price increases were caused by debasements of the coinage. Debasements were often necessitated by wars and were not undertaken for the purpose of raising prices.

The same is true about more recent instances of paper money inflation and credit inflation. In the majority of instances there was no question of any deliberate policy aiming at raising the price level. The State authority was merely prepared to put up with such a rise as the inevitable consequence of monetary expansion undertaken to finance wars, or for other purposes. Indeed, it seems reasonable to believe that very often the State authority drifted into inflation without knowing in advance the consequences of its actions. Inflation was usually due to decisions taken outside the realms of monetary policy, such as a declaration of war or measures of defence against enemy invasion. Monetary policy had to adapt itself in the best way it could to the consequences of such non-monetary decisions.

Monetary experience after the Second World War provides several instances of stabilization policies with a bias in favour of inflation. It was certainly not the aim of the United

States authorities to cause a rise in the price level. They wanted to maintain stable prices. On the other hand, they were even more anxious to avoid a slump than to avoid inflation. For this reason they preferred to err on the safe side by following a policy which resulted in a relatively moderate rise in prices, as an insurance against a much-dreaded fall in prices.

The experience of the thirties provides instances of reflationary efforts to restore prices to their pre-slump levels. This was the declared aim of President Roosevelt's monetary policy. The United States and other countries, having suffered gravely through the slump, were anxious to restore prices to their 1929 level.

Need for reduction of the excessive burden of debts figured prominently from very early times among the considerations determining monetary policy. The devaluation of the drachma by Solon in the sixth century B.C. served that purpose. Some economists are in favour of the secular trend of rising prices as the only possible way in which the otherwise intolerable increase in the burden of public debt can be offset. A policy aiming at a decline in the purchasing power of money is sometimes also advocated as a means for reducing the burden of private indebtedness. Consciously or otherwise, monetary policy may be influenced by such pressure which tends to weaken the will to resist the rising trend of prices.

Desire to undersell exporters of other countries is apt to be tempered by unwillingness to sell the national products at unduly low prices. If the prices of exports are unnecessarily low it means that larger quantities have to be exported in order to secure the same quantity of imports. In other words, the 'terms of trade' are unfavourable to the country concerned. One way of correcting this is by allowing domestic prices to rise for the sake of improving the terms of trade. This is done when there is full employment, because in such a situation there is no possibility of increasing employment through selling larger quantities abroad. It is advantageous when there is predominantly a 'sellers' market' – that is a state of affairs in which sellers can virtually dictate their terms – so that it is comparatively easy to export in spite of the higher prices. The post-War period provides instances of non-resistance to rising trends of prices for considerations of improving the terms of trade.

By far the most important motive of the policy of higher prices is the desire to stimulate production. Indeed, moderate inflation has come to be widely regarded as being inseparable from economic progress both as a cause and as an effect. More and more money is undoubtedly needed to finance an expanding volume of output and an increasingly complex production, and also to meet higher consumers' requirements due to the higher standard of living of a growing population. Admittedly in theory there is no cause for a rise in prices if the volume of goods increases to the same extent as the volume of money. In practice, however, it is necessary first to increase the volume of money in order to be able to produce more, and the monetary expansion is apt to affect prices before the additional goods become available. This is true to a particularly high degree concerning the production of capital goods.

Prosperous periods are usually accompanied by rising prices, while depressions are accompanied by falling prices. It is difficult to achieve prosperity through an expanding economy unless the monetary authorities are prepared to put up with some rise in prices. Prosperity is achieved partly through monetary expansion and partly through the stimulating effect of the rise in prices it causes. Some inflationists regard the rise as a necessary evil which has to be accepted in order to reap the benefits of expansion. Others go further by maintaining that a moderate rise in prices is worth having for its own sake, because of its stimulating effect on production and consumption. Indeed, they feel that a credit expansion could not be effective unless there is a rising trend of prices without which producers would be reluctant to avail themselves of the larger credit facilities offered to them. Rising prices are favoured because they mean the prospect of higher turnovers, higher profits, and lower risks. They mean a sellers' market in which almost anything that is produced can be unloaded, thanks to the ability and eagerness of consumers to buy.

It is true that higher profits earned as a result of rising prices are apt to be largely fictitious. For by the time the producers are able to dispose of their goods their cost of production may have risen to such an extent that the replacement cost of the goods sold is much higher than their cost of production had been a few months earlier. Many producers discovered after a few years of rise in prices that, although they had made handsome book-keeping profits, on balance they were worse off than before, because they had to contract large bank debts in order to finance their production at a higher cost and because their equipment had to be renewed at a higher cost. Notwithstanding this producers are apt to be hypnotized by the prospects of higher nominal profits. They are eager to produce to the limit of their capacity when prices are rising and to spend freely on capital expenditure in order to expand their productive capacity. If the Government wishes to encourage such expansion, that end can be achieved through causing prices to rise, or at any rate allowing them to rise. A rising price level is indeed a very powerful stimulus to trade.

During 1945–51 rising prices in Britain largely contributed towards the increase of industrial output. This explains why industrialists, in spite of their dissatisfaction with high taxation, interference with business by controls, and the Government's anti-capitalist attitude, continued to increase their output and their capacity. Although the Labour Government did not deliberately aim at a rise in prices for the sake of inducing private enterprise to function satisfactorily under a Socialist regime, this is how it worked out in practice. Some Socialist spokesmen candidly favoured the moderate non-stop rise in prices as a stimulus to production. Similar views were expressed during the long depression of the thirties by many non-Socialist economists. Although few Governments would ever admit that they favoured a policy of deliberately raising the price level for the sake of stimulating production, there can be no doubt that this consideration is apt to weaken resistance to an upward trend of prices.

Rising prices stimulate not only production, but also consumption. While high prices may in given circumstances discourage buying, increasing prices tend to induce producers, wholesalers, retailers, and consumers to buy before a further rise occurs. The pursuit of a policy of higher prices is therefore apt to kill two birds with one stone. It not only ensures an increase of the output, but secures a market for the larger output, without which over-production is liable to occur.

Temptation to stimulate production and consumption with the aid of a policy of 'creeping inflation' is tempered by the many obvious disadvantages of a depreciation of money. Those capable of seeing beyond the immediate future are bound to be concerned by the dangers that lie ahead. In the past every rising trend of prices has come to an end sooner or later, to be followed not by stability, but by a slump. The longer the rise continues the graver the dangers of a sharp reaction are apt to become. It is true, a policy of rising prices may have for its aim the perpetuation of a moderate rising trend, precisely in order to avoid a slump. The difficulty is that once it is widely realized that the rise is perpetual it is not likely to remain moderate. More and more people will be inclined to anticipate further rises, by making purchases before things become more expensive, and the pressure of their demand for goods is liable to accentuate the upward movement.

Needless to say, once inflation has reached an advanced stage its constructive aspects disappear and its destructive aspects become prominent. One of the reasons why a policy of moderate inflation finds favour in many quarters in the Anglo-Saxon world is that neither the United States nor Britain nor the Commonwealth has experienced runaway inflation, at any rate in the lifetime of the present generation. The United States had her dose of advanced inflation during the War of Independence and during the Civil War, but the memory of those experiences is too remote to be an effective deterrent. In countries such as Germany which experienced advanced inflation after the First World War a policy of inflation, however moderate, is seldom advocated from responsible quarters.

Even on the assumption that a moderate rise in prices need not be followed either by a slump or by an advanced inflation, the policy has many weighty disadvantages. One of them is that it tends to discourage saving and encourage extravagance on the part of both consumers and producers. There is no inducement for the latter to keep down their costs of production, since in a sellers' market they are able to pass on to the consumer any increases of their costs. What is perhaps even worse, there is little inducement for producers to exercise their judgement, since in a period of a non-stop rise in prices they can sell almost anything they produce. For this reason quality may become a secondary consideration. Producers are liable to make mistakes in misjudging their market, but amidst rising prices such mistakes may only mean a slower turnover and smaller profits. In one word, a policy of rising prices is apt to create not only a fool's paradise where producers work for fictitious bookkeeping profits, but also a more or less foolproof system where mistakes escape their penalty.

It would be easy to multiply the arguments for and against a policy of rising prices. Practical administrators cannot afford to be dogmatic about it. It is their duty to be fully aware of the sacrifices and the risks involved and to decide the extent of currency depreciation which may be regarded as justifiable in given circumstances notwithstanding those risks and sacrifices. It should be all a matter of degree rather than one of rigid principle.

CHAPTER TEN

Raising the Value of Money

THROUGHOUT monetary history the upward trend in prices was often interrupted by periods of decline. Documentary evidence shows that the purchasing power of silver had its ups as well as its downs in the chequered monetary history of Babylonia and Assyria. The inflation that resulted from the dispersal of the Persian gold hoard by Alexander the Great was followed, twenty years after the conqueror's death, by half a century of decline in prices throughout the area of the Eastern Mediterranean civilization. In modern times, too, price trends have shown some long periods of decline. Nevertheless, Feaveryear was right in saying in the concluding section of his standard work, *The Pound Sterling*: 'There is no doubt that the world's history can afford no example of a monetary unit which has been allowed for any very long period to appreciate.'

From time to time, however, Governments did pursue monetary policies which not only allowed the monetary unit to appreciate, but even deliberately caused it to appreciate. In this chapter we are concerned solely with the fall in prices deliberately aimed at by monetary policy. We are not concerned here with price declines which take place spontaneously or incidentally as a result of monetary actions pursuing other aims, or with declines which monetary authorities were unable to prevent. Official action to lower the price level is liable to be taken as a matter of deliberate policy for the following reasons –

(1) Pursuit of a stabilization policy with a deflationary bias, in order to safeguard the community against the risk of inflation by means of excessive anti-inflationary measures.

(2) Resistance to the adjustment of the volume of money to a previous increase in prices caused by non-monetary factors.

(3) Compliance with consumers' clamour for returning to the 'good old days' of low prices.

(4) Allowing lower cost of production caused by technological progress to produce its effect on prices.

(5) Restoration of confidence in a depreciated and discredited currency through a deliberate raising of its purchasing power.

(6) Efforts to check a speculative boom and to enforce the liquidation of unsound ventures that had developed under the influence of prolonged inflation.

(7) The favouring of creditors and encouragement of saving.

(8) The lowering of the cost of production in order to stimulate exports and discourage imports.

(9) Reduction of the cost of living in order to avoid wages demands and industrial disputes.

It is impracticable to strike a happy medium exactly halfway between inflation and deflation. Monetary trends cannot be regulated with absolute accuracy for any length of time. We saw in the last chapter that even though the official policy may aim at stability it is sometimes inclined to have an anti-deflationary bias and is prepared to cause a moderate rise in prices rather than risk a fall. Conversely monetary policy may have an anti-inflationary bias, which means that for the sake of making sure that inflation is avoided it aims at a slight reduction of prices. If a Government is more afraid of inflation than of deflation it may consider it expedient to adopt disinflationary measures as soon as there is the slightest indication of inflation. It may be inclined to apply deliberately excessive doses of that remedy in order to prevent the development of the disease. A Government with a strong anti-inflationary bias may even consider it expedient to adopt preventive anti-inflationary measures in anticipation of the appearance of the first symptoms of inflation.

A fall in prices may be caused as a matter of deliberate policy through preventing the volume of money from adjusting itself to a previous rise in prices. Such a rise may have occurred for a very wide variety of reasons other than a previous increase in the volume of money. It may have been caused, for instance, by an increase of prices abroad, or by a devaluation of the national currency, or by excessive wage demands not warranted by a previous rise in the cost of living. It may even have been caused by an anticipation of a further rise in prices by buyers anxious to cover their requirements. Whatever may be the cause, the effect is an increase of the requirements for money in order to finance the same volume of production and consumption on the basis of the higher level of prices.

More often than not the monetary authorities yield to the pressure and allow the volume of currency and credit to adjust itself to the higher level of prices. This was what happened to a very large degree in Britain during the post-War period. From time to time prices rose, not in consequence of any previous monetary expansion, but owing to the devaluation of sterling, or an all-round increase of wages, or the boom in commodities abroad in 1950–51. The rise could have been reversed if the Government had firmly prevented the adjustment of the volume of money to the higher requirements caused by the rise in prices. This was not done, however, and the rise in prices became confirmed and consolidated through a corresponding monetary expansion which was regarded in these cases as the effect and not the cause of the rise in prices. It was not until 1952 that an attempt was made to reverse the movement by preventing the adjustment of the volume of money to the higher price level. Although the rising trend in prices was arrested the policy of preventing a monetary expansion was not carried sufficiently far to reverse it.

A policy aiming at a reduction of prices may be adopted in order to satisfy popular clamour for lowering the cost of living. There is reason to believe that, subconsciously at any rate, the restoration of sterling to its pre-war parity in 1925 was largely inspired by a desire to restore the pre-war price level. By 1931, however, the Macmillan Committee arrived at the conclusion that if any downward adjustment of the price level must exceed 10 per cent 'the game is not worth the candle'.

Seen from the consumers' point of view, it is tempting to regard the lowering of prices as the ideal end of a monetary policy. It has always been a habit of the older generation to feel nostalgic about the good old days when things were so much cheaper. The fact that in those days many people were unable to buy much more than bare necessities in spite of the low prices is apt to be overlooked by those to whom a low cost of living has come to be regarded as synonymous with universal happiness. During and after the First World War, when prices were rising, it was a widespread conception that this was bound to be a temporary abnormal phenomenon and that it was the Government's duty to aim at restoring the 'normal' pre-1914 price level. After a while such wishful thinking was abandoned and the rise in prices was accepted as permanent. During the Second World War most people knew better than to expect a return to the 1939 price level. Tempting as it may be for Governments to aim at assisting consumers by a policy favouring a decline of prices, they have to bear in mind the effect of such a policy on producers, merchants, and debtors. It is well to remember that when in 1933 prices in the United States declined to their pre-1914 level the result was a crisis without precedent. The return to pre-war prices brought happiness to very few people.

A downward trend of prices should be a normal consequence of technological progress. New inventions, the application of labour-saving mechanical devices, and a more efficient organization of production and distribution tend to reduce costs. In a competitive economic system producers tend to pass on to the consumer at least a great part of the benefit of their economies in the form of lower prices. In a world of monopolies producers may be inclined to keep for themselves all or most of such benefit. When the balance of power is in favour of employees under conditions of over-full employment, employers may have to cede most of the economies to the employees in the form of higher wages and salaries, or shorter working hours, in which case prices can not decline in proportion to the savings effected. On the whole the chances are that technological progress tends to lower the price level to some extent at any rate, unless its influence is offset by monetary expansion.

The question is, what aim monetary policy should pursue in face of such a natural declining trend. The monetary authorities are in a position, should they wish to do so, to maintain a stable price level in spite of a decline in the cost of production of a large number of goods. The alternative would be to allow a decline in prices to take place. This would necessarily mean great hardship to a large proportion of producers unable to lower their costs sufficiently.

Any substantial lowering of prices through the reduction of costs would set in operation the ruthless principle of 'the survival of the fittest.' Only the most efficient producers would be able to make an adequate profit on the basis of the lower prices and the less efficient units would have to go out of business. In the opinion of many people this is an argument in favour of the policy of allowing lower costs to produce their full effect on prices. The elimination of less efficient units would tend to increase production, especially during periods of full employment when the more efficient units are unable to expand sufficiently for lack of man power. It is, however, a cruel doctrine that smaller units which have not the advantage of being able to achieve economies through mass production must be condemned to extinction.

During periods of rising price levels cuts in individual prices would be relatively moderate because in a sellers' market there is no need for the producers to pass on to the consumers the whole benefit of their economies. Even so, it would mean smaller profits for the less efficient units, but most of them would stand a chance of surviving somehow. During periods of declining prices they are doomed to extinction. This may be in accordance with the requirements of efficiency. Efficiency, however, is not an end itself, but merely a means to the supreme end of human happiness. Many people feel that the extermination of small firms would be a matter for regret. Production would become less individual and more stereotyped. There is, within reason, a great deal to be said for allowing the moderately fit to survive.

In any case if the process of elimination through a decline in prices were allowed to continue long enough even efficient big units might eventually become its victims, because there is always a possibility that some other unit will become even more efficient and produce at even lower costs. For one thing, it is impossible for established firms to scrap their costly capital equipment each time a new labour-saving device is invented, so that the latest arrival in the trade is at an advantage because he can equip his plant with the very latest machinery. The elimination of units, big or small, producing at a higher cost is necessarily a painful process involving heavy losses of invested capital and inflicting hardship on employees who may find it difficult to secure equally suitable new employment.

If the monetary authorities are opposed to the full application of the doctrine of the survival of the fittest they can pursue an expansionary monetary policy causing prices to rise, to counteract the declining trend of prices brought about by lower costs of production. If those responsible for monetary policy are in favour of a decline of prices, all they have to do in the circumstances is to adopt a 'neutral' attitude towards the effect of the decline in costs.

Much has been written by economists about the question whether or not the monetary authorities should allow declining costs to produce their natural effect on the price level. In our days this dilemma seldom arises. Throughout modern history there has been an uninterrupted technological progress. It is reasonable to assume that ever since the beginning of the industrial revolution in the middle of the eighteenth century the cost of goods in terms of human effort has been declining. Nevertheless, temporary intervals apart, prices have been increasing. This is due in part to the rise in real wages that has been going on throughout the ages. Labour-saving devices cannot always lead to corresponding reductions in prices. In the long run the wages bill of the smaller number of workmen required for the production of certain goods tends to be higher than that of the larger number of workmen had been prior to the adoption of labour-saving devices. The standard of living of employees and their wages requirements tend to rise simultaneously with technological progress and to absorb a large part of the savings in costs achieved as a result of that progress. Working hours tend to be shorter, and restrictive practices are apt to limit the output.

Another reason why technological progress has failed to reduce prices is that, relatively brief intervals apart, the monetary trend has been distinctly inflationary. It is reasonable to assume that but for the decline in the cost of production through technical progress the rise in prices would have been even more pronounced during the past fifty years. The decline in costs has been unable to cause a fall in prices, but has to some extent moderated their rise. From time to time it has actually led to provisional setbacks in prices. For instance, during the inter-War period the mechanization of agriculture through the widespread use of tractors, combine harvesters, etc., brought about a declining trend in the price level. The monetary authorities sought to counteract this and aimed at maintaining a stable price level. The result was over-production which played a decisive part in the series of crises and the long depression of the 'thirties. Owing to the change in the balance of power between employers and employees since the Second World War it seems probable that in future the effect of lower costs of production on the price level will be largely offset by higher wages and social benefits and by more favourable working conditions.

After a period of prolonged currency depreciation the Governments may favour a policy of deliberate fall of prices in order to restore confidence in a currency discredited by prolonged inflation. The choice is between trying to stabilize the value of money at the level to which it has declined or bringing about a partial recovery before stabilizing it. There are many instances of both policies in the monetary experience of the periods that followed the First and Second World Wars. In cases of runaway inflation it may be necessary to reverse the trend instead of merely halting it before stabilization of the value of money can be attempted with a fair chance of success.

A policy aiming at lower prices may be decided upon in an attempt to check a speculative boom. During the course of a prolonged boom a number of unsound ventures are bound to come into existence, and it is to the interest of the community that a large proportion of these should be forced into liquidation. A policy aiming at a lower price level automatically eliminates mushroom growths which have no *raison d'être* except during periods of boom. Unfortunately it also tends to eliminate well-established units working with a relatively high cost of production, as we saw above.

A reversal of non-stop increases in prices may be favoured not only for the sake of eliminating unsound units, but also for that of discouraging unsound wasteful practices. Occasional elimination of the thoroughly unfit through a period of declining prices may be favoured for the sake of better utilization of productive capacity.

A policy aiming at lowering the price level is often suspected, rightly or wrongly, of being due to a desire to favour creditors at the expense of debtors. Beyond doubt such a consideration played an important part in many primitive communities. They chose their monetary objects with a view to ensuring a perpetual scarcity of money for the benefit of the ruling classes, which were the principal holders of money and the principal creditors. In modern times, however, there can be little ground for such suspicion. Advantages derived by creditors from a decline in prices are liable to be offset by wholesale defaults or repudiations on the part of debtors affected by the increase in the burden of their debts brought about by lower prices. It may become necessary to consent to a moratorium or to legislation involving a reduction of the interest and capital of the claim. Creditors may have to pay a high price for the advantage of an increase in the commodity value of their claims. While their influence may be effective in inducing Governments to resist an inflationary rise in prices, they are hardly likely to persuade any Government to pursue a policy of lowering prices for their special benefit.

A much more realistic reason for which a policy of lower

prices may be favoured is that it tends to improve the balance of payments. If the price level is higher than that of other countries, then this disequilibrium may be corrected either by causing a decline in the price level or by reducing the exchange value of the currency. If the discrepancy is not very pronounced the former alternative is likely to be found preferable, as it is hardly worth while to disorganize the national economy by a devaluation of, say, five per cent.

Situations may arise in which the Government may resort to a policy aiming at a lowering of the price level in order to avoid an epidemic of wage disputes or a wave of wage increases leading to a rise in the price level. Wage claims may be disarmed through evidence being produced of a fall in the cost of living. It was with this object in view that the French Government in 1948 enforced a uniform cut in prices.

One of the main arguments against a policy of deliberately lowering the price level is that once a deflationary spiral is initiated the Government may find it very difficult to check it. The fall is liable to proceed well beyond the extent to which it is considered expedient for the purpose that inspired the adoption of the policy. Since falling prices are usually accompanied by an increase of unemployment the pursuit of a policy of falling prices has become politically and socially more difficult since the Second World War. Such a policy is liable to encounter much political opposition not only on the part of workers fearing unemployment but also on that of industrial and commercial firms who stand to lose through a business depression. During 1952 there was evidence of much discontent with the British Government's anti-inflationary policy even among business men who politically supported the Government. The United States had a similar experience when in 1953 the Republican Administration attempted to pursue a policy aimed at reversing the rise in prices. The case for such a policy has to be very strong indeed before any Government will decide that it is necessary to expose itself to unpopularity by its adoption.

CHAPTER ELEVEN

Accumulating and Safeguarding Monetary Reserves

ACCUMULATION of stocks of monetary metals by the State authority has always been an important end of monetary policy. In our days of inconvertible currencies the object of building up and safeguarding gold stocks is to provide the country with a substantial foreign exchange reserve to meet adverse trade balances and other international requirements. During the days of the gold standard the object, in addition to this, was the provision of adequate security for the monetary system of the country. Since the volume of money depended on the amount of the gold reserve, it was necessary to accumulate enough gold to be able to satisfy essential demands for currency and credit.

In earlier centuries the kings and their advisers aimed at building up gold or silver reserves largely from the point of view of sound public finance. The extent to which they were able to raise money through borrowing was limited. It was necessary to accumulate a cash reserve in the Treasury to meet future deficiencies in receipts as compared with expenditure. In countries which had gold or silver mines, or which ruled over colonies possessing such resources, the need to accumulate reserves called for measures of mining policy rather than of monetary policy, though even such countries had to resort to devices of monetary policy in order to retain a sufficient amount of the precious metals. Mediaeval England, being almost entirely devoid of gold or silver deposits, had to depend on devices of monetary policy for attracting and retaining a metallic reserve.

The significance of being able to accumulate and retain a large gold and silver stock in the Treasury was political as well as financial and economic. It was a most important means of establishing and maintaining the supremacy of the monarch's power within the country. A king with a considerable reserve in coin and bullion was in a strong position to assert his authority against the feudal lords, or against any pretender coveting his throne. Externally too, he was in a much better position to wage defensive or aggressive wars, to secure allies, or to equip expeditions for securing colonies. He was in a strong negotiating position in the frequent disagreements between Church and State. He was not so dependent on supplies voted by Parliament and did not have to pledge valuable domains as securities for loans. That the advantages of possessing large cash reserves were duly realized is indicated by the fact that contemporary historians, and even more recent authorities, judged rulers according to whether they were able to keep their Treasury well filled. History speaks of Henry VII in terms of the highest praise largely because he was able to leave a substantial monetary reserve to his successor.

Even in our days the possession of a large monetary reserve makes for political prestige at home and abroad. The inadequacy of the Sterling Area gold reserve during the late forties and early fifties materially weakened Britain's power to pull her full weight in international affairs, dependent as she was on external support for economic stability.

Early writers on monetary policy were strongly influenced by the realization of the need for a large and increasing metallic reserve. During the late mediaeval period and the two centuries that followed the mercantilist school, according to whom it was the principal task of Governments to secure an influx and prevent an efflux of money and monetary metals, reigned supreme. Administrators resorted to a variety of devices to attract precious metals. The object of these policies was not only to procure monetary reserves for the Treasuries but also to secure an expanding circulation of coins to meet expanding commercial needs. Even so the desire to fill the Treasuries played an important part, especially in England where all imported bullion and foreign coins had to be sold to the Royal Exchanger who had a monopoly of dealing in precious metals other than English coins. To achieve the desired end the kings adopted measures which gravely handicapped foreign trade. They engaged in competitive currency debasement in order to attract gold or silver to the country. A fair proportion of it was bound to find its way to their Treasuries.

As a reaction to the mercantilist policies a school of thought developed in the eighteenth century advocating a diametrically opposite policy. It favoured the removal of all obstacles to foreign trade. Under the influence of Adam Smith this school of thought gained growing ascendancy during the nineteenth century and succeeded in determining the policy of Britain and other countries. British economists during the nineteenth century ridiculed their forerunners' desire to safeguard monetary reserves by means of restricting trade. They held the view that all a country had to do was to import freely and lend abroad freely, and the rest would take care of itself. They were indeed right – amidst the unusual conditions of prosperity prevailing in nineteenth-century Britain. There was no need for British statesmen of that period to worry about the gold reserve. As the British industrial revolution was well ahead of that of other countries Britain certainly held most of the trumps and could afford to be liberal. In the case of countries as in that of individuals the rich always stands a better chance of earning more. 'To him that hath shall be given and from him that hath not shall be taken away.' Other countries which were less favourably placed had to make an effort to safeguard and increase their gold reserves with the aid of import duties and other devices at their disposal. Britain on the other hand managed with a relatively small gold reserve, relying on her ability to attract more gold when needed with the aid of an increase of the Bank Rate. She did not have to pursue a policy of accumulating a large permanent gold reserve but left it to the operation of the automatic gold standard to secure additional gold when required.

As a result of the First World War this situation underwent a fundamental change. Britain no longer held all the trumps in the sphere of international trade and finance. She could no longer rely on the automatic working of the system. However, British monetary policy refused to recognize the change and continued to work on the assumption that Britain could afford to uphold free trade with the aid of a gold reserve that was a fraction of the American and even of the French gold reserve. It was not until the run on the pound in 1931 that the need for a substantial gold reserve came to be realized in Britain. Throughout the thirties up to the outbreak of the War it was one of the main objectives of the activities of the Exchange Equalization Fund and of British monetary policy in general to build up a gold reserve commensurate with the country's importance in world trade and world finance. It was realized that, amidst the prevailing instability, the policy of keeping barely enough gold for immediate requirements was no longer satisfactory. In particular it was realized that a gold reserve representing a fraction of the foreign short-term claims on Britain was inadequate. The experience of 1931 showed that foreign balances were liable to be withdrawn on a large scale at short notice. It brought home the necessity for building up a sufficiently large reserve to meet such withdrawals in addition to meeting adverse trade balances and any temporary losses due to persistent speculative pressure.

The experience of 1931 taught Britain and other countries yet another lesson – that a monetary reserve, in order to be usable, must be liquid. At the time of the gold standard crisis, when the Bank of England's gold reserve was practically exhausted, Britain held overseas investments to a value of some £3,500 million. In normal times the realization of a fraction of these holdings – in addition to the recalling of the short-term credits of some £150 million – would have been sufficient to restore stability and confidence. Amidst a world-wide crisis, however, these investments became utterly immobilized and were quite useless for immediate requirements. Even the greater part of short-term claims on foreign countries became frozen owing to

the insolvency of the debtor countries if not of the individual debtors. A 'standstill' was imposed on all short-term
claims on Germany, Austria, and Hungary. Many other
debtor foreign countries stopped the transfer of credit
repayments abroad.

Evidently the aims of monetary policy in respect of the
building up of monetary reserves had to be reconsidered.
Already during the First World War an important secondary
reserve, represented by coins in circulation, a large part of
which could be withdrawn through the banking system,
ceased to operate. During the thirties Britain had to relinquish her easy-going policy, pursued successfully in the
more stable and prosperous conditions of the past, of relying
for foreign exchange requirements largely on the liquidity
of short-term claims and even of long-term investments.
It became evident that nothing short of gold or holdings of
'hard' currencies is really suitable for serving as monetary
reserves.

Amidst the unstable conditions that both preceded and
succeeded the Second World War, monetary policy had to
aim at maintaining a large and liquid monetary reserve.
Hence the conclusion of a large dollar loan in 1945. But
the ease with which the proceeds of that loan became depleted in a matter of months shows that amidst unstable
post-war world conditions even an exceptionally large and
absolutely liquid monetary reserve is liable to fail to achieve
its end. Evidently no reserve is inexhaustible. It is possible to
visualize conditions in which even the gigantic gold reserve
of the United States might become inadequate to meet prolonged and persistent adverse pressure. Indeed, although
that gold reserve is obviously far in excess of immediate and
predictable requirements, each time it declines by more
than a few hundred million dollars there is evidence of a
certain amount of concern in American opinion. Amidst
the prevailing instability even the United States could
hardly afford to abstain from conducting her monetary
policy from time to time with an eye on the monetary
reserve. In his book *The Dollar*, Harrod urges the United

States to increase the dollar price of gold, in order to be able to write up the *value* of her gold reserve, and thus to ensure that it is adequate in case of another major War.

The fact that no monetary reserve is inexhaustible is an additional reason for concentrating much thought and effort on its reinforcement. Monetary policies pursuing directly that end should be supplemented by monetary and economic policies making for sound internal conditions. Even the biggest gold reserve is liable to disappear if pressure on it is justified by over-inflated conditions at home; by inadequate production and excessive consumption; by inadequate saving and excessive spending; by maladjustment of production, over-ambitious capital investment, etc. It would be a mistake to imagine that once the monetary policy aimed at building up a large gold reserve has achieved its end we can afford to over-spend or over-lend or relax our productive effort, trusting, as we did before 1914, that the automatic working of natural tendencies will correct the situation if and when correction is needed. A big gold reserve must be regarded as the means to the end of safeguarding the stability and the prosperity of the national economy against the ups and downs of the trade balance and other uncontrollable international factors. Behind the shielding wall of an adequate gold reserve the nation fortunate enough to possess it should be wise enough to know how to safeguard its strength by maintaining a well-balanced production and resisting the temptation of excessive consumption.

Monetary policy aiming at a large gold reserve is complementary to monetary policy aiming at expanding production. Situations may arise, however, in which the two aims may come into conflict with each other. Such situations are apt to come about when full employment is reached and any further monetary expansion is liable to produce inflationary effects. The aim of maintaining full employment may demand the continuation of the expansionary monetary policy. On the other hand the aim of safeguarding the monetary reserve may call for disinflation. In the days of the gold standard the end of safeguarding the gold reserve was placed above everything else – if for no other reason, because any loss of gold would automatically have caused a contraction of credit resulting in unemployment. Now that there is no direct and obvious connexion between the volume of monetary reserve and that of currency and credit it is tempting to adopt the view that considerations of full employment must in all circumstances prevail over considerations of safeguarding the gold reserve. It is widely believed that full employment could now be maintained independently of the size of the gold reserve. This may be true for a country which is essentially self-sufficient. It is not true, however, for a country which, like Britain, depends largely on imported raw materials. A depletion of the British gold reserve would inevitably bring about large-scale unemployment, not by causing an automatic contraction of credit as under the gold standard, but by reducing raw material imports for lack of foreign exchange. Because of this, even though Britain is no longer on the gold standard, any substantial decline of her gold reserve is liable to lead to a contraction of credit as a result of official disinflationary measures aiming at the improvement of the balance of payments.

It is doubtful whether British opinion has realized this aspect of the problem to a sufficient extent. In the crises of sterling in 1947, 1949, and 1951, the drain was stopped in time before it could affect materially the import of essential raw materials. For this reason there may be a widespread impression that we can inflate with impunity. Any restrictionist monetary measure undertaken for the sake of safeguarding the gold reserve is, therefore, widely condemned on account of its adverse effect on employment. Beyond doubt the supreme end of avoiding large-scale unemployment must always be borne in mind. When there is a run on the gold reserve, however, the question is not whether employment should be sacrificed for the sake of the gold reserve but whether employment can be better maintained through safeguarding the gold reserve with the aid of credit restrictions even at the cost of causing thereby some relatively moderate temporary unemployment, or whether unemployment should be deferred until the gold reserve is exhausted, in which case when it does come as a result of a scarcity of imported raw materials, it is liable to be extensive and lasting. It is dangerous to dogmatize about this question as indeed about any subject relating to monetary policy.

The requirements of external monetary stability may, in given situations, conflict with those of safeguarding or increasing the gold reserve. In 1931 the gold standard was abandoned and sterling was allowed to depreciate in order to replenish the depleted gold reserve. The devaluation of 1949 pursued the same end. The agitation in favour of a 'floating' pound that developed during the fifties was largely based on the assumption that, by allowing sterling 'to find its own level' instead of supporting it against an adverse pressure, it would be possible to avoid unduly heavy losses of gold.

Hitherto we have been dealing with the international aspects of monetary policy aiming at the accumulation and maintenance of monetary reserves. It has, however, also important domestic aspects. Monetary reserves were liable to changes not only through imports and exports of monetary metals but also through increases or decreases of private holdings of such metals. For many centuries privately held gold plate was regarded as an important secondary monetary reserve of England. Demand for bullion for the manufacture of plate absorbed a large proportion of the available monetary metals, to the detriment of the Mint. On the other hand, from time to time it provided an important domestic source out of which the Mint was able to secure monetary metals. In more recent times the private holdings of gold coins were regarded as a kind of secondary gold reserve. Indeed de-hoarded sovereigns came in very useful to the Government after 1931 and again at the beginning of the Second World War. In other countries too hoarded gold or silver coins provide a useful secondary reserve, especially in India where de-hoarding became an important factor after 1931.

The disadvantage of the dispersal of gold by the hoarding of coins among private individuals is that the gold cannot necessarily be made available in sufficient quantities when needed. Monetary policy has only a limited influence over movements of gold between private hoards and public reserves. The authorities are usually in a position to increase private holdings at the expense of public holdings through the issue of coins. Movements in the opposite sense depend, however, largely on the willingness of private holders to surrender their holdings. Nevertheless, the authorities have various means at their disposal with the aid of which they can pursue the end of concentrating a large proportion of privately held gold in their own hands.

The modern trend of monetary policy is decidedly in favour of ensuring the concentration of gold hoardings in the hands of the authorities. The issue of gold coins has practically ceased and coins issued in the past gradually find their way into monetary reserves. Unfortunately from the point of view of the adequacy of monetary reserves a large part of the gold output after the Second World War found its way to hoards, in spite of the efforts of the International Monetary Fund to prevent such dispersal of the monetary metal. Between the World Wars the need for safeguarding the largest possible proportion of gold supplies for monetary pruposes was already generally realized. Monetary policy in various countries aimed at attracting gold both from abroad and from internal holdings.

Between the Wars an influential school of thought developed under the leadership of Keynes, according to which it was a mistake for monetary policy to aim at the accumulation and maintenance of a gold reserve. Although Keynes influenced the trend of monetary policy in many other ways he entirely failed to influence it in this respect. In spite of the radical changes in the monetary system that have taken place during the last two decades the accumulation and maintenance of a gold reserve has remained one of the most important ends of monetary policy.

CHAPTER TWELVE

Influencing Foreign Trade

WE saw in the last chapter that the aim of monetary policy to accumulate and maintain a substantial monetary reserve is attained largely through measures in the sphere of foreign trade. Accumulation and maintenance of a metallic or foreign exchange reserve is not, however, the only object of influencing exports and imports with the aid of monetary policy devices. From an early period the State authority endeavoured also to encourage exports and to discourage imports for the purpose of attracting money from abroad to meet the financial requirements of domestic production and trade. A third purpose for which exports are stimulated is to provide the means with which to pay for essential imports. A fourth object of monetary policy aiming at influencing foreign trade is to create additional demand for domestic products as a means for increasing the prosperity of producers and for creating employment.

Already in early mediaeval mercantilist literature there is a tendency towards favouring exports as an exceptionally worthwhile type of trade. Various authors throughout the sixteenth and seventeenth centuries emphasized that export trade was more important than domestic trade. They said that the latter merely amounted to taking in each other's washing – a process by which one individual may profit at the expense of another, but the nation as a whole does not stand to gain. On the other hand they claimed that in foreign trade there was a possibility of their nation making a profit at the expense of other nations. This primitive view is the beginning of the *mystique* that surrounds foreign trade right up to our day. Exaltation of foreign trade over home trade is not confined to the mercantilists. Their opponents, the Free Traders, adopted the same cult, even though they arrived at it on totally different grounds.

Whatever may be the reason for this preference in favour of foreign trade, it is bound to influence monetary policy. The encouragement of foreign trade was one of the objectives of mercantilist policy and remained one of the objectives of nineteenth century liberal policy. The liberal view favoured exports not for the sake of any influx of money it might produce but for the sake of furthering international division of labour under which everything is produced in the country where it can be produced in the most favourable conditions and at the lowest cost. This aspect of it was not appreciated until Adam Smith and his successors of the liberal school.

The original reason for favouring export trade, apart from increasing the monetary reserve of Treasuries and the monetary circulation of the countries, was that its proceeds provided the means for buying much sought-after imports. Even though the prevailing policy was to discourage imports, especially luxuries, the need for certain imports had always been realized. Exports were favoured in order to be able to pay for essential raw materials, for food, or for certain much-coveted manufactures which could not be produced within the country.

It was not until a later stage that the need for encouraging export trade and reducing import trade for the sake of stimulating home production came to be realized. It was the consequence of the development of mass production calling for extensive foreign markets. Technical progress and the increase of the population enabled both industrial and agricultural countries to produce large surpluses available for export. This increased productive capacity could not be fully utilized without the danger of over-production unless foreign markets could be secured. Once this stage was reached the motive for assisting export trade through devices of monetary policy became considerably stronger. In particular with the advent of large-scale industrial unemployment the possibility of 'exporting unemployment' with the aid of monetary devices came to be realized.

The aim of stimulating export trade can, of course, be

approached through various non-monetary means which are outside the scope of this book. Monetary policy, however, can be very helpful to an export drive. The manipulation of exchange rates to stimulate exports has been a device that was frequently resorted to in earlier centuries and again since the First World War. Various devices of domestic policy, too, can be placed at the service of an export drive. That end can be pursued by curtailing domestic consumption and reducing the cost of production with the aid of deflation, but also by stimulating the expansion of exporting or import-saving industries by means of a certain degree of inflation. To that end discriminatory credit facilities can be applied in order to divert productive resources to capital investment in industries producing largely for export or to those capable of replacing imports.

The same devices of monetary policy may serve all the objectives of expanding exports. An export surplus achieved with their aid can increase the monetary reserve and the monetary circulation at the same time as providing means for increasing imports and stimulating the development of home production. This does not mean, however, that these various considerations never come into conflict with each other. In mediaeval times the State authority was primarily concerned with filling the Treasury through attracting bullion and coin by imposing customs duties on exports as well as on imports. Obviously export duties tended to discourage export trade to the same extent as import duties tended to handicap import trade. Nevertheless, the kings of that period were satisfied that they stood to gain both on the swings and on the roundabouts by levying and collecting substantial duties on goods entering and leaving the country. By forgoing their claim on export duties they could have assisted export trade and could have improved the trade balance, which would have meant a larger amount of coin for the requirements of their subjects. Since, however, they were primarily concerned with their own Treasury they resorted to a policy which they expected would help to accumulate treasure even though this was to be to the detriment of export trade and of the domestic monetary circulation. They did not ignore, however, the latter consideration. By means of bans on the export of precious metals and Statutes of Employment under which the proceeds of imports from abroad had to be spent in England, they endeavoured to maintain a balance between exports and imports and avoid a drain on the monetary circulation. This, however, was a secondary objective. The main purpose of most measures was to keep the precious metals at home for the benefit of the Treasury.

This narrow concept gradually gave way during the sixteenth and seventeenth centuries to a policy which aimed at securing an export surplus not so much for the sake of the benefit of the Treasury as in order to provide trade with an adequate money supply. This attitude gained ground with the progress of the merchant and manufacturer classes and the decline of the absolute power of the rulers. For some time, however, it was considered of relatively small importance whether the much-desired export surplus was achieved through a curtailment of imports or an expansion of exports. In this respect again the development of industrial production with its growing requirements of imported raw materials played a decisive part in influencing the ends of monetary policy. Once the need for large imports came to be realized, import restrictions had to be relaxed. In order to be able to pay for growing imports the volume of exports had to be increased.

An outstanding example of a conflict between the ends of monetary policy in the sphere of foreign trade was provided in Great Britain after the Second World War. The execution of extensive domestic capital development schemes entailed inflation. Yet it was necessary in the interests of Britain's future exporting capacity, for the sake of which plants had to be modernized and expanded, new industries had to be created, and additional electric power supplies had to be provided. On the other hand, the urgent claims of export trade called for a curtailment of domestic demand for capital equipment so as to enable and induce

E

heavy industries to produce largely for export. When there was large-scale unemployment in Great Britain before the Second World War this conflict did not arise in an acute form. There was ample productive capacity for satisfying the requirements of capital investment and also those of domestic consumption, and there was an ample capacity for producing larger exportable surpluses. Even then an ambitious capital investment programme meant a rising trend in prices which was liable to discourage exports. The difficulty of overcoming this handicap, however, was not insuperable.

On the other hand, after the Second World War, with the virtual disappearance of unemployment, the British authorities were confronted with the choice between reducing their capital investment programme and accepting an adverse trade balance. To a large extent the solution was found in the financing of the adverse trade balance out of American aid. But from time to time it was found necessary to make drastic cuts in the investment programme because of the decline of the gold reserve due to an adverse balance of payments in excess of the proceeds of dollar aid. Inflation had to be curtailed from time to time, and this was done largely by cutting investment expenditure. Even though this was detrimental to Britain's future capacity to export, it was considered inevitable in order to cope with the immediate problem of the adverse balance of payments.

Stimulating exports is not the only foreign trade objective pursued with the aid of monetary policy devices for monetary ends. In given circumstances such devices are apt to be applied also for the purpose of stimulating imports. Immediately after the Second World War, when there was a world-wide scarcity of many essential commodities, the mercantilist principle was reversed. Instead of competing for each other's gold and silver, the Governments were competing for the scarce supplies of essential raw materials, food, capital equipment, etc. In order to be able to pay high prices for these goods without unduly raising their prices in terms of domestic currency, the monetary policy of several countries aimed at raising the exchange value of the national currency, or at any rate at maintaining it at a high level.

While before the War there was competitive currency depreciation to stimulate exports, after the War the volume of exportable surpluses was limited. Countries possessing essential goods endeavoured to obtain the maximum of foreign exchange for them and to that end a high exchange value of the national currency was called for. There were indications of a competitive currency *appreciation*, though it did not proceed very far.

Another instance of a monetary policy aiming at the encouragement of imports rather than exports was provided by Germany under the Nazi regime. One of the best known 'Schachtian' devices was to compel countries under German occupation or under German influence to accept the reichmark at an abnormally high exchange value in payment for their exports to Germany. By such means Germany secured the necessary imports at a low price in terms of reichsmarks or indeed in terms of German goods exported to the countries concerned. The same practice was pursued by the U.S.S.R. after the Second World War in the satellite States, which had to accept the rouble at an excessively high value in payment for their exports to Soviet Russia.

Monetary policy may also pursue the end of stimulating re-export trade and various international commercial and financial activities. In order that a country should be able to fulfil the functions of an international commercial, banking, insurance, etc. centre it has to possess a stable and convertible currency. Its monetary policy is liable to be influenced considerably by the desire to serve the requirements of these activities. It was one of the major considerations which induced the British Governments in the early twenties to adopt a monetary policy aiming at the restoration of the gold standard. This was achieved in 1925, but the appreciation of sterling to $4.86 imposed a grave handicap on both home trade and export trade. Although the restoration and maintenance of London's international position was not the sole end of that policy, it undoubtedly played a very important part in it. Likewise, after the Second World War various premature attempts at convertibility were largely inspired by the desire to secure the benefits of 'invisible exports' represented by earnings from international commercial and financial activities.

Beyond doubt monetary policy can play an important part in encouraging international trade by aiming at facilitating international payments. Free trade is inconceivable without free transfers. During the nineteenth century, when exchange restrictions were virtually unknown, high tariffs were considered to be the main obstacles to a really free international interchange of goods. In more recent times free traders have discovered that the most formidable enemy is not the tariff wall but import quotas, embargoes on imports, and exchange restrictions. Under the experience of the last twenty years trade has come to be regarded as being relatively free if it has to cope with nothing worse than high tariffs. By making the allocation of foreign exchanges to importers subject to licence the authorities have in fact imposed a watertight control over imports, far more effective than any tariff wall. A monetary policy aiming at free trade has to remove exchange restrictions, at any rate as far as current commericial payments are concerned. This principle may sound very simple; in reality its application gives rise to difficult dilemmas. In time of peace it is usually possible for a well-governed country to do without exchange restriction in the interests of free trading. Indeed, the adoption and maintenance of a stable and convertible currency is a very effective contribution of monetary policy towards an expansion of international trade. But very often this end can only be achieved by sacrificing other monetary ends.

Monetary policy may aim at overcoming transfer difficulties that hamper free international trade by means of international monetary arrangements. This subject will be dealt with in detail in a later chapter.

CHAPTER THIRTEEN

Fiscal Objectives

ONE of the earliest ends of monetary policy must have been to serve the financial interests of the State authority. Indeed it seems reasonable to assume that in many instances money owes its origin to the desire of primitive rulers to further the aims of their treasuries. At an early stage of economic evolution the subjects of these rulers contributed their dues in kind, surrendering a proportion of their products. The accumulation of an odd assortment of objects in the primitive treasuries, however, presented grave problems. Ancient Egyptian history provides much evidence about such treasuries which had to store a wide range of industrial and agricultural products, including such incongruous objects as furniture, grain, wine, cattle, etc. For some reason which is difficult to understand the Egyptians were prepared to put up with the clumsiness and costliness of the system even after having reached an advanced stage of civilization and statecraft. Other communities must have felt at a much earlier stage of their development the need for standardizing the contributions to tribal or national treasuries.

Even before the means in which compulsory gifts to the tribal authority, tributes, fines, or taxes had to be discharged became standardized, there was bound to be some unit of account on the basis of which the relative value of the various contributions in kind could be reckoned. The primitive State authority, having realized the inconvenience of accumulating and distributing its treasure in kind, sooner or later imposed on its subjects its rules about the standardized form in which payments must be made, leaving it to the subjects to convert their sundry possessions into that form before making payments.

It is, of course, impossible to form an opinion about the relative part played by this factor in the adoption of monetary systems and the gradual improvement that was achieved largely in order that they should serve better the convenience of the treasuries. It seems probable, however, that this consideration played an important part in influencing early decisions of monetary policy. However this may be, sooner or later the State authority came to regulate and operate its monetary system largely from the point of view of fiscal advantages. Monetary policy was placed at the service of public finance.

The fiscal ends monetary policy can pursue can be manifold. Kings or their treasurers in the past and their modern equivalents in more recent times found many ingenious ways in which they could use their power over the monetary system for the benefit of their treasuries.

The royal prerogative to issue money and to determine the metallic content and face value of the coinage has been for many centuries an important direct source of revenue. Indeed, from the early origins of the monetary system the issue of coins was apt to be regarded as being largely, if not exclusively, a revenue-producing device. The State often secured for itself the monopoly of producing or importing the monetary material. Thus in many countries the mining of precious metals was made a State monopoly. The mints, whether run by the State or farmed out to private enterprise against substantial payment, charged a seignorage for the benefit of the treasury, varying during the Middle Ages between two and twelve per cent. For this reason alone the treasury had a vested interest in ensuring that the mints were kept busy. This consideration influenced mediaeval monetary policy to no slight degree and was responsible for many debasement decisions. Whenever the mint stood idle because the market value of gold or silver at home or abroad was higher than the mint price, the kings were always inclined to ensure an increased activity through raising the mint price of the metals. In these instances – and they were many – the fiscal ends of monetary policy outweighed other ends.

Debasement served fiscal interests also through securing a profit for the kings on the re-coinage of the coins in circulation on the basis of a lower metallic content of the monetary unit. Contemporary writers frequently argued that even from a purely fiscal point of view this was a very short-sighted policy. It is true, the kings collected on each occasion a handsome immediate profit. But they were also obliged to collect their revenue thereafter in a currency of an inferior value. Admittedly, during the mediaeval period prices were rather inelastic, so that it took some time before the princes came to feel the full disadvantages of debasement in the form of higher prices and the resulting higher expenditure. Rising prices worked out, however, in the long run to their disadvantage, because feudal dues had been rigidly fixed and revenue from the royal domains was also inclined to lag far behind the rise in prices. Nevertheless, many monarchs found it difficult to resist the temptation of an immediate profit on debasement.

The adoption of paper currency opened new possibilities for treasuries to secure large financial resources with the aid of monetary policy devices. This was done on a gigantic scale during various major wars in modern times. It was also resorted to by many Governments to a more moderate but substantial extent even between wars. In countries where the paper currency was issued by State banks the treasuries had a direct and unlimited control over the printing press. In countries where Central Banks were in charge of the note issue it was necessary for the treasuries to induce these institutions to grant them advances. This was usually done in return for the granting or renewal of their charter. Though in many instances Central Banks resisted such inflationary borrowing they usually yielded eventually. Their loans to the treasuries were in many cases never repaid.

Another way in which paper money was used to serve fiscal ends was through its devaluation, as a result of which the book-keeping value of the gold reserves of Central Banks was written up and the profit surrendered to the Treasury.

As a result of the nationalization of many Central Banks after the Second World War the extent of the control of treasuries over the printing press increased. There is, there-fore, more temptation and more opportunity to use the note issue for fiscal ends. Nevertheless, thanks to the broadening of the responsibilities of the Treasury in Britain and other countries – it has now come to be regarded as being res-ponsible not only for public finance but for the entire national economy – Finance Ministers are now liable to think twice before embarking on crude monetary inflation unless it is under pressure of extreme emergency. In any event in advanced countries inflation through the operation of the printing press has now been replaced by more sophis-ticated versions of monetary policy pursuing fiscal ends.

We saw above that the adoption of a standardized means of payment and the improvement of its form were in themselves calculated to help the State authority in the col-lection of taxation revenue. The power of the State auth-ority to influence the quantity of money was also often used in the interests of revenue. In his *Essay on the Nature of Trade*, published more than two centuries ago, Cantillon remarked: 'The revenues of the State are raised more easily and in comparatively much larger amounts where money abounds'. It was to the interests of rulers, however despotic and selfish, to endeavour to ensure plentiful mone-tary supplies in their countries if only in order to be able to take away a great part of it by high taxation. Beyond a certain limit the increase in the volume of currency is apt, however, to react, unfavourably on public revenue. One of the causes of the weakening of royal authority in England during the seventeenth century was that the rise in prices resulting from the influx of precious metals from the New World reduced the purchasing power of the largely inflexible royal revenues from Crown domains. Kings were no longer able even in times of peace to live on the proceeds of their domains, and became increasingly dependent on the voting of supplies by Parliaments. In earlier periods, however, their capacity to collect taxation was often reduced not through an inflationary depreciation of the coinage but through the inadequate volume of coins in circulation. In such situations it was to their interest to do everything possible to attract precious metals to the country, not only for the sake of their revenue derived from the Mint or from the collection of customs duties, but also because the increase in the circulation of coins made it easier to collect revenue.

In modern times, too, a moderate degree of inflation may assist treasuries in solving their Budgetary problems by automatically raising the yield of taxes. Advanced inflation, however, is liable to operate in the opposite direction because the increase of expenditure may well outdistance that of revenue. Much depends, of course, on the system of taxation in force and on the relative extent of tax evasion. While in Britain after the Second World War the rise in prices produced a series of unexpectedly large revenue surpluses, in France it resulted in a perennial Budgetary deficit owing to the high degree of resistance of the French public to taxation. This is an instance to illustrate that the same rule does not necessarily meet the requirements of monetary policy in different countries even though the ends of their monetary policies may be identical. Moderate inflation may serve the purpose of augmenting revenue in countries where the yield of taxation is elastic while the expenditure is relatively inelastic. The existence of a large public debt also tends to increase the advantages of currency depreciation from a fiscal point of view, because the burden of interest charges does not rise in proportion to other items of public expenditure. On the other hand in countries where the public is inflation-conscious wages are apt to become adapted quickly to the rise in prices, especially if they are linked with the cost of living index. Consequently, public expenditure is apt to rise in sympathy with the price level.

Because of the uncertainty of the relative effect of higher prices on revenue and expenditure it is always risky to pursue fiscal ends by means of a deliberate policy of inflation. Likewise it would be a leap in the dark to embark on deflation for the sake of securing Budgetary advantages. It is impossible to see how a fall in prices is liable to affect revenue and expenditure respectively. Its disadvantages from a fiscal point of view are obvious when there is a large public debt, the burden of which will increase through a fall in prices. If the national income is reduced as a result of deflation, while the cost of the debt service remains unchanged, a higher proportion of the revenue has to be devoted to it.

Hitherto we have been dealing mainly with Budgetary ends of monetary policy. Another equally important fiscal end which monetary policy has to pursue is that of facilitating Government borrowing and the management of public debt. It is the duty of Treasuries to prepare the financial markets for the issue of new Government loans in order to ensure favourable terms and a satisfactory response by subscribers. To that end the creation of easy money conditions is naturally helpful. On the other hand in this respect as in respect of facilitating the collection of revenue, monetary expansionism is a double-edged weapon. If it leads to a persistent rising trend of prices it might discourage demand for fixed interest bearing securities unless interest rates are raised sufficiently to compensate investors for the prospective decline in the purchasing power of their investment income. It is, of course, possible for some time to ensure a satisfactory response to Government issues on terms favourable to the Treasury by means of further monetary expansion causing an increase in the volume of funds seeking investment. This is, however, a vicious circle which cannot be operated with impunity beyond a certain point. When it is eventually brought to an end the prices of Government securities are bound to fall heavily. This is what happened in Britain after the policy of bolstering up the gilt-edged market came to end in 1947.

Taking a long view monetary policy can assist treasuries very effectively in their task of financing Government deficits on favourable terms by ensuring monetary stability and strengthening confidence in the national currency instead of 'rigging the market' for Government loans. The benefits of such a policy, though less spectacular than those of stimulating investment demand artificially by monetary expansion, are apt to be more valuable in the long run.

Even so in special circumstances such as a war or a rearmament drive it may be found expedient to resort temporarily to the system of creating easy money conditions in order to ensure favourable terms during periods of heavy borrowing. A policy of cheap and plentiful money may also help Treasuries in their conversion operations. It tends to reduce or keep down the cost of the existing public debt. This consideration is of particular importance when a large proportion of the public debt is floating debt or is due to mature in the near future.

Under the modern currency and credit system the Treasuries are placed in the enviable position of being able to determine to a large degree the rate of interest at which they borrow. The end of economizing in public debt charges is apt, however, to conflict with other ends of monetary policy. Very often it may appear advisable to raise money rates in order to discourage inflation or a speculative boom. Until recently it was generally assumed that this could only be done at the expense of increasing the burden of interest on the public debt. After the Second World War, however, attempts were made in a number of countries to insulate interest charges on Government debt from those payable by the private section of the national economy. The methods employed to that end will be described in detail in chapters dealing with the means of monetary policy. We propose to show that to some extent at any rate some of these experiments were successful. It has proved to be possible in this sphere to eat our cake and have it. Several Treasuries resorted to credit restrictions in the sphere of the private section of the national economy in order to resist inflation. In spite of this they were able to avoid corresponding increases in interest rates on the Government debt. In so far as such results were achieved by inflationary means sooner or later the experiment had to be abandoned. There are, however, insulating devices which are not inflationary. In this sphere as in many others there is ample scope for further progress in scientific monetary management.

CHAPTER FOURTEEN

Monetary Isolation

IN nineteenth century economic literature it was generally assumed that economic internationalism must necessarily be the end pursued by monetary policy. Until recently few people realized the possibility that monetary policy might pursue the opposite end – that of economic isolationism. Even in our days the great majority of economists confine themselves to presenting the case against it, ignoring any arguments in its favour or in its mitigation. Since, however, monetary policy has served isolationist ends in a large number of instances during the last two decades, it is our duty to examine the monetary policies pursuing the end of economic isolationism and to take into account arguments both for and against. It is true that the pursuit of sound economic policies would obviate the need for monetary isolationism. This is, however, an imperfect world in which the pursuit of sound economic policies is often politically impracticable.

There were two sets of circumstances which induced various Governments to resort to monetary isolationism as part of a programme of economic isolation. In many instances they felt impelled to do so as a result of the inadequacy of their gold and foreign exchange reserves with which to maintain a system of free exchanges. In other instances they adopted or maintained a policy of isolationism in order to be able to expand their production or consumption with comparative impunity behind the shelter of an isolated monetary system.

Under an internationalist system any increase in domestic price level resulting from an expansionist policy, or any increase in domestic consumption that takes place as a result of artificially preventing an expansion of purchasing power from causing an increase of prices, is liable to bring its retribution in the form of an adverse balance of payments. Beyond doubt, the perpetuation of disequilibrium by preventing an increase of demand from causing an increase of the price level has proved to be feasible up to a point, as a result of the application of rationing and other control devices. If carried too far, the system is liable to break down sooner or later, apart altogether from its effect on the balance of payments. Even Stalin in his much-quoted article that appeared in the *Bolshevik*, just before the Communist Party Congress of 1952, admitted with considerable emphasis that in the U.S.S.R. economic laws could not be ignored indefinitely and to an unlimited extent. Nevertheless, even in countries which have not isolated themselves economically to such an extent as the U.S.S.R., it is possible to defy economic laws for a while so far as the internal economy is concerned.

The penalty for ignoring economic laws is apt to come much more swiftly in the sphere of the balance of payments than in internal economy. Monetary expansion in an already fully employed domestic economy necessarily means that too large a proportion of the products is used up for domestic capital investment or consumption, and that import requirements for both purposes tend to increase, while the volume of exportable supplies declines and their prices increase. In the absence of water-tight and comprehensive price control there is a rise in the domestic price level which tends to handicap exports and stimulate imports. Given freedom of trade and of international payments, the adverse balance thus created is liable to deplete the gold reserve, especially in the conditions after the Second World War, when the gold reserve of most countries was very small relative to their foreign trade turnover. Foreign aid may bolster up the situation for some time, but it cannot be depended upon to continue indefinitely. Nor is the devaluation or depreciation of the national currency liable to provide more than temporary relief. If it is resorted to too frequently the extent of relief it provides is likely to be diminishing, because domestic prices will tend to catch up more quickly with the depreciating exchange. A non-stop depreciation or a too frequent repetition of devaluations tends to produce an all-round demoralizing effect.

Nor is it practicable, under conditions of free international trade, to defend the balance of payments against the effects of inflation by means of price controls and physical controls. It is true the domestic price level may be kept artificially low, and this would maintain or even increase the competitive capacity of exporters. On the other hand the surplus purchasing power which is not spent on necessities owing to their low prices and their rationing is likely to be spent on imported goods or on goods which might otherwise be exported; or the inflated domestic demand might induce industries to produce for the home market in preference to producing for export. Nothing short of a completely watertight control on the domestic economy – something on the lines practised in the Inca Empire – would provide a solution under free international trading. Such a degree of control is impracticable in times of peace in democratic countries.

It is not surprising, therefore, that whenever a Government is reluctant to maintain or improve the balance of payments in the hard way by means of painful deflationary devices, it is inclined to try to reduce the effect of inflationary domestic disequilibrium on the balance of payments by means of an isolationist policy. With the aid of isolationist measures it is possible to defy economic laws with comparative impunity for a much longer time.

There are many historical instances of more or less advanced economic isolation. The mediaeval baronial estates constituted independent economic units. Until the second half of the nineteenth century Japan isolated herself completely from the rest of the world and carried on no foreign trade whatsoever. In these and other instances of economic isolationism, however, considerations of monetary policy did not arise. On the other hand in the case of the Soviet Union, economic isolation from non-Communist countries, achieved by drastic political and economic measures, is accompanied by a watertight system of exchange control. No payment to and from abroad can take place except through the authorities. This system completes the political control on contact with the outside world and the foreign trade monopoly with which isolation was enforced. Even in the absence of exchange control the State authority would be in a position to control import and export prices independently of the exchange rates. Under the Communist system it is possible to reserve for export trade any goods selected for that purpose and it would be possible to sell them even at a permanent loss if necessary in order to secure markets for them. Likewise, goods are imported not because they are cheaper abroad or because consumers demand it, but because the State authority deems it necessary to import them irrespective of considerations of price. A Communist State is like a big business firm which may deliberately incur losses in one of its departments for the sake of the overall profits of the whole firm. Nevertheless, as is indicated by Stalin's article, there are limits to the extent to which even a Communist State is prepared and able to disregard economic laws.

Many non-Communist States, too, have resorted to a high degree of economic isolation in recent decades. During the Second World War relative prices played a very subordinate part in determining the international flow of goods. As in the U.S.S.R., it was the Governments of belligerent countries that decided what to export and to import, and to or from which countries. In the absence of free interchange of goods and of free foreign exchange markets the price levels of various countries lost touch with each other. Thanks to the adoption of a policy of economic isolation there was no need for the Governments to worry about the growing discrepancies between price levels at home and abroad or to take inopportune measures of deflation – which might have interfered with the economic war effort – for the sake of restoring equilibrium. This state of disequilibrium between price levels continued for some time after the War, though to a diminishing extent. The price levels remained out of touch with each other and in most instances the Governments were reluctant to adjust the exchange rates to offset the discrepancies between the price levels. They were even more reluctant to adopt drastic deflationary measures in order to lower their price levels to those of other countries. Indeed they were even reluctant to resist pressure in favour of extending social services and increasing capital investment, although by yielding to such pressure they tended to accentuate the rise in their price level and to widen the disequilibrium with the price levels of other countries. Fortunately for them most other countries also pursued expansionary monetary policies, so that the world level of prices was rising, even if the extent of the rise varied from country to country. In order to be able to avoid unpopular measures for the sake of adjusting their price levels to those of other countries, they maintained to a large extent their wartime isolationist policies.

Economic isolation can be attained through physical control over imports and exports or through controls over financial transfers in payment for imports and exports. On the face of it it would seem that effective control over foreign trade would in itself suffice, since the extent of the circumvention of such control by means of smuggling must be negligible. In reality it is essential to supplement physical trade controls with monetary devices, not only in order to make circumvention of trade controls more difficult but also to prevent unwanted transfers of funds for purposes unconnected with current trade.

This brings us to the other main object of isolation. Gold reserves can be exhausted, not only through adverse balances of payment, but also through a large-scale or persistent capital outflow. From time to time under the gold standard the domestic trade of a country found itself penalized through no fault of its own, as a result of a crisis or a boom in some other part of the world, which caused heavy withdrawals of funds. To check such withdrawals the country concerned had to raise its Bank rate even though domestic trade conditions did not necessitate or justify such a change. Such experience provided a strong argument in favour of isolationism by means of monetary policy devices.

During the late twenties Poincaré's success in stabilizing the franc resulted in a large-scale repatriation of French capital from London. This caused acute embarrassment to Britain, especially as it coincided with a large-scale drain of capital attracted to the United States by the Wall Street boom. Many similar instances could be quoted to show how embarrassing international movements of capital are liable to be. Throughout the thirties large funds were being shifted from one country to another in order to avoid anticipated devaluations or depreciations. These movements of funds were a source of trouble, not only to the country which was losing them, but also for the country which was receiving them. It was justly remarked at the time that such funds are like teeth – they are a nuisance when they come, they are apt to be a nuisance when they are there, and they are a nuisance when they go.

Although after 1931 many of the financially weaker countries resorted to exchange restrictions in order to check such unwanted capital movements, the financially stronger countries allowed them to proceed unhampered. British monetary policy in the thirties aimed at discouraging an unwanted outflow of foreign balances by allowing sterling to depreciate, and at discouraging an unwanted inflow of foreign balances by allowing sterling to appreciate. It was not until the outbreak of the Second World War that international capital movements came to be checked by isolationist monetary measures.

In Germany, on the other hand, a watertight exchange control and trade control was adopted after the advent of the Hitler regime. The country became economically isolated from the outside world. This, together with effective measures of control over internal economic activities, made it possible for Germany to follow a policy of fairly advanced monetary expansion in connexion with the rearmament drive of 1933–39, without having to pay the full price in the form of deterioration of the balance of payments and an enforced curtailment of essential imports. Isolation went a long way towards enabling Nazi Germany to have guns *and* butter – or at any rate margarine.

Monetary isolationism is liable to be applied whenever a Government is engaged in economic experiments such as the adoption of a semi-Socialistic system in a capitalist country. If the basic system is changed into Communism then the problem of monetary isolationism against capital movements does not arise in a particularly acute form. Most liquid capital is confiscated by a stroke of the pen and cannot therefore be exported. In any case, as we saw above, a Communist State has other means of preventing a capital outflow. On the other hand, if the basic characteristics of the capitalist system are retained but the Government adopts an anti-capitalist policy by means of the nationalization of certain industries, very high taxation of profits, and advanced control of business activities, then monetary isolation is likely to be resorted to in order to prevent a large-scale flight of capital. But for the operation of exchange control in Britain during 1945–51 the outflow of capital trying to escape from Socialism and high taxation would have wiped out the gold reserves in a very short time and would have transferred the ownership of a very large proportion of British assets to holders resident overseas.

Large-scale flight of national capital may be caused also by fears of external aggression or internal upheavals. Many of those who can afford it would like to play for safety by accumulating nest-eggs in safer countries. The extent of such movements might well prove to be disastrous to the country menaced by aggression or civil disturbances. Considerations of national survival amply justify measures of monetary isolation to prevent such flights of capital.

There is yet another way in which a policy of monetary isolationism may be considered useful and necessary in given circumstances. It is useful for the prevention of strong countries from using the multilateral system of foreign trade and payments for unilateral purposes. Ever since the economic balance of power changed strongly in favour of the United States during the First World War one of the major sources of the world's economic troubles has been the unwillingness of the United States to import a sufficient quantity of goods to enable the debtors to pay for the American goods they import and to repay their debts owed to her. Whenever a foreign industry succeeded in creating a good market for its product in the United States the American interests affected mobilized all their political influence to induce their Administration to adopt protective measures against the imports in question. Although this undoubtedly served the sectional interests of specific American industries, in the long run it was detrimental to the interests of the United States as a whole as well as to the exporting countries, who were thus prevented from paying for their imports from the United States. The advantage of bilateralist methods under which a country would limit the amount of dollars expended in the United States to the amount of dollars earned in that country would be to make American opinion realize that in order to be able to export the United States has to import.

In practice such a bilateral monetary device would work out in the following way: the moment the big American exporting interests noticed that pressure was brought to bear on the Administration to exclude certain imports they would mobilize their influence to counteract such pressure. Under multilateral free trading they have no inducement for doing so, because it appears to them that there is no connexion between the volume of their exports and that of American purchases of imported goods. On the other hand if the adoption of bilateralist monetary devices makes them realize that a cut in American imports necessarily and immediately affects their capacity to export, they will take steps to prevent such a cut. The 'lobbies' operated by secondary American industries trying to seek protection against foreign competition would then find themselves confronted with the all-powerful tobacco lobby, Hollywood lobby, etc., each one of which is in a position to influence the Administration to a much larger extent than any combination of foreign Governments whose exports are threatened by the efforts of the lobbies of the secondary industries.

It seems, therefore, that measures of monetary isolationism are not necessarily detrimental to a free international interchange of goods. In given circumstances they may provide a welcome corrective to excessive and narrow economic nationalism leading to ultra-Protectionism in surplus countries which is liable to distort and gravely hinder the working of the multilateral trading system. Although technically the monetary measures adopted to cope with such situations isolate the country adopting them from the monetary effects of an adverse balance due to protection in other countries, in reality the choice is between two different kinds of interference with the natural international flow of goods.

Beyond doubt isolationist monetary policy is liable to entail grave disadvantages. It enables Governments to try to perpetuate disequilibrium. Nevertheless, without overlooking the disadvantages, it is necessary to bear in mind its advantages and to balance them against the arguments of those who are inclined to be dogmatically opposed to them.

It is arguable that monetary isolationism is fundamentally unsound and harmful, because it enables Governments to prolong the pursuit of unsound economic policies and to defer the inevitable day when realities have to be faced and unpopular measures have to be adopted to readjust the artificial situation. Even so, there are situations in which a policy of monetary isolation can serve useful ends. Like many other policies, it is liable to misuse. But its use in moderation may obviate worse evils or it may secure substantial benefits. Whether or not those who consider it a thousand pities that it has ever been invented are right, the policy is there for better or for worse, to be used or abused.

CHAPTER FIFTEEN

Monetary Policy and Business Cycles

ALTHOUGH in many circumstances monetary policy may aim at deliberately causing changes in price levels or exchange rates, in the majority of instances its end is to prevent such changes. Ironing out fluctuations constitutes the major objective of those in charge of monetary policy. They may direct their action against minor day-to-day movements in the money market, the foreign exchange market, or in the market for Government Loans. Or they may endeavour to offset seasonal and other medium-term movements in those markets. Above all they aim at preventing movements of prices and fluctuations in business activity over longer periods. The stabilizing functions of monetary policy in the sphere of prices and exchanges were dealt with in earlier chapters. Here we propose to confine ourselves to its functions as a stabilizing influence in respect of business cycles.

Business cycles are regarded as the worst effects of economic freedom. Their extent tends to grow bigger with the growth of quantities in our economic system – the figures of budgets, public and private debts, bank deposits, gold reserves, trade, production, etc. – and with the increasing complexity of that system. Indeed, it is widely believed that unless means can be found for dealing with business cycles they may endanger the very existence of the capitalist system and the democratic way of life. It is considered one of the duties of those in charge of monetary policy to adopt measures by which to mitigate the ups and downs of business cycles, even if they are unable to prevent them altogether. Ever since the development of the modern economic system periodically recurrent booms and slumps have been causing much concern to theoretical and practical experts.

Although these cycles may vary widely in detail, in substance they follow the same pattern. Whenever business shows signs of prolonged prosperity it gives rise to a wave of optimism resulting in excessive expenditure, both on capital investment and on consumption. Profits expand and there is an increase of demand for labour leading to a rising trend of wages. The resulting increase of purchasing power, accompanied by an expanding trend of bank credits, tends further to stimulate business activity until it assumes a boom-like character in many respects. The rising trend of prices encourages speculative buying of commodity stocks and of Stock Exchange securities and big vulnerable speculative positions are created. Company promoting and the issue of new securities is stimulated by indiscriminate demand, and there is a mushroom growth of new business firms of a doubtful stability. The insistent and indiscriminate character of demand encourages an expansion of production without regard to the long-range possibility of finding markets. A large and increasing proportion of business activities comes to be financed by means of short-term credits, creating many vulnerable commitments.

Such a speculative boom obviously cannot continue for ever. For a wide variety of reasons it must come to an end sooner or later, and a sharp reaction sets in. The pendulum then swings in the opposite direction. Holders of securities and commodity stocks hasten to liquidate their holdings, thereby accentuating the slump in the commodity markets on the Stock Exchange. Many firms incur heavy losses and get into difficulties. In so far as they finance their operations with the aid of commercial credits or bank credits they may become insolvent, thereby inflicting losses on many more firms and on banks. The over-buoyant optimism that characterized the boom period gives way to an equally exaggerated pessimism. On the top of the boom cautious people rightly assume that rises in prices had been exaggerated and play for safety. During the early phases of the downward movement of the cycle it comes to be widely assumed that the slump will continue for a long time.

Producers curtail their activity, traders reduce their stocks, consumers withhold their purchases in anticipation of lower prices and for fear of a decline of their incomes. They wish to preserve their liquid resources. Employment declines and the purchasing power of consumers contracts. The volume of credit becomes reduced, not only because banks want to play for safety and to curtail their commitments, but also because many credit-worthy business firms are reluctant to borrow.

Both boom and slump are cumulative processes. Apart altogether from the original causes that initiated them they tend to feed themselves as they proceed. After a while the unsound positions built up during the boom are liquidated and prices are at a more reasonable level. Nevertheless, business firms are reluctant to increase their activities. They then come to realize very gradually that it has become once more reasonably safe to increase their commitments. There is a cautious expansion of business activity, at first slow, then gradually gathering momentum, until it assumes once more a boom-like character. Another business cycle begins to take its course.

Throughout the nineteenth century business cycles re-curred with a disquieting regularity. Economists disagree about the average length of the period between one slump and another, but it has become a generally accepted concep-tion that the world is bound to experience a slump at inter-vals of between seven and eleven years. The losses incurred through such slumps by holders of stocks and securities, business firms and their employees have come to be regarded as the inevitable price mankind has to pay for the advan-tages derived from a competitive free economy. This fatal-ism contributed to no slight extent towards the progress of the Socialist movement and towards the tendency to the adoption of State control over economic activities as an alternative to booms and slumps.

Opinions differ widely about the causes of the business cycles. According to a large and influential school of thought they are largely if not entirely due to unwarranted credit expansion, which is responsible for the booms, leading to conditions in which a slump becomes inevitable. There are other explanations, such as the fluctuations of crops, the changes in the cost of production through inventions, etc. There can be no doubt, however, that even if business cycles are initiated by non-monetary factors they are supported and accentuated by monetary expansion during the boom and monetary contraction during the slump. For this reason it is only natural that many experts and intelligent laymen look towards monetary policy for relief from the curse of business cycles.

According to Hawtrey, the business cycle is entirely a monetary phenomenon and could be dealt with by the aid of timely and drastic monetary measures. Even those who do not share his belief in the exclusively monetary character of the business cycle are inclined to agree that measures of monetary policy could mitigate business cycles to a large degree. During the period of the automatic gold standard such measures were to a large degree automatic. Credit expansion brought about by a boom reduced the reserve ratios of Central Banks which were compelled under their statutes to take measures to maintain those ratios. This was done by an increase of the Bank Rate leading to a contraction of credit. Such an increase very frequently constituted the danger signal which pricked the bubble of the boom. With the decline of the demand for credit the reserve ratio tended to rise, and this was followed by a decline of interest rates. Although in theory the process was automatic, in practice there always had to be someone to take decisions leading to higher or lower interest rates. Nevertheless, these decisions were largely governed by the prevailing circumstances, and more often than not the monetary authorities followed the trend rather than trying to guide it.

To the extent to which the monetary system became less and less automatic after the Second World War, the responsibility of the monetary authorities for decisions taken in order to mitigate booms and slumps increased. Already during the twenties elaborate policies were pursued to that end, especially in the United States, where anti-business-cycle monetary policies were developed into a fine art following the establishment of the Federal Reserve System.

Before the First World War the figure of Central Bank reserve ratios and the trend of interest rates in the open markets was regarded as the main index to guide the action of the authority. During the twenties these indices were replaced by that of the trend of the price level. It was hoped to prevent a boom by resorting to adequate measures of credit restriction as soon as there was any indication of a rise in prices. Before very long events proved that this policy was far from ideal and failed to provide the much hoped-for solution. As a result of the decline in the cost of production, especially in agriculture, but also in industry, stable prices meant expanding profits and the development of a sweeping boom. The movement culminated in the Wall Street boom, leading to the disastrous slump of 1929, which was followed by a series of crises of unprecedented violence, and by a prolonged depression with declining prices and large-scale unemployment.

Needless to say, the above description of the boom and slump of the late twenties and early thirties necessarily over-simplifies a very complex phenomenon. What is essential is to realize that the devices of monetary policy were unable to prevent the business cycle from taking its course and from assuming unusually large proportions. The conclusion to be inferred from this experience is that the management of business cycles with the aid of monetary policy devices is not so simple as it appeared to experts in the twenties.

While in the twenties monetary policy was unable to prevent or regulate a boom, during the thirties it proved to be largely helpless in face of the slump and the prolonged depression. In addition to the time-honoured device of lowering interest rates and trying to expand credit facilities, other expansionary devices were adopted, such as the fiscal device of deficit financing, devaluations, etc. Eventually towards the middle thirties the slump and the depression came to an end and the business cycle showed signs of resuming its upward movement. The upswing proved to be very shortlived. It was followed by a mild trade recession in 1937. Then the Second World War broke out. War-time inflation which continued also after the war created a situation in which the traditional business cycle did not function, even though at times there were indications of a recession.

Notwithstanding the discouraging experience of the interwar period, expert opinion at the end of the war was practically unanimous in favouring the adoption of monetary policy measures against the recurrence of business cycles. Experts are sharply divided, however, between two schools of thought. According to the one, it should be possible to control the business cycle through the improved application of the monetary devices tried without conspicuous success in the twenties and in the thirties, supplemented by devices based on the Keynesian theory which connect trade trends with the ratio between saving and investment. According to the other school of thought, the only safe way of avoiding business cycles is by means of a monetary policy aiming at the perpetuation of moderate inflation and at the maintenance of full employment by every possible means. The fact that inflation has been proceeding almost without interruption ever since 1939 is quoted as evidence to prove that an expansionary monetary policy, coupled with social policies aiming at maintaining a high level of steady consumption, is capable of preventing a slump.

Those who oppose this monetary policy do so either on the ground that non-stop inflation is too high a price to pay for the elimination of the business cycle or on the ground that conditions since 1939 have been exceptional and that sooner or later the business cycle will resume its course in spite of the non-stop inflation – or possibly because of it. It must be admitted that the absence of a slump following the end of the Second World War came as a surprise to most people – not in the last place to the rulers of the Kremlin, who ever since the end of the war have been hoping for a gigantic slump that would undermine the resistance of the capitalist world.

Beyond doubt if it were certain that a policy of non-stop

'creeping' inflation could permanently eliminate slumps, it might be well worth while to put up with the grave inconvenience resulting from that policy. The results of the post-war experience are, however, far from conclusive. Hence the insistence of the anti-inflationary school on the adoption of disinflationary monetary devices for the sake of mitigating the disadvantages of non-stop inflation. Such measures are strongly opposed by the inflationary school on the ground that they entail very grave risks. For, should they initiate a deflationary spiral, the authorities might not be able to reverse or even mitigate it.

Under the influence of the disadvantages of creeping inflation during the late forties and early fifties doubts have arisen in some minds whether to make it an aim of monetary policy to eliminate business cycles is not, after all, fundamentally wrong. While appreciating the benefits of monetary expansion and of the absence of violent slumps and of large-scale unemployment, they claim that deflationary set-backs are an essential part of the competitive economic system and that in moderation they have their advantages. For although inflation tends to stimulate the full utilization of productive resources, they tend to be utilized in a wasteful form. We already have seen in Chapter 10 that deflationary reactions secure the elimination of inefficient units and ensure that productive capacity is employed to better advantage. It is only natural that after a prolonged inflationary experience the disadvantages of the recent trend should be felt keenly and the advantages of the trend of the more remote past should be missed. Possibly this attitude might grow stronger as and when an inflationary period continues for a long time without interruption. At the time of writing, however, elimination of business cycles remains an almost uncontested end of monetary policy. In the view of many economists and others, it takes precedence over various other ends. The monetary authorities in most countries seek to achieve this end by the 'foolproof' method of perpetuating a moderate inflationary boom rather than by the skilful application of Keynesian devices.

CHAPTER SIXTEEN

Full Employment

THE principle that the achievement and maintenance of full employment must be the foremost end of monetary policy is of recent origin. It arose as a reaction to the abnormal increase of unemployment during the early thirties. The change of attitude was largely the consequence of the replacement of the automatic monetary system by managed monetary systems between the two wars. So long as monetary policy was confined to the regulation of the automatically functioning gold standard, the objective of influencing the level of employment by monetary devices had no high priority. The rule that it is the foremost task of the authorities to maintain the gold standard was considered axiomatic. When the measures needed for maintaining the gold standard caused an increase of unemployment it was considered deplorable, but it was assumed to be inevitable. It was one of the fundamental rules of the gold standard game to raise interest rates and restrict credit whenever the exchange was weak. In fact to a large degree this happened automatically because there was an outflow of gold as soon as the exchange depreciated to its 'gold export point' – the rate at which it became profitable to withdraw gold from the Central Bank and export it. It would not have occurred to anybody in a responsible position to argue that, rather than lose gold or prevent its loss at the cost of creating unemployment, the exchange should be allowed to depreciate. It was considered a matter of course that a decline in the volume of gold should result in a decline in the volume of currency and credit. That this was detrimental to business and employment was regarded as an unfortunate necessity and very few people blamed the monetary author.ties or the monetary system for producing that result.

Once the automatic system was replaced by a managed

system it followed logically that the inevitability of restricting credit for the sake of defending the international stability of the currency would be called in question. Until then it was only contested by a handful of would-be monetary reformers who were unable to make headway against the prevailing orthodox conception. Even though men such as McKenna and Keynes lent their authority to the new school of thought during the twenties, it could not make an impression until after the gold standard had to be abandoned under the force of circumstances. Once monetary management became the established practice it was open for the authorities to adopt the rule that monetary policy must primarily aim at full employment. This was not done in fact until 1944, when the White Paper on Employment Policy announced the acceptance by the Government 'as one of their primary aims and responsibilities, the maintenance of a high and stable level of employment after the war.' The White Paper did not actually promise full employment, and it was open for anyone to interpret the meaning of 'high level of employment'. In fact, however, the White Paper is generally considered as an official recognition that monetary policy must aim at something like full employment.

In Britain the Government's obligation to maintain a high degree of employment rests merely on a declaration of policy, repeated in election pledges by the rival political parties. In the United States, on the other hand, it is embodied in the Employment Act, 1946, in which Congress declares that it is the Federal Government's responsibility, subject to certain reservations, to maintain conditions 'under which there will be afforded useful employment opportunities . . . and to promote maximum employment, production and purchasing power.'

The exact degree of employment which can be described as 'full' is largely a matter of opinion. Even the firmest supporters of the policy of full employment admit that there is always bound to be a small percentage of unemployed consisting of the unemployables and of those seasonally out of work or in transition between two jobs. Those in favour of 'a high level of employment' – as distinct from 'full employment' – are prepared to accept a certain amount of unemployment beyond that minimum, provided that it does not develop into large-scale unemployment. On the other hand, many people favour a state of affairs in which the number of unfilled vacancies far exceeds the number of those looking for employment. This latter state of affairs may be described as 'over-full employment.' It is distinctly inflationary because, human nature being what it is, it is difficult for employees to resist the temptation of taking advantage of their scarcity value. In order to be able to recruit and maintain their staffs, employers have to bid against each other for the limited supply of labour. Any new industry or expansion of existing industry can only solve its man-power problem by offering higher wages and thereby enticing the workers of other industries to come over to it. Private firms and public corporations are not in a good position to resist wages demands made under such circumstances, even if the demands are not justified by the extent of their profits. In order to be able to make a profit they have to add at least part of the wages increases to the prices of their products. The result is a rise in prices, which in turn leads to more wage demands.

In order to avoid sliding into non-stop inflation through the operation of the wages spiral monetary policy would have to aim at a prevention of over-full employment. This is, of course, easier said than done, because the borderline between full employment and over-full employment is very indistinct. British official statistics which do not give the full picture of the employment situation showed for a long time after the war a considerable excess of registered vacancies over registered unemployed. Whenever in such a situation a new factory or hydro-electric power station is brought into operation, the additional demand for labour can only be satisfied by withdrawing man-power from existing industries. The output does not increase through such changes. All that happens is that, while the new works add their output to the total, the established works have to quote longer delivery dates for lack of man-power. On the other hand, since the process entails a rise in wages, consumers' purchasing power increases. This, together with the higher cost of production through higher wages, accentuates the rising trend of prices.

The worst of it is that in the same country over-full employment can exist concurrently with local unemployment. This is because of the inelasticity of labour that has developed since the Second World War. Unemployed workers are reluctant to move to other districts – it is in any case difficult to do so owing to the housing shortage – or to switch over to another industry even in the same district. They are confident that, thanks to the new policy of full employment, there can be no unemployment except quite temporarily. They prefer, therefore, to await re-employment in their own district and in their own industry. There is indeed the utmost pressure brought to bear on the Government to pursue an inflationary monetary policy which would minimize local and temporary unemployment even in industries which have become largely redundant.

For example, in 1952 it became obvious that the Lancashire textile industry stood no chance of recovering many of its lost overseas markets. Notwithstanding this, unemployed textile workers refused to change over to aircraft industry which had many vacancies owing to rearmament requirements. They preferred to wait while Lancashire Members of Parliament on both sides of the House were pressing the Government to adopt monetary and other measures to increase domestic demand for textiles. Yet it should have been obvious that, in view of her balance of payments difficulties, Britain in 1952 could ill afford to stimulate artificially the domestic consumption of manufactures produced with the aid of imported raw materials.

In such circumstances a monetary policy aiming at full employment is liable to bolster up sections of industries which have become redundant and ought to be liquidated to release man-power for other industries which are short of labour. Had large-scale overall unemployment prevailed there would have been everything to be said in favour of keeping Lancashire going by means of inflationary financing, because the alternative would necessarily have been an increase of unemployment. Since, however, in the conditions existing in 1952 there was no difficulty in finding employment for the unemployed, all that the full employment policy achieved was the prevention of the transfer of manpower from redundant industries to vital industries. The engineering and shipbuilding industries had to lose foreign orders because, owing to shortage of man-power, they had to quote long delivery dates. On the other hand, domestic consumption of textiles was artificially stimulated, to the detriment of the balance of payments which had to provide for higher cotton imports for domestic requirements.

What was said above is not intended to make out a case against a monetary policy aiming at full employment. Nobody who remembers the experience of the thirties can object to the principle of that policy. But it is necessary to realize the need for a more elastic application of that principle in order to avoid its inflationary effects and to obviate the bolstering up of unsound industrial positions to the detriment of the national economy. It must be borne in mind that a persistently adverse trade balance, if increased through the consequences of inelasticity of labour, is liable to cause unemployment if the gold reserve declines to such an extent that the import of essential raw materials has to be cut.

With the above reservations the claim is justified that the new monetary policy tends to increase the productive capacity of the community. It avoids the waste of maintaining millions of idle workers as many countries did between the wars. It attracts into productive occupation a large number of those who had not hitherto been directly productive. Between the wars the inadequacy of the supply of credit resulting from a restrictive monetary policy compelled the banks to refuse loans for purposes which were financially secure, commercially profitable, and socially useful. This they had to do in innumerable instances in spite of the existence of at least one and a half million unemployed. Amidst large-scale unemployment productivity was low because of the widespread fear among workers that if they exerted themselves they would work themselves out of employment. On the assumption that only a limited amount of work was available, they endeavoured to spread it out as much as possible. Hence the restrictive regulations adopted by many unions, as a result of which even those workers who were able and willing to work harder were compelled to limit their output.

One of the main arguments used in favour of a monetary policy aiming at full employment is that it tends to increase productivity by doing away with the need for restrictive practices by Trade Unions, and with the workers' inclination to go slow for fear of working themselves out of employment. Since under the new policy the threat of unemployment has declined considerably, there was every reason for abandoning such practices. Unfortunately, judging by post-War experience, this was not done universally. The output per man-hour of those industries which did not have the benefit of increased mechanization showed actually a decline instead of increasing. This is particularly true of the building industry, even though in post-War Britain there was no ground for building workers to fear that they would work themselves out of employment. 'Feather-bedding' practices often prevented mechanization from leading to a corresponding reduction in the cost of production or a corresponding increase of the output. In many instances when newly-installed machinery reduced the number of hands required the workers insisted that the firms should continue none the less to employ the same number of workers. Dismissals through redundancy encountered strong resistance during a period when the workers who became superfluous through mechanization could easily find productive employment elsewhere where they were badly needed.

A great deal could be said about the bad effects of absenteeism and lack of industrial discipline on output under full employment. On balance, however, it is probably correct to

F

claim that, notwithstanding these and other obvious disadvantages, an intelligently managed monetary policy aiming at full employment is something well worth having, provided that its effect on the price level does not endanger the balance of payments.

This brings us to the international aspects of the full employment policy. Generally speaking it is true to say that its application is bound to be accompanied by a rising trend in the domestic price level. If the same policy were applied to approximately the same extent in all countries this inflation would not affect the balance of payments of any country. This was duly realized, and a vague international understanding was actually reached after the War under which the participating countries declared themselves willing to pursue a policy of full employment. The interpretation of that broad principle varies, however, from country to country. It is inevitable, therefore, that there should be discrepancies between the extent of the rise in the price level through monetary expansion aiming at full employment.

The result is a disequilibrium. The countries in which the policy of full employment is applied to a higher degree are liable to lose markets at home and abroad because their prices tend to become too high and their domestic consumption tend to increase too much. This tends to produce an adverse balance of payments which may in given circumstances endanger the very foundations of full employment. With a depleted gold reserve the country that applied the full employment policy excessively compared with other countries may reach a stage at which it can no longer afford to pay even for essential raw material imports. This may mean that although the domestic financial resources for producing to capacity remain available and the consumers have both the willingness and the purchasing power necessary to pay for the goods, production may have to be curtailed for lack of raw materials.

Even if it were possible to apply the full employment policy to an equal degree everywhere, the risk of unemployment through lack of raw materials could not be ruled out. Unplanned expansion of certain industries over-stimulated by the world-wide application of the new policy is liable to create 'bottlenecks' on an international scale. Total world demand for certain raw materials is liable to exceed world supply. The countries producing these key materials would naturally want to reserve for themselves as much as they need, which necessarily means that less favourably placed countries would have to go short. This is actually what happened in 1951. Though the immediate cause of raw material shortages was the additional demand caused by re-armament, unplanned and uncoordinated monetary policies aiming at full employment prepared the ground for the situation that developed following on the outbreak of the Korean war.

It is necessary to realize these dangers and to avoid the development of a new orthodoxy fully as complacent as that of the nineteenth century economists who firmly believed that if only economic factors were allowed to operate without interference things would necessarily work out for the best. Uncritical enthusiasts of the full employment policy, too, are inclined to believe that all that is needed is to adopt the policy of non-stop inflation for the sake of full and over-full employment, and mankind could live happily for ever after. Unfortunately things are not so simple in real life. A great deal more is needed than the dogmatic application of an over-simplified formula.

There is indeed a grave danger in the new dogmatism. It came as a not unnatural reaction to the old dogmatism under which everything was naturally expected to be sacrificed for the sake of upholding the stable international value of the currency. No sacrifice was considered too great to that end. Under the new conception Governments are expected to be willing to sacrifice any other consideration for the sake of full employment. Beyond doubt large-scale unemployment is an evil which it should be sought to avoid and for the avoidance of which it is well worth while to sacrifice other ends of monetary policy. It must not, however, be the only consideration which the monetary authorities have to bear in mind in determining the needs of their monetary policy. They have to avoid adopting courses which would eventually defeat the ends of their full employment policy owing to the effect of domestic inflation on the balance of payments. They also have to make up their mind about the degree of inflation they are prepared to accept as a price of full employment. The policy is still in an experimental stage, and its principles will have to be established through trial and error.

The need to reconcile full employment policy with other vital policies was clearly expressed in the American Employment Act of 1946. This declared it to be the duty of the Federal Government 'to use all practical means consistent with its needs and obligations and other essential considerations of national policy' for the purpose of creating and maintaining maximum employment in a manner calculated 'to foster and promote free competitive enterprise and the general welfare.' Under the wording of this passage the United States Government would not be under an obligation, for instance, to introduce controls for the sake of achieving or maintaining full employment. Many people would not endorse this formula, which is quoted here as an example of the dilemma those responsible for major monetary policy decisions have to face. It is liable to arise in connexion with the restoration or maintenance of the convertibility of currencies. The gold standard might have been maintained in 1931 at the cost of timely and drastic deflationary measures leading to a further increase of the existing large-scale unemployment. Even convertibility into other currencies may only be achieved or maintained in given circumstances at the cost of increased unemployment. The Government has to decide in such situations whether convertibility is worth the price that has to be paid for it.

In his evidence before the Congressional Committee on Monetary Policy and the Management of the Public Debt in 1952, Mr John W. Snyder, Secretary of the Treasury, said that the Declaration of Policy referred to above would have been better if it had included among the reservations the maintence of general price stability. He remarked that if measures undertaken to promote maximum employment, production, and purchasing power are prosecuted fully they are capable of producing undesirable increases in the general price level. Yet, he declared, the prevention of sharp changes in the general price level in either direction is an essential condition of national policy and of the general welfare.

This remark shows the kind of conflicts that are liable to arise between the end of full employment and other ends of monetary policy. While the need for sacrificing other ends to a large degree for the sake of full employment is now widely realized, it would be clearly going too far to lay down as an absolute principle that for the sake of full employment all other ends must be sacrificed in all circumstances. Situations may arise in which moderate increases in unemployment, regrettable as they are, have to be considered as a lesser evil than a runaway inflation or a complete depletion of the gold reserve.

CHAPTER SEVENTEEN

Social Objectives

THE ends of monetary policy dealt with in previous chapters may themselves be means to broader ends. A monetary policy aiming at lower prices, for instance, may envisage economic prosperity or social welfare or in given circumstances even political advantages as its ultimate end. In the present chapter we are concerned with the ultimate social ends monetary policy pursues through the intermediary of its various immediate ends.

Money is intended to serve not only economic needs but also social ones. By this we mean needs arising from non-economic aspects of human relationships, and also economic needs in so far as they concern the relative position of social classes. In the origin and early evolution of money this aspect was predominant. Money was adopted largely for the purpose of satisfying requirements arising from primitive religion, political relationships, marriage, etc. It was adopted as a means for establishing and accentuating distinctions between social classes. Such deliberate monetary policy as was pursued at those early stages must have served primarily such non-commercial ends. Money was adopted largely in order to provide a standardized means by which contributions to religious ceremonies, tribute, blood money, bride price, etc., were discharged and in which wealth, the possession of which conferred on its owner social distinction and political power, was accumulated. In a number of known instances, however, the social factor operated in the opposite direction. In many communities the State authority resisted the development of the monetary system or the replacement of a primitive money by some more advanced form of money. Rightly or wrongly the State authority took the view that the social upheaval resulting from a departure from a natural economy or from a primitive monetary

economy would entail disadvantages which would outweigh
the commercial advantages of a new monetary system. This
may have been the cause of the resistance of the State
authority in ancient Egypt to the development of a monetary economy. We encounter many instances of resistance to
the trend to replace payments in kind by payments in money
in various countries in mediaeval Europe. In Japan too, until
comparatively recently, the State authority discouraged the
replacement of rice currency by modern money in everyday
use.

In all these instances the object of the official attitude was
to preserve the existing social order. This aim may have
been pursued for two diametrically opposite reasons. Many
communities at the dawn of history must have feared that
the adoption of a monetary economy might accentuate
social inequality by facilitating the accumulation of wealth
on the one hand and the enslavement of the poorer classes
on the other. This aspect of the adoption of money was
noticeable in ancient Greece, where it had led to the
replacement of a patriarchal mode of life by a system of pronounced class distinctions between employers and employees. In the ancient period and for many centuries afterwards,
default on debts entailed enslavement, so that the stimulus
given to the practice of lending and borrowing by the development of a monetary system was a major factor in the
extension of slavery in formerly free communities. Too much
weight should not be attached to this argument, however,
in view of the fact that slavery and class distinctions had
existed to a very pronounced degree in ancient Egypt in
spite of the absence of a monetary system.

It is much more probable that in many communities
during the Ancient and Middle Ages the State authority resisted the adoption of a monetary economy and its progress
because this was against the interests of the ruling classes.
Generally speaking it is probably true that on balance the
abandonment of natural economy was against the interests
of landowners and served those of the rising merchant
classes and industrialists. This was particularly evident

during the mediaeval period when scarcity of metals, which gravely handicapped industry and commerce, was not unduly inconvenient to landowners, for rents and agricultural wages could usually be paid in kind. The depreciation of the monetary unit after the discovery of the gold and silver resources of America was gravely detrimental to the princes and the land-owning classes in general. They had to accept rents in depreciated currency once rents ceased to be paid in kind, because tenants were now in a position to exercise their option to pay in cash. In Japan the feudal system was endangered by the replacement of rice currency by metallic currency; hence the resistance of the ruling classes to such development.

The evolution of modern money has largely contributed towards the evolution of the present social system. It has contributed greatly to the creation of a society based on division of labour and competitive private enterprise. The primary economic objective of a better utilization of natural resources, man-power, and human inventive genius could not have achieved such advanced stages had it not been for the adoption and modernization of money. It was inevitable that this evolution should be accompanied by social developments such as the accentuation of class differences and the relative increase in the numerical proportion of low-income classes. During recent times more and more attention has been paid to this aspect of our monetary system. Whether this is happening through the awakening of a social conscience on the part of the higher-income classes or through the growing political power of the lower-income classes, the result is that Governments to-day can ill afford to disregard altogether the clamour for social welfare and for a levelling down of inequalities of wealth and income. Irrespective of the political orientation of the Government, monetary policy which formerly was placed almost entirely at the service of economic objectives is now being placed increasingly at that of social objectives. Fortunately the two often overlap to a large degree. An increase in the volume of goods produced is a social as well as an economic objective, because it increases the means with which to relieve poverty. Nevertheless, economic and social considerations influencing the aims of monetary policy are liable to conflict with each other. In a competitive economic system a monetary policy aiming at an extreme equalization of all incomes serves as a disincentive and is economically disadvantageous because it discourages invention and initiative, and tends to prevent an increase of output. In spite of this it may appear to be socially advantageous, at any rate in the short run, from the point of view of the standard of living of the lower-income classes.

By raising or lowering the price level monetary policy can produce far-reaching social effects. Very often these social effects are the purely incidental results of policies aiming at higher or lower prices for economic ends. A policy of raising or lowering prices can also be pursued, however, primarily if not exclusively for the sake of the social effects of the changes involved. Any substantial changes in the price level are a highly effective method of bringing about a re-distribution of wealth. It is much more effective than taxation and is liable to operate much more speedily.

Equalitarian monetary policy can be pursued very effectively through a deliberate depreciation of currency, which process is calculated to go a long way towards wiping out the fortunes of the upper classes and reducing the economic strength of the middle classes. It does not necessarily follow that inflationary policy will produce such a social effect. Much depends on the degree and speed of inflation and the ability of the upper and middle classes to 'hedge' against currency depreciation. There is also a possibility that a large number of people may not only succeed in preserving their fortunes during an inflationary period but even manage to accumulate new fortunes through a skilful and unscrupulous exploitation of price increases. Quite possibly wealthy classes as such do not disappear, but the fortunes pass into other hands. This would mean that if the inflationary policy aims at levelling down inequalities it would not altogether succeed in its objective. On paper there may appear to be fewer rich people. In practice this may only mean that the new rich are more skilful in evading taxation, being unencumbered by a standard of behaviour which the *noblesse oblige* principle imposed on the former wealthy classes. Nevertheless, by and large inflationary policy is likely to succeed in levelling down incomes. In particular higher grades of salaries and professional earnings are not adjusted to rising prices to the same extent as lower grades of wages.

Inflation is a most effective way of helping the debtor classes, the relief of which may be an important social end of monetary policy. In many instances in the course of history had it not been for currency depreciations the position of certain debtor classes, such as farmers or owner-occupiers of houses bought on mortgage, might have become intolerable. In such situations currency depreciation may be considered to be a painless alternative to waves of bankruptcies, spelling widespread ruin and discontent, and leading to social unrest.

Conversely, a deflationary monetary policy aiming at lower prices may have for its social objective a consolidation of the position of the 'ruling classes' in their capacity of creditors. While a deflationary policy is not likely to be adopted deliberately for that purpose, a community might slide into deflation by pursuing a policy of stabilization and exaggerating the anti-inflationary measures in order to safeguard the interests of the creditor classes.

One of the frequent objectives, declared or undeclared, of the pursuit of monetary stability is to maintain the social *status quo*. Creditor classes and recipients of fixed incomes are inclined to use their political influence for opposing any inflationary policy or any policy which, though aiming at stability, is not sufficiently anti-inflationary to safeguard against unintentional currency depreciation.

The development and extension of social services constitutes a most important objective of contemporary monetary policy in most modern countries. A rapid extension of the Welfare State is usually accompanied by a rising trend of prices, though this rise is not deliberate but merely incidental. On the other hand a Government determined to expand social service benefits substantially within a brief space of time is likely to be inclined to avoid committing itself to a too rigid system of monetary stability such as had existed under the gold standard. The maintenance of such a system necessarily limits the Government's freedom of action in the sphere of social services. In 1931 the National Government in Britain felt impelled actually to cut down social services for the sake of saving the gold standard which had come under fire. These cuts and other economic measures were retained and even reinforced after the suspension of the gold standard for the sake of preventing an excessive depreciation of sterling. Any Government is liable to be confronted with such dilemmas unless its monetary system is so fluid that the maintenance of internal or external stability of its currency has a very low priority.

Rigidly stabilized exchange parity, or determination to prevent the rise in the domestic price level, or, in the case of an elastic currency, determination to prevent an unduly heavy depreciation, is apt to come into conflict with the policy aiming at an expansion of social services. Each Government has to make up its mind about the priority or the degree of priority of social services over other requirements of monetary policy. If a Government adopts the line that social services are sacrosanct and must in no circumstances be cut for the sake of a disinflationary policy, that attitude is liable to set a limit to the possible degree of deflation and is even liable to jeopardize monetary stability through inflation. The Government may feel impelled to abstain from resisting inflation too rigidly if it wishes to maintain its social services intact.

On the other hand, monetary policy may pursue the end of preventing or moderating inflation for the sake of maintaining the purchasing power of pensions and other social service benefits. It is true, it is possible to link such payments to a cost of living index in order to prevent a decline of their purchasing power through inflation. In practice the adjustment of payments to a rise in prices through the operation of the cost of living clause is always subject to a time lag during which the purchasing power of the beneficiaries is bound to suffer. In periods of fairly sharp and continuous price increases the time lag is apt to be continuous because, by the time the payments are adjusted on the basis of the cost of living index for the previous month or quarter, prices may have risen further. For this reason once beneficiaries of social services realize how a rise in price affects them they may be inclined to join forces with the rentier classes in using their influence to induce the Government to resist inflation.

The extent to which monetary policy can pursue social objectives is not without limits. It cannot achieve distribution of more than is available for distribution, though it can increase the total volume of goods available for distribution by the pursuit of an expansionary policy. What monetary policy can do is to distribute an increased volume of purchasing power conveying the fictitious appearance of prosperity without an actual increase in the volume of goods available for distribution.

One of the social objectives of the monetary system is to secure a wide freedom of choice. Even under an advanced system of rationing everything is not rationed, and in any event the rations represent only a maximum limit of the goods available. Consumers are in a position to abstain from taking up their full rations and to apply their purchasing power for the acquisition of unrationed goods instead. Under a moneyless system, like that of the Inca Empire, the consumers had no alternative to taking up their rations. Since a certain degree of freedom of choice constitutes an important social requirement in any community that is above the bare subsistence level, even in an advanced Communist society the monetary system is retained for that purpose.

Economic planning operating with the aid of financial and physical control devices may aim at reducing the dependence of production and consumption on the automatic operation of the price system. The object of economic planners is to create a system in which considerations of social utility and not those of cost of production and selling price should determine what is to be produced. Even where the social objective prevails monetary policy remains important as a means for achieving that objective. Economic planning pursues its ends partly through monetary measures. This is so even in the Soviet Union, where the monetary system was repeatedly manipulated after the Second World War, in the interests of social ends of economic planning.

In capitalist countries monetary policy is used for social ends to an increasing degree. There is a growing realization of the fact that neither the increase of wealth nor the maintenance of stability are ends in themselves but merely means to the end of human happiness. Monetary policy has to serve that ultimate end, and it is not always possible to do this by serving the intermediate ends of increasing wealth or maintaining stability. Nevertheless, more often than not, the means of achieving social ends are in the long run identical with the means of achieving economic ends. Enlightened self-interest on the part of the lower-income classes may induce them sooner or later to find a compromise between social and economic ends instead of insisting on the absolute priority of the former.

CHAPTER EIGHTEEN

Political Objectives

MONEY has always been an important factor both in the sphere of domestic politics and in that of international affairs. From its earliest origins monetary policy pursued political ends to a large degree. Even before money came to be used sytematically as a medium of exchange it served as a means for safeguarding, consolidating, and increasing the political powers of tribal chiefs or rulers and those of the ruling classes. In present-day and recent primitive communities secret societies played a prominent rôle as the controlling political factor. In communities with such societies one of the main objects of the means of payment employed was to buy membership and promotion in the societies. Holding high rank in those societies meant social prestige and political power. Decisions of the tribal authority affecting the choice of the primitive means of payment or the regulation of its production and use often pursued a political end.

In external policy the possession of large supplies of some means of payment which was valued outside the community enabled the tribal authority to secure allies. This practice has often prevailed also in modern communities. Governments with strong monetary reserves were, and still are, in a position to secure the support of other Governments. During the ancient period certain types of money were adopted for the specific purpose of pursuing external wars. For instance Carthage adopted coinage for that purpose before it was adopted for internal circulation.

In innumerable instances throughout history belligerent countries have abandoned the policy of monetary stability for the sake of being able to finance their wars. It is arguable, however, whether in such cases monetary depreciation can be said to have necessarily come about in pursuance of a deliberate monetary policy. In most instances the countries concerned drifted into debasement or devaluation, the extent of which was not foreseen when it was decided to embark on a costly war. There were exceptions in which rulers are known to have been fully aware that they could only wage war if they decided to abandon monetary stability, and took deliberate decisions to that end.

An instance of monetary policy with a political objective was the well-known accumulation of gold by Germany shortly before the outbreak of the First World War. There was no pressing need for such accumulation for any economic or social purpose. It simply served the purpose of building up a reserve in anticipation of military requirements.

Money is an important instrument of political prestige. A strong and stable currency backed by a large monetary reserve confers prestige on a country. It is true that its authority is primarily economic. Countries such as Switzerland or Sweden with a strong currency enjoy a high economic prestige but their political power in the international field is limited. Nevertheless, a financially strong country is apt to carry much more weight in international politics than a financially weak and unstable country, given equal military strength. The weakening of the financial strength of a country tends to reduce its political power in the international sphere.

Britain's example after the Second World War clearly illustrates this. There have been very few instances in world history in which the relative political influence of a victorious Great Power suffered such a degree of decline as did that of Britain after 1945. To some extent this decline may be attributable to war-weariness as a result of which Britain reduced her armed strength to an undue degree. But, then, this was done also by the United States – at any rate as far as conventional arms were concerned – and yet she remained one of the two leading World Powers. It was done by Britain throughout her history after each victorious war, without suffering political eclipse in consequence. The main reason why after the Second World War Britain's political influence declined almost as much as if she had lost the war instead of winning it, was the decline of her economic power due to the weakening of sterling's position. Rightly or wrongly the Socialist Government of 1945–51 concentrated its efforts on the building up of the Welfare State in a very short time. This could not be achieved without rendering sterling vulnerable owing to the chronic balance of payments difficulties it entailed.

It is a matter of opinion whether it was worth Britain's while to sacrifice her position in the front rank of the great powers for the sake of raising the standard of living in six years instead of, say, twenty. We are only concerned here with the bare incontestable fact that the expansionary monetary policy which made possible the speedy building up of the Welfare State, and which maintained full and even over-full employment during most of the post-war period, necessarily precluded the restoration of the pre-war strength of sterling and of the pre-war influence of Britain in the sphere of international politics. Amidst her perennial balance of payments difficulties, due to living right up to the limit of her means and possibly a little beyond it, Britain became dependent on American aid. This fact alone made it impossible for her to make herself felt in the council of nations to a sufficient extent.

It seems reasonable to assume that those responsible for shaping Britain's destinies during the post-War period were aware that they could not have it both ways and that their decision to eat their cake in preference to having it was taken as a matter of deliberate policy. National greatness in the sense of political influence and prestige was sacrificed for the sake of national greatness in the sense of possessing advanced social institutions. If carried too far, however, this policy might mean getting the worst of both worlds. Freedom from fear cannot be sacrificed to freedom from want with impunity in the long run. Inadequate defences entail the risk of invasion. A defeated country is liable to be exploited by its conqueror, which would mean a considerable lowering of its living standard.

On occasions considerations of international prestige prevailed over considerations of standard of living and business prosperity. When in 1925 sterling was restored to its pre-War parity the main object was probably the determination to safeguard Britain's reputation for financial integrity irrespective of cost. The popular slogan that the 'pound must be able to look the dollar in the face' appears to imply, however, that considerations of political prestige were also involved.

Similarly, many of those in favour of the restoration and maintenance of the convertibility of sterling amidst difficult post-war conditions are inspired by considerations of prestige. But the possession of a freely convertible currency only makes for the economic and political prestige of a country if there is implicit confidence in its ability to maintain convertibility. Any distrust in the prospects of convertibility is liable to be damaging to its prestige and to its political power. In 1936 France sacrificed her security for the sake of maintaining the gold standard a little longer, by abstaining from taking military measures which could have prevented the remilitarization of the Rhineland by Hitler.

Much has been said in recent years about the so-called 'dollar diplomacy'. The term suggests that the monetary strength of the United States has been used for securing political influence. It has been alleged that one of the reasons why the United States refused to increase the dollar price of gold from the figure of $35 an ounce fixed in 1934 was that by adopting that monetary measure it would grant indiscriminate and automatic assistance to any foreign country possessing or producing gold. By maintaining the dollar price of gold at a level at which there is bound to be a world-wide shortage of dollars the United States was in a position to grant or withhold dollar aid according to the political, military, and economic policies of the Governments in need of it. To the extent to which the refusal to raise the price of gold was inspired by this consideration the monetary policy decision to maintain gold at $35 an ounce pursued political ends. It would be a mistake, however, to attach too much importance to this argument.

The establishment and maintenance of the Sterling Area pursued not only economic but also political objectives. The operation of any such currency area is apt to create political as well as monetary ties. It establishes a high degree of identity of interests between the countries of the same monetary area, and this cannot be lightly disregarded by the Governments in shaping their external policies.

Strong countries are often in a position to compel economically or politically oppressed countries to pursue monetary policies in accordance with the interests of the 'ruling race', The countries of South-Eastern Europe before the Second World War and practically the whole Continent during the years of German domination were forced to fix their exchange rates in accordance with the requirements of the Nazi Government's policy of exploitation. Germany was able to secure a large quantity of goods of the occupied or satellite countries by fixing a high exchange value for the reichsmark in terms of their currencies. Although the advantages thus gained were primarily economic, Imperialist exploitation of that type is essentially political in character and monetary policies pursued in its service followed therefore largely political objectives.

To some extent every Colonial power imposes its monetary policy on its colonies, but the political character of that policy is largely a matter of degree. It has always been a popular argument in American textbooks on history that the British policy in the eighteenth century aiming at the prevention of the development of coinage in the North American Colonies pursued the object of maintaining these colonies in a state of dependence on the mother country as well as exploiting them economically. It seems, however, that since the balance of payments of these undeveloped countries was bound to be strongly adverse during the phase of their rapid development – in the words of the American economist Horace White, 'they could not have both a metallic currency and an axe' – there was a trend for coins to be exported to England in any case. There would have been no sense in encouraging the issue and import of coins which the colonies could not in any event have retained in domestic circulation.

It has also been suggested that the arrangement under which the British Crown colonies in our time keep their monetary reserves in the form of sterling balances is inspired by political motives. Beyond doubt it strengthens the political links between the colonies and the mother country. It is justified, however, even on economic grounds, since the colonies transact most of their foreign trade with the United Kingdom and other countries of the Sterling Area, so that it is reasonable for them to keep their monetary reserves in sterling.

Hitherto we have been dealing with the external political aspects of monetary policy. In domestic politics too, monetary policy is apt to play an important and at times decisive rôle. Moderate inflation may be inspired by the desire of the ruling party to secure popularity. It is always tempting for governments to engage in costly public works schemes and to incur other expenditure liable to secure votes for them. Very often this can only be done at the cost of inflating the national currency. Such a monetary policy is condemned by the overwhelming majority of economists as inherently unsound and vicious. Beyond doubt in many instances their criticism is justified. Democracy is at its worst when the opposing political parties feel impelled to outbid each other in offering bribes to the electorate at the cost of debasing the currency. It would be a mistake, however, to be dogmatic in condemning an expansionary policy inspired by political considerations as being inherently wicked in all conceivable circumstances.

There are situations when monetary expansion, undertaken primarily for political ends, has a strong justification from an economic point of view. Let us take an instance. It is impossible to repair the large-scale devastations of a modern war within a short period without inflating the currency. The alternative is to spread the reconstruction over a long period of years and even decades. It goes without saying that speedy reconstruction is popular and that any Government with a programme of completing the task in five years is liable to defeat the party which wants to proceed cautiously and plans to complete the work in twenty. Even those statesmen who are aware of the inflationary consequences of a speedy reconstruction, and who may take the view that the economic disadvantages of the currency depreciation it entails would outweigh the disadvantages of delayed reconstruction, would be inclined to favour speedy reconstruction for the sake of the popularity of their party. In this instance the right thing would be done for the wrong reason. While it may be a matter of opinion whether it is worth while to sacrifice monetary stability and to put up with the disadvantages of inflation for the sake of industrializing a country within a brief period, or for the sake of completing an ambitious programme of public works, or even for the sake of establishing an advanced Welfare State in record time, there can be no two opinions about the urgency of restoring towns and villages ravaged by war. For delay in physical reconstruction would mean low output, and scarcity of goods is liable to cause a rise in prices, so that the choice rests between monetary inflation and price inflation.

The maintenance of the gold standard, or of the stable parities of an inconvertible paper currency, imposes a restraint on any political policies that would necessitate expenditure on a large scale. Indeed, according to many supporters of the gold standard and of stable parities, this is one of the greatest advantages of the system of their choice. In order to be able to proceed with costly political schemes it may become inevitable to discard the self-imposed restraint that is necessary so long as external monetary stability is maintained. For this reason, among others, it is broadly speaking true that Conservative regimes favour the gold standard or a rigidly stable money. The more deeply it is ingrained in the minds of the public that the maintenance of such a system is a matter of vital interest and of national prestige and honour the more the electorate is likely to support a Conservative regime.

From this it would appear that it is natural for Conservatives to favour a rigidly stabilized pound and for Socialists to favour an elastic pound. Yet in 1952–53 British Conservative circles were inclined to flirt with the idea of restoring the 'floating' pound for the sake of being able to restore convertibility. It is arguable that when the pound is kept artificially stable it does not function as a barometer that would react immediately to overspending by the Government or by the country. If sterling is allowed to fluctuate any excessive Government expenditure or deterioration of the balance of payments would result in a depreciation which would serve as a warning signal. Those who accept this argument may hold the opinion that in pursuing a political end the monetary policy of a Conservative Government should aim at restoring the floating pound on the assumption that the advent of a Socialist Government would cause a depreciation and that fear of such depreciation might influence the attitude of the electorate.

Supporters of this view point out that in 1931, when after the suspension of the gold standard sterling became an elastic currency, the British electorate was frightened into bringing in a large Conservative majority in the hope that a Conservative Government would be in a better position to moderate the depreciation of sterling. On the other hand those who believe that Conservative monetary policy ought to aim at rigid stability point out that had sterling been in the habit of fluctuating in August 1931, Ramsay MacDonald would not have been frightened by the prospects of its depreciation into deciding to form a National Government. The decision to allow sterling to depreciate would probably have been taken as a matter of administrative routine on an official level, possibly without even submitting it to the Cabinet. Nobody would have thought it to be out of the ordinary to witness a depreciation of sterling by twenty per cent or more. It was precisely because the importance of maintaining the gold standard and the stability of sterling around its parity of $4.86 was deeply ingrained in the minds of the British public that the threat of having to abandon the parity created such a profound impression.

From the foregoing it is evident that even if a Government wished to use its monetary policy for furthering the ends of domestic politics there would be room for fundamental disagreement about the way in which this end could be achieved. In given circumstances it may be largely a matter of opinion which of two diametrically opposite courses would produce the desired result.

One of the difficulties of pursuing a political objective by means of monetary policy is that there are no absolute rules determining relations between cause and effect in this sphere. On the one hand a devaluation is liable to undermine the prestige of a Government and damage its political prospects. On the other hand measures taken to resist devaluation are almost inevitably unpopular. Following on a prolonged deflationary depression, devaluation is liable to be welcomed with relief, and the Government, in deciding to devalue, stands to gain rather than lose politically. On the other hand a devaluation, and more especially repeated devaluations, during an inflationary period is liable to damage the Government's prestige, because it is rightly considered as a sign of weakness or an admission of having pursued mistaken policies. Well-timed devaluations may be useful politically as a 'shot in the arm' providing temporary relief before general elections.

Monetary policy may pursue a political objective also by conferring favour on some sectional interests. Pressure in favour of bimetallism in the United States during the nineties was inspired partly by the political end of securing the support of the silver-producing States. Even though it did not achieve its purpose it was found necessary to retain a limited monetary rôle for silver. To this day the United States Treasury is under obligation to buy silver, and its operations tend to produce some slight inflationary effect.

A policy of deliberate currency depreciation may be adopted by extreme Left regimes not only in pursuing the social objective of levelling down wealth and incomes, but also with the political objective of reducing the political power of undependable and hostile elements. Extreme Left regimes which consider it inexpedient to decree confiscation of private property without compensation can achieve the same end by more subtle devices of monetary policy. They can avoid uncompromising measures that are liable to encounter desperate resistance on the part of the owners of the confiscated property by paying them 'full' compensation in the form of Government Bonds which can subsequently be wiped out through a policy of progressive currency depreciation. On balance the effect of that policy is apt to be the same as that of nationalization without compensation, but its form may be considered to be politically more expedient by Left-wing Government which are not strong enough to pursue a frankly confiscatory policy.

Generally speaking the pursuit of political objectives with the aid of monetary policy is apt to be harmful rather than otherwise, both in the sphere of international affairs and in that of domestic politics. While there is much to be said in favour of placing monetary policy at the service of social progress, its use for political ends is very often indefensible. However, we live in an imperfect world in which those in power often yield to the temptation of misusing their control over monetary policy. Anyone examining the ends of monetary policy, not as they ought to be in an ideal world, but as they are, must pay due attention to open or concealed political motives without which his picture could not be complete.

CHAPTER NINETEEN

Other Objectives

THERE is an almost infinite variety of ends that monetary policy may pursue in addition to those dealt with in the foregoing chapters. Some of the ends of monetary policy dealt with briefly in this chapter are fully as important as most of those to which separate chapters were devoted. The reason why these ends are not dealt with here so extensively is that their subject-matter has been, or will be, covered in some other chapter from some different angle. For, to a large extent, most ends of monetary policy are liable to overlap with other ends. There is also much overlapping between ends and means.

From a very earlier period one of the objects of monetary policy was to ensure that the quantity of money at the disposal of the community should be adequate. Long before the connexion between an increase in the volume of money and the trend of prices or trade was realized it had been known that shortage of coins had been the source of many difficulties both to the ruler and to his subjects, and had hampered the normal functioning of the economic system. In a great many instances the object of debasement was to remedy the shortage. In modern times, too, during periods of runaway inflation when the rise in prices far exceeded the increase in the volume of money, and high prices necessitated a larger volume of money, the authorities decided to speed up the operation of the printing press for the purpose of meeting the increased monetary requirements. In emergency the status of money was conferred on various objects in order to overcome the grave difficulties caused by the inadequacy of monetary circulation. The quantity of money may be increased not in order to raise prices or to lower interest rates or to create employment, but solely for the sake of having enough money in circulation to satisfy the requirements of the community.

Reference was made in Chapter 12 to convertibility, whether in gold or in other currencies, as a means of expanding international trade. Convertibility may, however, be pursued also as an end of monetary policy for its own sake. A large section of expert opinion and public opinion is in favour of convertibility, not so much from the point of view of any advantages it may yield, but because it appears to symbolize economic freedom and the liberal way of life. Those who feel in such a way about it are convinced that the restoration and maintenance of the highest possible degree of convertibility should be made the foremost aim of monetary policy. In the United States this school of thought is represented by an influential group of economists favouring the restoration of the convertibility of the dollar into gold for domestic as well as international purposes, and even the resumption of the issue of gold coins. In Britain such an ambitious objective is considered clearly unattainable, but the restoration of the highest possible degree of convertibility of sterling into dollars and other 'hard' currencies is viewed with much favour in many quarters, even though it is strongly condemned in others.

The maintenance of stable interest rates may be an important objective of monetary policy. Instead of using changes in interest rates as means for affecting the volume of currency and credit or the tendency of exchange rates, various monetary devices may be applied for the purpose of preventing any fluctuations of interest rates. Such fluctuations are liable to disturb trade, and there are obvious advantages in keeping interest rates stable. French monetary policy for many years before the First World War attached considerable importance to the stability of the Bank Rate. The Bank of France resorted to various devices as an alternative to changing its re-discount rate, when the situation called for such changes. In given circumstances stable interest rates may have to be achieved at the cost of fluctuating price levels or fluctuating exchanges, or through the application of various controls or other devices. Usually the object of monetary policy is to keep interest rates stable at a low level. This policy of cheap money may also be an end in itself. All the anti-usury laws adopted everywhere for thousands of years pursued the end of cheap money for its own sake. There are many modern instances in which cheap money is the end of monetary policy. Since, however, cheap money is more frequently a means to other ends, we propose to deal with it in detail in a later chapter.

Influencing international capital movements is yet another possible objective of monetary policy. A capital influx may be encouraged not on account of its effect on exchange rates, gold reserves, or interest rates, but in order to secure capital resources unobtainable internally. A major objective of British monetary policy has always been the attraction of short-term funds to London in order to ensure international banking activity in which the City has specialized, and to stimulate international commercial activity which is assumed to result from London's prominence as an international banking centre. Amidst the difficulties of the inter-War period the British monetary authorities often sought to attract funds to London in order to strengthen sterling or to check an inconvenient decline of the gold reserve. In such instances the influencing of international capital movements was a means to an end. On the other hand when the object was to attract funds so as to enable the City to pursue its international financial functions then the influencing of capital movements may be considered to have been an end of monetary policy.

Monetary policy may aim not only at encouraging capital outflow, but also at discouraging it. It may place its devices at the service of encouraging or discouraging investment abroad. All these objectives are very often means to other ends, but not infrequently they are ends of monetary policy.

The maintenance or increase of the national income is another possible end of monetary policy. It is one of the recent additions to the list of monetary objectives. Until twenty years ago regulation of the size of the national income was not considered to be part of the functions of the Government. Indeed official national income statistics were in most countries non-existent. To-day most Governments possess elaborate statistical organizations for the purpose of calculating and estimating the national income. Even though much remains to be done in this respect the progress made since before the war has been truly remarkable.

The reason why national income has risen to prominence among objects of monetary policy is that under the conception that has developed in recent decades monetary trends largely depend on the size of national income. According to one school of thought, an increase in the volume of money would not in itself affect the price level were it not for its influence on the size of incomes. The idea did not make much headway during the twenties, when economic thought was largely dominated by the Quantity Theory of money which sought to establish arithmetical relations between the volume of money and the level of prices. During the thirties, however, increasing attention came to be paid to the connexion between monetary trends and the trends of national income. But it was not until after the Second World War that monetary policy in Britain and other countries came to be guided to some extent by the desire to influence the size of national income. More often than not this is a means to some other end. It is conceivable, however, that monetary measures may be taken mainly with the object of raising or lowering the national income.

Yet another end of monetary policy is the ironing out of minor fluctuations as distinct from the fight against major fluctuations such as business cycles or inflationary and deflationary trends. Monetary policy is very often employed for reducing minor fluctuations to a minimum, whether in the money market or the foreign exchange market. It is of course difficult to draw the dividing line between minor fluctuations and major trends. The monetary authorities may seek to counteract minor fluctuations because they are anxious to prevent them from developing into major movements. On other occasions, however, it is reasonably clear that there is no such danger, and the object of neutralizing minor fluctuations is to avoid such relatively minor disadvantages as they are liable to cause.

Seasonal fluctuations are among the movements which monetary policy may aim at preventing or moderating. In the old days when the Bank of England kept aloof from the foreign exchange market the dollar rate usually moved against sterling in the autumn as a result of seasonal demand in connexion with cotton imports and other crop movements. The fluctuations were limited by the operation of the gold points. Once the rate reached the figure at which it became profitable to ship gold it could not depreciate any further. Such restricted fluctuations did not cause much harm, as business firms were able to 'hedge' against them through forward exchange operations. Nevertheless, such seasonal movements, whether in exchange rates or interest rates, were liable to cause a certain inconvenience. Many Central Banks considered it their task to counteract them as far as possible by means of intervention in the foreign exchange market or the money market. From 1932 till 1951 it was the policy of the Bank of England to maintain discount rates virtually unchanged. From the outbreak of the Second World War until December, 1951, exchange rates were kept rigidly pegged. Since then sterling has been allowed to fluctuate within a narrow range. The discount rate policies pursued by various continental Central Banks aimed among other objectives at preventing a temporary rise in bill rates through seasonal demand during the busy seasons, such as the harvest period in predominantly agricultural countries.

Monetary policy may pursue ends of justice and equity. When a depreciation is unavoidable steps are taken occasionally to minimize the losses incurred by certain classes and the gains unjustifiably earned by other classes. This can be done through the operation of a sliding scale on the basis of which debts are valorized according to the value of currency at the time they were incurred. There can, of course, be no more than rough justice. The same may be said about arrangements under which wages, salaries, and other payments are linked to the cost of living index. Such devices usually pursue primarily social or economic, or even political ends. It is conceivable, however, that in some instances they were inspired largely by considerations of abstract justice and equity, irrespective of practical consequences.

With this chapter we have completed the examination of the ends of monetary policy. We have seen that the authorities, in deciding on their monetary measures, are in a position to pursue a wide variety of objectives. Our next task is to examine the wide variety of devices with the aid of which they may try to achieve the diverse ends of their monetary policies.

PART THREE

The Means of Monetary Policy

*

CHAPTER TWENTY

Alternative Means

THE foregoing chapters dealt with the ends which those responsible for decisions of monetary policy are in a position to pursue. In the following chapters we propose to deal with the means which are at their disposal and by which they may approach these ends.

Although certain means are frequently used to the same end, the same means may serve various ends and the same ends can be served by various means. Consequently the choice of the end does not necessarily pre-determine the choice of the means. There must be therefore two distinct sets of monetary policy decisions. The authorities must first decide the aims of their monetary policy and then the ways in which these aims could best be achieved. The deliberate choice of the ends of monetary policy is an essentially political decision and must always be taken on the highest level, even though the politicians ultimately responsible for the decisions may follow the advice of technical experts. The choice of means, on the other hand, is largely a technical decision and can often be taken on an administrative level. Nevertheless, even in this respect the political authority usually has the last word as far as major principles are concerned. For instance, it is for the Government and not the Central Bank or even the Treasury officials to decide whether a rise in prices should be prevented through price controls, credit restrictions, or a re-valuation of the currency or through some other means.

To the generation that has grown up since the suspension of the gold standard in 1931 it may appear almost incredible that a quarter of a century ago many Central Banks had practically a free hand in deciding the choice of the means of their country's monetary policy, and that very often they determined even its ends. To-day the only power left in the hands of Central Banks is the implementation of monetary policy decisions taken by Governments. It is only in the sphere of the technique of monetary practice that Central Banks still have a reasonably free hand. At the same time Treasuries are largely advised by Central Banks, and the latter thus retain a certain influence in the choice of means and, to a much less extent, even of ends.

The curtailment of the powers of Central Banks in respect of the choice of the means of monetary policy is to some extent due to the changed conception, under which monetary policy has come to be regarded as one of the Government's major responsibilities. To a very large extent, however, the change is due to the widening of the scope of monetary policy. A quarter of a century ago the range of the means among which Central Banks had to choose was limited. Tradition largely determined the devices to be applied in given situations. The choice of devices has widened remarkably in the lifetime of our generation. To-day it includes some means the application of which requires a major political decision. It is inconceivable, for instance, that the adoption or removal of exchange control or even its substantial modification could be decided upon by technical experts alone. Such decisions are necessarily taken on a Cabinet level. They are outside the sphere of Central Banks to the same extent as is the choice of the ultimate or intermediate ends which monetary policy must pursue. It is only when it comes to the actual application of the means selected by the Government that Central Banks still have a reasonably free hand.

In few economic spheres has there been such a remarkable change within the brief span of a quarter of a century as in that of monetary policy. We already saw in the foregoing chapters the extent to which the ends of monetary policy have become modified in our lifetime. Changes that have come about since the twenties in respect of the means of monetary policy have been if anything even more far-reaching. This is due to the coincidence of two influences. One of them was the realization through practical experience during the thirties that in given conditions traditional means of monetary policy are apt to be inadequate. The other was the influence of the teachings of Keynes, whose new monetary theories and practical monetary proposals have revolutionized the methods of monetary policy.

In the domestic sphere there were until recently relatively few alternative means to choose between. While they could choose between various techniques, the only policies which the monetary authorities had at their disposal were to regulate the quantity of money by direct intervention or by changing the level of interest rates. The application of these means was based on the assumption that demand was determined by the quantity of money and that price trends must therefore be influenced by determining the quantity of money. Most economists and monetary experts now regard this concept as out of date or at any rate over-simplified. It is now recognized that there are factors other than the total quantity of money which are liable to affect demand. The importance of the velocity of circulation of money has come to be realized by those responsible for decisions of monetary policy. They have also become aware that the effect of changes in the total volume of money is produced through the volume of the national income and its distribution, or the volume of saving and that of capital investment. To use Keynesian terminology, 'liquidity preference', affecting the volume of investment, and the 'propensity to consume', affecting the volume of consumer demand, are apt to play a decisive rôle.

It is no longer considered sufficient for the authorities to confine themselves to regulating the total quantity of money. It is now thought essential that they should endeavour to influence the volume of the national income – whether by influencing the volume of money or by some other means – and its distribution as between high and low income groups, as a means of determining the trend of prices. They are also expected to influence the trend of capital investment, not only its total but also its allocation as between the production of capital goods and consumer goods.

When the private sector of the national economy prefers to keep its funds in a liquid form official monetary policy may have to supplement private investment by public investment. When the propensity of the public to consume is inadequate monetary policy may have to apply devices to stimulate consumers' demand.

Monetary policy nowadays has to differentiate also between means stimulating production for the domestic market and production for exports. Indeed the authorities may even have to adopt means to encourage exports to certain areas and discourage them to other areas.

Even within the traditional sphere of determining the quantity of money, the means employed nowadays differ materially in many respects from those employed until comparatively recently. Changes in the Bank Rate no longer play such an essential part. On the other hand the relative importance of changing the volume of credit by means of open market operations has increased. In some countries such as the United States changes in the reserve requirements of commercial banks and adjustments of Treasury deposits play an important part.

In addition to determining the grand total of the volume of money, the new monetary policy tries to achieve its ends also by discriminating in favour of or against certain types of credits. There is a wide variety of devices of selective credit control. It is characteristic of the degree of encroachment of Governments on the preserves of Central Banks that even in respect of such administrative devices the decisions are now usually taken by the Treasuries.

The combination of financial controls with physical controls provided the authorities with a wide variety of new devices. The adoption and the application of such means is of course entirely a matter for the Government. It requires decisions on the highest level and very often the adoption or removal of controls also necessitates legislation.

Fiscal means of monetary policy are employed for determining the totals of incomes and their distribution, and also for encouraging or discouraging the production or consumption of certain types of goods. The Budget has come to be regarded as a most important means of monetary policy. Likewise Treasury operations are now among the weapons in its armoury. Throughout financial history monetary policy often served the end of facilitating Treasury operations. More recently relations have become reciprocal, and as often as not the timing and terms of Treasury issues serve the ends of monetary policy.

Various economic policies are adopted and followed with an eye on their effects on the monetary situation. Such policies may affect production, foreign trade, wages, etc. Indeed generally speaking it is true to say that most decisions in the sphere of economic policy are now taken with an eye on their monetary effects.

In the international sphere too the choice of a means of monetary policy has widened considerably. Under the gold standard the Bank Rate was supposed to be the only weapon, though some continental countries practised for many decades an elaborate *Devisen-Politik*, employing a variety of means. Even the Bank of England resorted at times to some special devices to discourage withdrawals of gold and to encourage gold imports. However, such measures were exceptional. During the thirties exchange control made its appearance, with its almost infinite variety of devices. A relatively recent development has been the adoption of international means of monetary policy by co-operation with monetary authorities of other countries or by the conclusion of international agreements and the operation of some international institution.

The choice of means of monetary policy is fully as controversial as the choice of its ends. There is the unending struggle between traditionalists and progressives. The trend is, however, towards the adjustment of traditionalist attitude to changing requirements. 'Orthodoxy keeps catching me up,' remarked Keynes in 1941 on the occasion of his election to the Court of Directors of the Bank of England. The former 'heretic', whose views on monetary policy had been for many years the main target of all traditionalist critics, was made one of the high priests of the temple of monetary orthodoxy, not because he recanted his heresies, but because they had been largely accepted by 1941 as part of the official creed.

CHAPTER TWENTY-ONE

The Quantity of Money

DETERMINATION of the quantity of money has always been regarded as one of the most important means of monetary policy. In the absence of official intervention to influence the quantity of money it is liable to be affected by a wide variety of factors, often not to the advantage of the community. The volume of money may become excessive or it may become inadequate to meet requirements. It is one of the supreme tasks of the monetary authorities to ensure that their community should have the correct quantity of money – that is, the quantity which the authorities rightly or wrongly consider to be correct in view of the ends which their monetary policy rightly or wrongly follows.

The maintenance or adjustment of the quantity of money may pursue many different ends. The most obvious end is to provide the community with the volume of money required for the smooth functioning of its economy. It is determined by the volume of business at the prevailing level of prices. Other ends, notably that of influencing the price level, have overshadowed the end of meeting the communities' normal monetary requirements. As we saw, however, in Chapter 19, the endeavour to satisfy the monetary requirements of the community influenced monetary policy long before the connexion between the quantity of money and its value was adequately realized. Kings and governments were unaware until comparatively recently that inadequacy of the quantity of money was liable to cause a fall in prices. They assumed that the rise in prices that followed debasements of coinage was entirely due to the lowering of the metallic value of the coins and not to the increase of their quantity.

Monetary action to prevent an increase in prices by preventing an increase in the quantity of money is a comparatively modern development. It is true it is encountered in a rudimentary form in primitive communities which, in many instances, selected monetary objects in order to ensure chronic monetary scarcity. They also sought to prevent an increase in the volume of money by the aid of religious taboos. For example, in certain communities monetary objects could only be collected at certain phases of the moon. In many instances surplus quantities of the monetary material were systematically eliminated through their destruction by means of religious sacrifices, or were hoarded as ornaments in places of worship or palaces.

The State authority was often confronted with problems arising from an excessive volume of debased coins. Generally speaking, however, until the advent of paper money with its unlimited possibilities of increasing the supply of currency, the problem of Governments was not to keep down the volume of money, but to raise it. It is true that from time to time re-coinage transactions resulted in a deliberate reduction in the volume of currency. This was, however, merely an incidental result of the policy aiming at an improvement of the quality of currency by increasing its metallic content.

The discovery that changes in the quantity of money are liable to affect prices is generally attributed to Jean Baudin, who put forward his theory to that effect in 1568. In fact he was preceded by Copernicus, who in his treatise on debasement remarked in 1526 that money tends to depreciate when it becomes too abundant. It took a long time from the discovery of this truth before the monetary authorities came to adopt deliberate policies aiming at influencing the trend of prices by changing the volume of money.

During the paper currency inflations of the eighteenth century the European Governments had to learn through bitter experience the effect of an increase in the volume of paper money on the level of prices – a lesson which Chinese rulers had learnt and had forgotten again and again some centuries earlier. They adopted policies endeavouring to limit the expansion of the note issue, though under the pressure of military requirements these limits had to be raised. Systematic intervention to regulate the volume of currency and credit in the interest of maintaining a stable price level did not make its appearance until the nineteenth century. It has been brought to a fine art during the present century. The aim of such intervention to influence prices by regulating the quantity of money was not necessarily the maintenance of stability. During the thirties the declared policy of the United States and other countries was one of 'reflation', aiming at raising the price level, in order to correct some of the bad effects of the preceding slump, partly by deliberately increasing the volume of money. In much more frequent instances the authorities adopted a policy of deliberately reducing the volume of money in an effort to lower the price level.

Another object monetary policy has often pursued by influencing the volume of money is the safeguarding of the balance of payments. If the price level in a country is too high compared with other countries, it is liable to handicap exports and stimulate imports, because foreign competitors at home and abroad are able to quote lower prices. The result is an adverse trade balance causing a weak trend of the exchange value of the currency and a decline of the gold or foreign exchange reserve. One of the ways in which this situation can be remedied is by forcing down the domestic price level by deflation, that is, by reducing the volume of money.

Yet another object that can be pursued by means of influencing the volume of money is the maintenance, increase, or reduction of interest rates. Relations between the level of interest rates and the quantity of money are, of course, reciprocal. The quantity of money can be influenced by raising or lowering interest rates, because there is more inducement to borrow at low than at high rates. On the other hand, interest rates can be caused to rise by reducing the volume of money and they can be caused to fall by increasing monetary supplies in accordance with the law of supply and demand. The monetary authorities are in a position to decide at which end they should initiate their intervention. Often it is initiated simultaneously at both ends.

Determination of the quantity of money is a most important means to the end of controlling business cycles. The trend of trade responds to changes in the volume of money in three ways. An increase in the volume of money tends to stimulate business activities by providing the means for financing an expansion; by encouraging production and the purchase of goods through causing prices to rise; and by creating an atmosphere of optimism. A reduction in the volume of money tends to produce the opposite effect by curtailing the financial facilities available for business; by discouraging production and consumers' demand as a result of a falling trend in prices; and by generating an atmosphere of pessimism.

A policy of monetary expansion is one of the most effective means of achieving and maintaining full employment. By itself it is not always capable of attaining that end. An increase in the volume of money available for producers and consumers does not necessarily mean that producers and consumers will take advantage of the increased facilities offered. In given circumstances monetary expansion has to be supplemented by other employment-creating devices. Even so, most such additional devices involve an increase in monetary requirements, so that they can only be carried out through an increase in the volume of money. Monetary expansion must accompany an increase of employment, whether as its cause or its effect. More money is required to finance a larger volume of employment. If the authorities prevent an increase in the volume of money to meet the increased requirements a scarcity of money is liable to develop and to cause a fall in employment.

In mediaeval times the State authority often endeavoured to bring about an increase in the volume of coinage in order to facilitate revenue collection. This means of expanding the volume of money in the interests of the Treasury exists in modern times to an even higher degree. While during the Middle Ages it was in many instances possible to collect revenue partly in kind, this solution is inconceivable in modern conditions. A policy of moderate monetary expansion is found useful for ensuring an increase of taxation receipts without having to resort to increasing the rates of taxation. Treasuries may also favour from time to time an increase in the volume of money in order to facilitate the issue of Government loans, or the conversion of maturing loans, or the funding of floating debt on favourable terms.

The device of increasing the volume of money can be used effectively for a wide variety of social or political ends. It is possible to step up the pace of the development of the Welfare State provided that the Government is prepared to embark on monetary expansion. The same means can serve in a different way the ends of equalitarian social policy; an increase in the volume of money causes its value to depreciate, and this tends to level down wealth. In the political sphere monetary expansion is a preliminary condition of a rearmament drive on any substantial scale. Modern wars are inconceivable without monetary expansion to finance increased military requirements. In domestic policies it is possible to achieve popularity by increasing Government spending through creating real or fictitious prosperity by means of monetary expansion.

Hitherto we have been dealing with the device of determining the volume of money in a general way, with only casual references to the type of money concerned. Until the end of the seventeenth century money meant in Europe almost exclusively coins and any monetary policy had to concern itself with determining the volume of coinage. Paper money became more or less universally adopted in Europe during the eighteenth century. Until the First World War notes circulated jointly with coins, and it was one of the most important tasks of monetary policy to regulate their issue. This task came to be increasingly overshadowed during the nineteenth century by the task of regulating the volume of credit. There are still even now a number of countries in which currency plays a more important part than credit. These include the comparatively backward countries with no adequately developed credit system, but also some highly-advanced countries such as France, with a widespread habit of hoarding notes in preference to keeping bank accounts. On the other hand, in Britain, the United States, and many other countries it is the volume of credit rather than that of notes – coins have disappeared from circulation except as token money – that matters from the point of view of monetary policy. In such countries the volume of notes is largely determined not by the authorities, but by the public, who draw on their bank balances if they need more cash and pay into their accounts any superfluous notes. The control of the volume of credit has come to be regarded in such countries as by far the most important means at the disposal of the monetary authorities.

Changes in the volume of money must be related to changes in the requirements of the community. The same amount of money may be inadequate at a given moment and may become adequate or even excessive through changes in requirements. Such changes may be due to an increase or decrease of the population or of the territory on which the money is used. The size of requirements may be affected by changes in the scope within which money fulfils its functions. Any change from natural economy to money economy or *vice versa* affects requirements. So does the extension or reduction of the rôle played by money in its various capacities. The employment of devices resulting in economies in the use of money or their abandonment materially influences requirements.

Monetary requirements bear a close relation to the volume of goods. Any increase in the volume of goods offered for sale calls for a corresponding increase in the quantity of money if the authorities wish to maintain the same degree of relative scarcity or abundance of money, and if they want to avoid a change in the price level. In given circumstances the maintenance of the volume of money at the same level may mean the creation of scarcity or abundance as a result of changes in the requirements due to changes in the volume of goods or to any of the circumstances mentioned above. This means that the quantity of money can be changed in the absolute sense by altering its actual amount or in a relative sense by leaving its actual amount unchanged in face of changed requirements.

The increase in the volume of money is not necessarily inflationary. It may be due to an increased desire to hold cash, such as developed in the U.S.A. after the Wall Street slump, and after the banking crisis of 1933. The Second World War resulted in an increase of the cash holdings of the public in Britain owing to the possibility of a destruction of banks through air raids. Any grave uncertainty, political or economic, is liable to produce the same result. Such increase in the volume of money does not in itself mean inflation. The cash or deposits may be held not for the purpose of immediate expenditure, but as a liquid form of capital. But the possession of relatively large liquid assets increases the temptation of, and opportunity for, spending, and is therefore a potential source of inflation.

CHAPTER TWENTY-TWO

The Monetary Circulation

IN communities which have no modern banking system, or in which the public has not acquired the banking habit to a very high degree, the device of regulating the quantity of money is practised mainly by regulating the quantity of currency, that is notes, coins or such other objects as may serve for monetary purposes. Originally the volume of currency was determined by factors largely outside the control of the State authorities. Primitive commodity currencies were often produced or imported on private initiative. Moreover, it was usually possible to switch monetary objects from non-monetary to monetary use or *vice versa*. The quantity of commodity-currencies was liable to become reduced through wastage or export. In many instances, however, we encounter at an early stage intervention on the part of the State authority to determine the volume of circulating media. The production or import of monetary objects was made the monopoly of the tribal authority, or the increase of that quantity on private initiative was prevented by tribal laws or religious taboos.

The rôle of the State in determining the quantity of currency became particularly important with the advent of coinage, which in the early period of monetary history was usually a State monopoly. The minting of coins was the prerogative of kings, or of the authorities of City States, though coins of other States were often allowed to circulate within the community. Coins were minted when the authorities considered it necessary. During later centuries, however, this monopoly became relaxed. Free coinage developed either by a cession of the rights of coinage to private mints, or at any rate by making it possible for anyone in possession of monetary metals to have them coined at the Mint. Under such a system there could be no absolute official control over the quantity of new coins. Nevertheless, the State authority possessed various means with which to influence the monetary circulation. It was in a position to encourage or discourage the mining of monetary metals. In many countries this was actually a State monopoly. Elsewhere the State was in a position to forbid or stimulate the working of privately owned metal resources. Colonial powers were able to assist in the development of the mining resources in their colonies. They could import the stocks of precious metals seized in conquered territories. On the other hand, there are also instances of official discouragement of the mining of precious metals. This was done by some rulers in ancient China, where precious metal deposits were only worked during periods when the Government wanted to increase the quantity of money.

Another way in which the State authority sought to influence the quantity of coin was by preventing the export of coin and of precious metals in general. In England such restrictions were in force from the early Plantagenet period right to the beginning of the nineteenth century. They will be dealt with in the chapter on exchange restrictions. According to contemporary opinion they were largely ineffective in preventing the outflow of monetary metals. Other legislative measures endeavoured to ensure that the proceeds of certain exports were repatriated in the form of precious metals.

Debasements were a very important device frequently resorted to by kings for the purpose of preventing a decline in the volume of money or securing its increase. Admittedly debasements could also pursue other objectives such as securing a revenue for the king in the form of profit on re-coinage. In a large proportion of instances, however, debasements were undertaken mainly if not exclusively for the purpose of checking the outflow of coins and their disappearance through melting down and hoarding. Whenever there was an adverse trade balance it resulted in a drain on the monetary resources of the country. The full-weighted coins were exported in payment for goods imported. The price of the monetary metal – whether gold or silver – tended to rise above the official mint price, and no metals were brought to the mint, so that the issue of new coins came to a stand-still. As a result of debasements abroad foreign mints offered nominally higher prices for the monetary metals. There was, moreover, always a tendency for good coins to disappear in melting-pots and in hoards, leaving clipped and worn coins in circulation. Bad money tended to drive out good money.

Very often the Government resorted to the remedy of raising the mint price of the monetary metals in order to check the drain, and to attract more metals to the mint both through import and through de-hoarding. This device was condemned almost universally by early writers on the sub-ject, largely on the ground that, taking a long view, debase-ments could not make much difference to the import and export of monetary metals which depended on the balance of payments in the long run. In reality debasements were helpful from the point of view of stimulating exports and discouraging imports. This was because of the inelasticity of domestic price levels. The lowering of the metallic value of the national currency was not followed immediately by a corresponding rise in prices. Consequently the goods of the country which had recently debased its currency were cheap for foreigners and foreign goods became relatively ex-pensive for domestic consumers. The balance of payments tended to improve, temporarily at any rate, until domestic prices had adjusted themselves to the debased value of the currency or – what occurred much more frequently – until other countries in turn also debased their currencies. Throughout the Middle Ages and the centuries that fol-lowed there was a competitive debasement race. Before the heavy inflow of precious metals from the newly-discovered America during the sixteenth and seventeenth centuries, the declared object of this currency depreciation race was to participate in the international scramble for the inadequate stock of monetary metals.

Measures taken by governments to increase the volume of money through the trade balance were not confined to debasements. One of the main objects of the mercantilist policy, which remained dominant right to the second half of the eighteenth century, was to ensure an adequate monetary supply by securing a big export surplus. Even in modern times right up to our days, governments which would emphatically disclaim pursuing mercantilist policies seek to secure a favourable balance of payments for the sake of strengthening the gold reserves. Although since the suspension of the gold standard the quantity of currency no longer depends on the amount of gold holdings, a decline of the gold reserve is liable to force the Government to adopt credit restrictions in order to improve the balance of payments and thus to improve its gold position.

Yet another means by which governments endeavoured to maintain or increase the quantity of currency was by attracting foreign capital. This was done to a relatively moderate degree until the nineteenth century, when it became one of the principal means for countries with adverse trade balances to maintain or increase their monetary stock. By that time it was not so much the volume of coins that mattered as the amount of notes that could be increased under the rules of metallic standards by means of importing monetary metal out of the proceeds of foreign loans.

Governments sought on many occasions to remedy the evils of currency shortage by encouraging or confirming the use of substitute currencies whenever this was considered inevitable. The North American colonies and the West Indies which suffered from a particularly troublesome and chronic shortage of coins had tried to solve their problem by the monetary use of a wide variety of commodities. Usually the staple products of the country were adopted for that purpose. Although in many instances their adoption as currencies was spontaneous, the State authority usually officially recognized them sooner or later, and regulated their monetary use. Tobacco, skins, and furs, cereals, pork, beef, timber, hemp, sugar, rum, cotton, etc., were made legal tender at one time or another in various North American colonies or in the West Indies. Although the use of such commodity-currencies had obvious disadvantages, it certainly relieved the scarcity of currency which would otherwise have gravely handicapped the development of these countries. In many instances the volume of these commodity-currencies increased to an embarrassing extent as a result of their monetary use, and the Governments felt compelled to intervene in order to curtail their production. This was done repeatedly and unsuccessfully in Virginia and other tobacco-growing colonies where tobacco was used as a currency.

The most effective method by which Governments came to be able to determine the volume of currency after the beginning of the eighteenth century was the issue of paper money. When the Bank of England was established it began to operate as a bank of issue. To a large degree, however, the issue of paper money was confined in England before the Napoleonic Wars to providing a convenient substitute for metallic currency rather than increasing substantially the total volume of currency. On the other hand France, the United States, and other countries soon discovered unlimited possibilities of increasing the volume of money with the aid of the printing press.

After some disastrous experiments in paper money inflation the advanced countries settled down during the relatively stable period of the nineteenth century to systems of restricted note issues. Under the established practices of metallic standards there was a self-imposed limitation on the quantity of notes to be issued. The Central Banks which in most countries were put in charge of the note issue had to maintain a certain percentage of note cover in the form of precious metals or eligible foreign exchanges. The size of these reserves set a natural if elastic limit to the extent to which it was possible to increase the volume of currency. In other countries such as Britain the banks of issue were authorized to issue notes up to a certain fixed amount in excess of their metallic reserves. Within the limits set by these various regulations the Central Banks or the Governments were in a position to pursue their monetary policies by determining the volume of currency.

After the adoption of paper money and before the development of the modern credit system the regulation of the volume of notes in circulation constituted one of the most important devices of monetary policy. While the regulation of the quantity of coins throughout many centuries consisted mostly of efforts to increase the volume in order to meet requirements the regulation of the note circulation consisted mostly of efforts to keep down or reduce the volume. The temptation to over-issue was very strong ever since paper money was first invented. Apart altogether from note issues for the purpose of financing wars, there was always pressure on Governments to relax the self-imposed limitations of note issues. Until the end of the Napoleonic Wars those opposed to currency inflation were fighting a losing battle in most countries.

It was largely during the nineteenth century that a system emerged under which note issues came under automatic limitation. Whatever anybody may say against the gold standard it must be admitted that it played an important historical rôle in compelling Governments to discipline themselves in respect of the use of the printing press. The solution of budgetary problems by means of paper money inflation was too easy, much easier than debasements in earlier centuries. There was strong temptation to take the line of least resistance. The adoption of the gold standard – or for that matter the bimetallic standard that operated in the majority of countries during the greater part of the nineteenth century – compelled Governments to exercise a certain degree of self-denial in order to maintain the metallic standard in operation. Most Governments went considerably out of their way to avoid the suspension of the convertibility of their notes, and their Central Banks pursued cautious policies to that end. Treasuries abstained as far as possible from drawing on the Central Banks in time of peace and Central Banks kept the private sector of the economy permanently on short ration.

This over-cautious attitude of most Central Banks during the reign of the gold standard has been subject to much criticism. Beyond doubt it handicapped economic progress during periods when the output of gold and silver was low. It was also detrimental from the point of view of social welfare. Nevertheless, viewed from the perspective of history it must be admitted that this was a useful and necessary phase in the evolution of monetary policy. Owing to the novelty of the device of paper currency and bank-credit money it was essential that Governments and public opinion should be made to realize the need for self-restraint in the use of this device. It was necessary to educate mankind how to use paper currency and bank credit without grossly abusing it, and the gold standard was very useful from this point of view.

The self-imposed limitations aimed at preventing excessive issue of notes assumed various forms. Convertibility into gold and/or silver was a powerful deterrent from unlimited increase of quantity. Indeed the original idea of paper money in Britain was that it was merely a more convenient medium of exchange than coins, and that notes issued by the Bank of England and other banks of issue must have full metallic cover. Then the 'fiduciary issue' – an amount by which the note issue was allowed to exceed the gold reserve – made its appearance. Originally very small, the fiduciary issue increased materially from the late twenties, and especially during and after the Second World War. From 1928 it became possible to raise the limit by administrative action. Increases of £50 million or more were a frequent occurrence and hardly attracted any attention. Any self-imposed limitation of the note issue has relative value only, since Governments with a majority in Parliament are always in a position to amend legislation and increase the ceiling of the note issue.

Nor was the alternative system under which there had to be a certain percentage of metallic cover any more effective except during normal and stable periods. Whenever there was pressure in favour of raising the note issue it was always possible for Governments and Parliaments to set aside or relax the provisions regarding reserve requirements.

Another method by which it was sought to limit the note issue was through the establishment of more or less independent privately-owned Central Banks. Their relations with Treasuries were governed by the terms of their charter which was granted for a definite period and confirmed by Acts of Parliament. Although there were many instances of Central Banks resisting the Government's demand for inflationary note issues, generally speaking they had been subservient to Treasuries. In any case many of them lost their legal independence after the War through nationalization.

Beyond doubt technically and politically it is much easier to-day for Governments to inflate the note issues than it was during the nineteenth century or even during the inter-War period. The notes are no longer convertible into gold, and such reserve requirements or ceilings of note issues as are in force are much more elastic. Notwithstanding this, the evil of currency inflation as such has not increased, because in the meantime credit inflation has become the principal danger as a result of the development of the credit system in the financially advanced countries. Monetary inflation in such countries no longer assumes the form of Government borrowing from the Central Bank and putting the borrowed notes into circulation. That crude form of inflation has been replaced by a much more subtle and sophisiticated form of credit inflation to be dealt with in the next chapter.

The volume of currency continues to play an important part as a means of monetary policy in countries which either do not possess a well-developed banking system or where the habit of keeping bank accounts is not widely adopted. In particular in British colonies with Currency Boards instead of Central Banks the size of the note issue is of the utmost importance from the point of view of economic trends. The disadvantage of that system is that the authorities cannot control adequately the size of the note issue. Notes are issued against the surrender of sterling to the Currency Board. They remain in circulation until demand for sterling by importers and others absorbs them. The monetary authorities have no direct means of neutralizing an excessive increase or decrease of the note issue.

In countries with a well-developed deposit banking system the size of the note issue is a passive rather than an active factor. An increase of the note issue is usually the effect rather than the cause of the rise in prices or of the expansion of business activity. In possession of large bank deposits the private sector of the economy is always in a position to satisfy its increased requirements of notes by drawing on these deposits. Conversely, whenever the note issue is in excess of requirements the surplus automatically finds its way back into the banks and increases the size of the deposits. If the monetary authorities wish to stimulate trade by increasing the volume of money they do so usually by causing an expansion credit rather than by increasing their note issue. Conversely if they want to discourage an inflationary rise of prices or a speculative boom, their means to that end is a curtailment of the volume of credit and not a cut in the note issue.

Nevertheless, situations are apt to arise which call for intervention in the sphere of the note circulation. In a number of Continental countries the note circulation increased considerably during the Second World War and continued to increase after it. As a drastic deflationary measure a number of Governments decreed the exchange or stamping of the notes, and blocked a large percentage of the notes surrendered, or retained it in the form of a levy or a compulsory loan. Such mopping-up operations were necessary to correct a currency inflation which would otherwise have caused much difficulty. Generally speaking, however, regulation of the note issue plays a secondary part in advanced countries among the means with which monetary authorities seek to control trends. While it still represents an important proportion of the liquid resources of the community the monetary authorities find it more convenient to concentrate on the regulation of the volume of credit on the assumption that the note issue automatically adjusts itself to changes brought about by credit restrictions or expansions.

Even so, the importance of the amount of currency should not be underrated. It is a very useful index showing the general trend. Although the authorities do not as a rule initiate a change in the volume of money by increasing or reducing the note issue, the figures of the note issue indicate whether or not such action is called for. They also show whether the Government's action has been successful.

CHAPTER TWENTY-THREE

The Volume of Credit

IN modern communities determination of the volume of credit plays such an important part among the means of monetary policy that many people when writing about monetary policy can think only in terms of official intervention to expand, maintain, or restrict credit. Yet, although regulation of the volume of credit played some part in monetary policy in earlier centuries, until modern times the possibilities of increasing or decreasing the volume of money by means of expanding or contracting bank credits were limited. Banking consisted largely of re-lending the moneys represented by the coins left with the banks on deposit. Facilities to increase the volume of credit beyond that of the coins on deposit were limited. Indeed, since the owners of these coins were in a position to withdraw their deposits their bankers had to retain a fairly high percentage of cash reserve in order to meet such withdrawals. There had been early instances of modern banking credit, but as a general rule all that the banker had done in earlier periods of banking history was to lend part of the coins whose owner temporarily relinquished their use.

The system under which it is possible to create large quantities of money through the operation of bank credits and deposits is a modern development. It owes its existence to two fundamental changes. One is the increased confidence of the public in the banks, as a result of which the latter need not keep more than a small fraction of their assets in the form of cash. Before banks became strong and confidence-inspiring they had to keep a large proportion of their assets in a liquid form in order to be able to meet any possible sudden withdrawals. As and when confidence in their solvency and liquidity increased, they were able gradually to lend a larger and larger proportion of their resources and to reduce the proportion of their liquid reserves without running undue risks. Moreover, as the banks grew bigger it became increasingly evident that insolvency of any one of them was liable to produce a run on other banks with disastrous consequences. For this reason there was an increasing degree of co-operation between banks and also between the banks and the monetary authorities. Thanks to such co-operation it became safer to reduce the ratio of cash reserve, because banks could reasonably rely on being supported by other banks or by the authorities in case of sudden heavy withdrawals of deposits. As a result of all these influences the banks are now in a position to lend or invest amounts many times larger than their own capital and reserves or their cash holdings.

The other change that has contributed to the development of the modern credit system with its capacity to expand the volume of money is the widespread adoption of the practice of keeping banking accounts. So long as the number of firms or individuals who possess banking accounts was relatively small the power of banks to create additional money was limited. The larger part of the money they had lent was withdrawn in the form of notes which did not find their way back to banks so that they could not be re-lent to other borrowers. It was only as and when most members of the business community and a fair proportion of private individuals came to possess bank accounts that the banks acquired their present remarkable power of adding to the total volume of money.

In countries such as France where the banking habit is not so widespread much of the proceeds of a bank loan is liable to be hoarded and the notes do not find their way back to the bank. In Britain, on the other hand, even if the recipients of the payments made through a bank credit do not themselves possess bank accounts, the money sooner or later – usually sooner – finds its way to someone with a bank account. Before the notes issued to some recipient without account change hands many times, most of them are paid to someone who pays them into a bank account.

They thus become once more available for re-lending. This is the explanation of the development of the process aptly described by Whittlesey in his *Readings in Money and Banking* as 'one of the marvels of a complex financial society'. What happens is that the amounts lent by banks return to them again and again in the form of additional deposits and become available for being lent again and again. The fact that the proceeds of a bank loan need not necessarily return to the same bank makes no difference so long as the banking system as a whole gets it.

Moreover, in many countries it is the practice of banks that, when they grant an overdraft to a customer, they credit his account with its amount. The overdraft immediately assumes the form of an additional deposit even before it is spent.

From the foregoing it might appear that banks have unlimited power to increase the volume of credit. This would be so in the absence of any rule that a certain proportion of deposits has to be kept in a liquid form. Even though the proportion is now smaller than it was in the past, the necessity of observing the rules tends to handicap banks in expanding credit. If as a result of credit expansion the total volume of deposits increases while the amount of total cash is unaffected, the ratio of cash to deposits declines. Although in Britain as in many other countries there is no statutory limit below which the cash ratio of banks is not allowed to decline, in practice the British banks regard eight per cent as the minimum. This means that banks are in a position to extend credit until the increase of their deposits is about twelve-and-a-half times the amount of their cash, the latter item including also their balances with the Bank of England. Although eight per cent is the conventional minimum for practical purposes it is also the approximate maximum. For it is to the interest of the banks to employ profitably the largest possible proportion of their resources and to keep down their idle cash reserves to the lowest possible figure compatible with the recognized rules of liquidity. They adhere therefore very closely to the traditional cash ratio which in their experience is sufficient to meet any with-drawals that may reasonably be expected to occur at short notice. As a result of this practice there is a tendency for the volume of bank credits to fluctuate in sympathy with the bank cash.

It is because of these characteristics of the system that the monetary authorities have in practice a very close control over the volume of credit. For they are in a position to in-crease or lower at will the amount of the total cash reserves of the banking system, thereby causing a rise or fall in the total volume of bank credits and bank deposits.

Under the gold standard the banks' cash reserves were liable to fluctuations that were not initiated by the mone-tary authorities. An inflow of gold increased the volume of bank cash and an outflow reduced it. Central Banking under that system consisted largely of influencing gold movements and the volume of credit by means of raising and lowering the Bank Rate, thereby discouraging or en-couraging the demand for credit. Until comparatively recently direct intervention of the monetary authorities to regulate the volume of credit through determining the volume of bank cash played a relatively subordinate part. The Bank Rate was the principal instrument with the aid of which Central Banks sought to cause an expansion or contraction of credit. They increased or reduced re-dis-counting and other lending facilities to supplement their Bank Rate policy. Generally speaking, however, they en-deavoured to achieve their end largely through the psycho-logical effect of the Bank Rate changes. Official intervention to control the volume of credit was rather vague and in-direct under that system. The authorities engaged from time to time in open market operations, but it is only during the last thirty years or so that the system of direct and more precise control of the volume of credit has developed.

The main causes of the development of direct credit con-trol may be summarized as follows:

(1) International monetary and economic instability fol-lowed the First World War. The degree of equilibrium that

existed before 1914 was never restored for any length of
time after 1918. During the twenties, when some form of
gold standard operated in a large number of countries,
gold reserves and foreign exchange reserves which served
as the basis of the credit structure were exposed to sudden
and substantial fluctuations. Under the old system this
would have led to very considerable contractions and expansions of credit, causing sharp falls and rises of the price
level and of employment. It was considered necessary,
therefore, to adopt a managed form of gold standard under
which the effects of the fluctuations on the metallic reserve
on the volume of credit were largely offset.

(2) Simultaneously with this change and not unconnected with it, monetary science made considerable progress. A new generation of Central Bankers and Treasury
officials was both able and willing to depart from the automatic system practised by their predecessors. Although
their progress towards the adoption of scientific monetary
management was not so rapid as radical monetary reformers such as Keynes would have liked it to be, nevertheless, viewed from the perspective of history, it must now
be regarded as having been almost revolutionary.

(3) The suspension of the gold standard in most countries
during the thirties removed the link between the volume of
metallic reserve and that of credit. It became necessary for
the monetary authorities to elaborate new practices with
which to determine the volume of credit instead of leaving
it to the free play of natural trends.

(4) From the thirties onwards monetary policy came to
pursue to an increasing degree broader economic and social
ends calling for low and stable interest rates. To that end
it became necessary for the monetary authorities to take
an active hand in determining the supply of credit as a
means for maintaining interest rates at the desired level.

One of the older devices that has been used more extensively since the War is the fixing of a rediscount ceiling by
which the extent to which the banks can automatically draw
upon the facilities of the Central Bank is limited. This device

was applied in France, where, in October 1948, a rediscount ceiling was established for each commercial bank in addition to the overall maximum fixed for the banking system as a whole. Once a bank exhausted its limit it was not granted any further rediscount facilities by the Bank of France. This measure was not so severe, however, as may appear at first sight. The ceiling was fixed at something like 20 per cent above the actual figures of rediscounts at the time of its imposition. Moreover, the ceiling was repeatedly increased as and when the volume of rediscounts approached it. Above all, certain types of bills were exempted from the ceiling, and this provided a loophole through which the attempted credit restriction was circumvented.

In Germany, too, a ceiling was introduced, not to rediscount facilities but to the total of acceptance credits the banks were allowed to grant. The amount fixed in October, 1950, was reduced by 10 per cent in the following month. Denmark was another country which adopted a rediscount ceiling at the time of the Korean War. In 1951 Germany introduced drastic regulations limiting overall commercial bank credits and compelling commercial banks to reduce the amount of credits within three months in accordance with quotas fixed by the Government. A variant of this device was applied in some countries in the form of fixing statutory ratios between the liabilities and liquid assets of the banks or between their liabilities and their capital resources.

In respect of statutory reserve requirements the United States adopted an elaborate system which played a prominent part in American monetary policy for the last thirty years. Member banks of the Federal Reserve System are required to hold on deposit with the Federal Reserve Banks a percentage of their deposits. The Federal Reserve Board is authorized to change, within prescribed limits, the percentage of these requirements. In order to restrict credit the Federal Reserve Board raises the percentage of Reserve requirements and it takes the opposite course when it considers it expedient to expand credit.

The example of the United States was followed by South Africa, New Zealand, India, and some Latin American countries before the Second World War. Indeed in recent years statutory authority for Central Banks to fix and change reserve requirements has become a widely adopted feature in new Central Bank legislation. Belgium, Sweden, and Western Germany are among the countries that adopted the system after the War. The original idea behind the system was to safeguard the interests of depositors. Subsequently it was discovered that the power to adjust reserve requirements constitutes a very effective means of monetary policy because it was liable to influence the volume of credit. It was used extensively by a number of countries during the inflation that followed the outbreak of the Korean War. In the United States its use has long become a matter of normal routine.

In India all banks have to maintain minimum reserves with the Central Bank. In many countries the reserves may assume the form of Government securities held on deposit with the Central Bank. In some countries the device takes the form of making it compulsory for banks to hold additional reserves against increases of their deposits. This system was adopted in Australia in 1941. Commercial banks have to maintain a certain proportion of their new assets on special account with the Commonwealth Bank. During the War almost the total of increases over 1939 had to be deposited with the Commonwealth Bank, but after the War the proportion was reduced to 45 per cent, only to be increased again to 60 after the outbreak of the Korean War. Similar measures were adopted by France, Italy, the Netherlands, and some Latin-American countries.

In addition to these various measures affecting the total volume of credit many countries employed devices limiting credits for specific purposes. We propose to deal with these devices in a later chapter.

By far the most important means for regulating the volume of credit is direct intervention to increase or reduce the amount of cash in the hands of banks, by means of official operations in Government securities. These operations are usually known under the name of open market policy, even though they do not necessarily assume the form of buying or selling of Government securities in the open market on official account. As we shall see in the chapter dealing with Treasury operations, the management of the public debt provides Treasuries with the opportunity for increasing or reducing the volume of publicly-held Government securities by the timing of the issues and maturities. If this is not sufficient to achieve the desired end of expanding or restricting credit it can be supplemented by open market operations proper. Central Banks can buy or sell Government securities in order to bring about the desired change in the volume of credit. Any purchase of Government securities by the authorities places additional money in the hands of the private sector of the national economy, increases the amount of the banks' cash reserves, and enables the banks to expand credit to an amount that is a multiple of that increase. Any sale of Government securities by the authorities withdraws money from the private sector of the national economy. It reduces the amount of the banks' cash reserves and enforces a contraction of credit amounting to a multiple of the amounts involved in the sale.

In addition to this highly powerful weapon the United States Government is in a position to adjust the volume of bank cash with the aid of a very simple device – that of changing the volume of its deposits held in commercial banks. This device does not exist in Britain. It is true that the commercial banks are used as channels for collection and remittance of funds by the Revenue Departments, and the spending Departments keep accounts with these banks where the Bank of England has no branches. Large amounts are always in the pipeline, but they simply serve the convenience of the Departments concerned. It is not the British practice to adjust these amounts in accordance with considerations of monetary policy. On the contrary, between 1940 and 1951 the reverse of this device was applied in Britain. Under the system of Treasury Deposits the commercial banks were compelled to surrender to the authorities each week an amount prescribed by the Treasury. With the aid of this device the Treasury was in a position to adjust the volume of bank cash. It involved a high degree of compulsion, and it was abandoned by the Conservative Government soon after assuming office in 1951. Indeed even the Socialist Government had intended to abandon it in due course.

We have seen above that Treasuries and Central Banks possess very extensive powers for determining the volume of credit. This does not necessarily mean that they always make full use of their powers. For various reasons they may think it expedient to relinquish the initiative for determining the volume of credit systematically and confine themselves to intervening for special purposes only. For instance the rigid pursuit of a policy of cheap money meant that, for the sake of keeping interest rates stabilized at a low level, the authorities automatically provided any amount of money that was needed in order to avoid a tightening of credit conditions. If for no matter what reason credit requirements increased in the London market during the period between the outbreak of the Second World War and November, 1951, the additional financial resources were automatically provided by the authorities in order to avoid an increase of Treasury Bill rates above the level at which the official policy wanted it to remain.

Another way in which the authorities can relinquish the initiative is by the issue of Government Loans which are 'on tap', that is, to which the public can subscribe at any time, and the total of which is not fixed. Such issues in Britain are the Savings Certificates and Defence Bonds. It is true that if the amount subscribed mops up too much or too little of credit resources, the authorities are in a position to adjust the situation through increasing or reducing the weekly amounts of Treasury Bills issued by tenders or through open market operations, or by other means at their disposal.

By pursuing the end of maintaining short-term interest

rates at a fixed level the authorities relinquish the scientific device of adjusting the volume of money in accordance with the requirements of stability. If the agents acting on behalf of the Government are always prepared to buy Government securities at a more or less fixed price this enables the banks to increase their cash reserves by turning into cash – 'monetizing' is the technical term – their Treasury Bills and other Government securities. In the absence of Government intervention if banks or other private holders want to sell Government securities they have to find private buyers who are willing to buy at a price, and the money paid for the securities merely changes hands between private holders without affecting the total amount of bank cash. If, however, the Government agent appears on the market each time there are no private buyers at the level fixed by the Government, then the volume of bank cash is liable to increase whenever there is no private demand for the securities at the officially fixed price. Conversely if banks or other private holders want to buy Government securities and are unable to find a seller willing to sell at the officially pegged price, then the authorities must provide a counterpart if they want to prevent an appreciation of their securities. The result of such operations is that some of the bank cash is mopped up.

What is important to bear in mind is that if the Government is determined to maintain Treasury Bill rates or the prices of Government securities at a pegged level, the volume of bank cash is liable to change on the initiative of the banks. They can always increase their cash reserve if they want to expand credit by selling some securities to the official buyer.

In order to be able to determine the volume of credit the authorities have to renounce their ambition of maintaining bill rates or the prices of Government securities rigidly pegged. If these rates and prices are allowed to fluctuate then there is no need for the authorities to buy or sell securities unless they want to influence the volume of bank cash in order to determine the volume of credit.

H

It would be a mistake to imagine, however, that even in such circumstances their power to determine the volume of credit is unlimited. They are in a position to extend the maximum limit of credit facilities, but whether the actual volume of credit conforms to their policy depends not only on the willingness and ability of lenders to lend but also on the willingness of borrowers to borrow. The experience of the thirties when the United States and many other countries found that it was impossible to bring about the desired degree of monetary expansion made the monetary authorities realize the limitation of their power to regulate the volume of credit. Neither producers nor consumers are likely to avail themselves of the facilities placed at their disposal if rightly or wrongly they expect a decline of prices or a business depression. In such situations the only way in which the authorities are in a position to expand credit is through deficit financing. This method will be dealt with in a later chapter.

In theory there is no limit to the powers of the monetary authorities to enforce a contraction of credit. In practice, however, unduly sharp contraction is liable to produce grave financial, economic, social, and political consequences. A stage is likely to be reached at which the authorities may feel compelled to check or reverse their policy no matter how firmly they are convinced that a further contraction of credit is necessary.

CHAPTER TWENTY-FOUR

Selective Credit Control

CREDIT control may be general or selective according to whether the authorities confine themselves to determining the total volume of credit or discriminate between various categories of borrowers. Until recently general credit control was all but universally in operation. One of its main disadvantages is that it tends to affect indiscriminately all sections of the national economy in so far as they depend on credit. If the monetary authorities, by reducing the volume of bank cash, compel the banking system to curtail substantially the total volume of credit, all categories of borrowers are liable to be affected irrespective of whether or not the specific conditions in their particular sphere call for any credit reductions. If the monetary authorities bring about a general expansion of credit it is liable to stimulate not only those industries which are in need of encouragement but also those which are over-trading and should be discouraged rather than encouraged.

This defect of indiscriminate general credit control has long been realized and has often been denounced as one of the weakest spots of the orthodox monetary system with which it had been associated. To some extent the disadvantages were mitigated by informal official advice given to the banks about their attitude towards particular types of loans. Such advice was usually followed to a considerable extent by most banks even in the absence of statutory powers to enforce it. There was a long way to go, however, from this informal system to the system of selective credit control which appeared after the Second World War.

During the War it was of vital importance to all belligerent countries that industrial resources should be reserved for the production of war materials and of essential civilian goods. The operation of extensive physical controls made it unnecessary for banks to discourage the production of superfluous goods with the aid of a discriminatory credit control. The system of rationing and allocations was a more effective way of influencing production and consumption than even the most advanced system of selective credit control could possibly claim to be. After all, producers and consumers have financial resources of their own, with the aid of which they are in a position to engage in production or purchases disapproved of by the authorities even if no credits are granted to them for such purposes. It was after the War, as and when physical controls were removed, that the need for the more extensive selective credit control became evident. In 1945 when the Bank of England was nationalized, the Treasury was given power to issue directions to the banks through the intermediary of the Bank of England. These powers have not been used, however, to any noteworthy extent for enforcing selective credit controls. From time to time the banks were requested to discriminate in favour of or against certain categories of credits. In particular they were requested from 1951 onward to discriminate in favour of credits for rearmament and export trade, and to increase such credits in spite of the reduction of the total volume of credit due to the general policy of credit restrictions.

A type of selective credit control which was frequently resorted to even before the War in most countries was pressure on the banks to abstain from granting credits for speculative purposes. In Britain in 1945, immediately after the end of the War in Europe, the banks were requested to abstain from granting large credits for financing speculative buying, and also for the satisfaction of personal needs and for financing holdings of securities or of commodity stocks. When Sir Stafford Cripps became Chancellor of the Exchequer in 1947 he caused the Bank of England to request the banks to discourage loans for the purchase of real property and not to expand credits for financing instalment buying of consumer goods. When pressure on sterling developed in 1949 the banks were requested to curtail credits in general but to make exceptions in favour of those producing goods for export to 'hard currency' markets or producers of goods which would otherwise have to be imported from 'hard currency' countries.

Britain is particularly well placed for the application of such selective controls owing to the fact that most of her banking activities is concentrated in the hands of a very small number of big banks with very well established traditions of co-operation with the Bank of England. In addition Britain possesses a well-established institution for the purpose of enforcing effective credit control. The Capital Issues Committee was created some years before the War for the purpose of controlling public issues on the London market. Under the chairmanship of Lord Kennet it succeeded in creating one of the few watertight controls in existence. After the War its sphere was extended from public issues to bank loans in excess of £50,000. The banks have to submit any such loans for approval to the Capital Issues Committee, which is thus in a position to exercise a very advanced form of selective credit control, even though loans of smaller amounts remain outside its scope.

Selective credit control was applied in a high degree in the United States after the War. In particular selling on the instalment system is subject there to far-reaching discriminatory control. The percentage of initial payments is fixed for each trade and also for real property deals. By changing that percentage the Government is in a position to influence the volume of transactions. The length of the period over which deferred payments can be allowed is also subject to statutory regulations. Similar measures were adopted in a less advanced form in Britain as a result of the sterling crisis in 1951.

France introduced in 1947 a rule under which commercial banks were to discriminate against borrowers who were expected to be able to raise the necessary funds through increased sales efforts, through liquidating excessive stocks, through using the owners' personal financial resources or by making public issues. This system has proved to be largely ineffective, as there are many ways in which the rule can be circumvented.

In Australia, New Zealand, and Canada bank loans for the purpose of capital expenditure are officially discouraged in order to compel potential borrowers to raise the necessary funds in the capital market.

Selective credit control need not necessarily assume the form of a ban on unwanted types of operations or a discrimination in favour of types enjoying priority. In Belgium the National Bank applies differential rediscount rates according to the type of the transaction financed by the Bills presented for rediscount. Its rules of eligibility for rediscount also take into account a list of priorities. During periods of adverse balance of payments the rediscount rates for bills financing imports can be raised above those for bills financing exports. Conversely, when there is an export surplus this practice can be reversed.

As a general rule selective credit controls are not established in detail by legislation. They are usually adopted in broad outline and are adjusted by means of informal agreements between the authorities and the banks. In countries where commercial banks are nationalized selective credit control is of course on an official basis. In some other countries, too, the Central Banks have statutory authority to determine the purposes for which loans can be granted. They have no power, however, to discriminate in favour of or against individual borrowers. Such countries include Australia, New Zealand, India, the Philippines, and some Latin American countries.

Selective credit control constitutes a means of monetary policy in so far as it affects the total volume of money. The distribution of credit resources within the various categories is a matter of credit policy rather than monetary policy, unless the steps taken aim at influencing the monetary situation. In most instances of post-war selective credit control the aim was to reduce or keep down the grand total by means of discriminating against what were considered unessential or less essential types of credit.

Another widely accepted purpose for which selective credit control was applied was to discourage excessive consumers' demand. Such control serves a monetary end in that it tends to moderate inflationary buying pressure. It has been an idea of long standing to seek to control business trends by encouraging or discouraging instalment buying. During periods when the purchasing power in consumers' hands is already excessive it is considered inexpedient to encourage them to use their future earnings in advance for immediate purchases. On the other hand, during periods when trade is handicapped by deficiency of consumers' purchasing power it can be usefully supplemented by facilitating the spending in advance of future earnings with the aid of deferred payments arrangements. Regulation of the terms of the instalment system therefore constitutes a highly serviceable means of monetary policy. The same end can be achieved not only by prescribing the terms on which industrial and commercial firms may sell on the instalment system, but also by inducing the banks to limit or expand the amount of credits made available for that purpose. The difficulty about this latter method is that it is not easy for banks to ascertain the extent to which loans granted to merchants or manufacturers are used for financing instalment buying. And even if some form of watertight control could be devised there would be nothing to prevent borrowers from diverting their other resources to the financing of instalment business, thanks to bank loans for other purposes which would release those resources.

Discrimination affecting credits for financing capital investment also constitutes a useful means of monetary policy. Thanks to Keynes the important rôle played by the extent of capital investment in the monetary situation is now generally realized, and the need for regulating the volume of capital investment as a means for influencing monetary trends has become a normal part of monetary policy. The immediate effect of diverting financial and physical resources towards the erection of factories is that less is produced for immediate consumption. The prices of consumer goods tend to increase or their decline is checked or slowed down. Cuts in capital investments tend to produce the opposite effect. Capital investment is of course largely financed out of capital resources rather than bank credits. It can be financed either out of the capital and undistributed profits of the firms concerned or by means of public issues, or borrowing on mortgage from non-banking sources. Selective credit control in this sphere cannot claim to be comprehensive so long as it is confined to banking loans. While public issues are subject to control, smaller loans by insurance companies, building societies, trust funds, etc., are outside the scope of monetary policy in most countries.

Yet another direction in which selective credit control constitutes a means of monetary policy is in its effect on the balance of payments. A persistent import or export surplus is liable to affect the monetary position and it calls for official intervention. One way in which the foreign exchange can be strengthened is by discriminating in favour of export industries in the allocation of credit or in rediscounting facilities. We saw above that this is done in several countries.

It is essential to realize the limitations of the influence of a selective credit control as a monetary device, in so far as it consists of diverting credit expansion into specific spheres. It is necessary to bear in mind that the purchasing power represented by the additional credits granted for specific purposes does not vanish into thin air once the money is spent for those purposes. Recipients of the money are in a position to spend it once more. Even though part of it is taken away in taxation or disappears from circulation through hoarding or through the acquisition of newly-issued Government Loans, part of it is bound to be spent again and again. Each time it is spent it tends to produce the same effect on the monetary situation as it did when it was spent the first time. This is what is called the 'multiplier effect', the total of which is probably several times the effect of the original transaction. After the first transaction the authorities have no longer any control over the purpose for which the additional purchasing power is used.

It is because of this limitation of the effect of selective credit controls that indiscriminate quantitative credit controls cannot be dispensed with. If the authorities are anxious to avoid inflation they cannot give banks a free hand to lend to industries which need encouragement unless at the same time the grand total of credit is subject to limitation. They may find that the purchasing power originating from credits granted for specific approved purposes may work its way round into demand of an entirely unwanted character. Nothing short of quantitative restrictions could safeguard against such demand. For this reason it is a mistake to imagine that general restrictions are an old-fashioned device which is liable to be superseded completely by more scientific methods of selective restriction. The two methods should complete each other.

Selective credit control can play an important part in a policy aiming at an insulation of loans to the Government from loans to the private sector of the national economy. Owing to the large size of the public debt most Governments are reluctant to raise interest rates in order to discourage over-trading or a rising trend of prices. Dear money is a costly device from the taxpayer's point of view. Thanks to the device of insulation, however, it is possible to some extent to safeguard the public debt against having to bear the full burden of an increase of interest rates. About this more will be said in Chapter 27.

CHAPTER TWENTY-FIVE

Influencing Interest Rates

FROM the dawn of history the State authority has been concerned with the level of interest rates. The policy of cheap money was not invented by Keynes; it is almost as old as the monetary system itself. Throughout the ages tribal laws, religious laws, and more advanced legislation have tried to set a limit to interest rates. There were such attempts in the Code of Hammurabi and in other ancient codes of law. The ancient Jews went so far as to forbid altogether the charging of interest on loans. The same principle is also found in the Koran and many strict Mohammedans observe it to this day. Many ecclesiastical writers come out strongly against the charging of interest, or at any rate against usury.

The enforcement of cheap money by means of anti-usury laws was never very effective. Its circumvention was the rule and its observance the exception. In Babylonia the statutory rate was a modest twenty per cent, but according to Woolley it was usual to charge twenty-five per cent on loans in silver and thirty-three and one third per cent on loans in grain. In backward countries even in our days interest is quoted per month or even per day, because the figure of the annual rate would be too staggering. Writers on money from Aristotle onwards condemned usury. St Thomas Aquinas laid down the maxim that 'money breeds no money' in support of his arguments against usury. Notwithstanding the severity of penalties, interest rates remained most of the time above the legal maximum, under the influence of the almost perpetual scarcity of money.

The State authority took it on itself from time to time to fight high money rates by means other than those of the largely ineffective anti-usury laws. For example in the Roman Empire Antoninus Pius and Alexander Severus reduced interest rates by lending public money on mortgage.

Although economic considerations must have influenced the efforts to lower interest rates, these were inspired first and foremost by social and political considerations. Measures against high interest rates may be considered to fall within our definition of monetary policy even if their object is not to expand currency or stimulate trade, but to allay the misery and discontent of the debtor classes.

It was only quite recently that intervention to influence interest rates has become a means of monetary policy in the more restricted sense of the term. Modern Central Banking did not develop until the nineteenth century. With it developed the Bank Rate policy which was for over a hundred years – and according to many economists still is – by far the most important weapon at the disposal of State authorities in the monetary sphere. It is a curious fact worth remembering that the first move towards adopting that weapon in Britain was the repeal of the anti-usury laws.

Beyond doubt the Bank Rate has played a most important part over a long period in the economic life of all modern countries. It largely determined the whole structure of interest rates, especially those on short-term loans. Monetary policy in the popular sense of the term is concerned mainly with short-term interest rates such as discount rates, rates on day-to-day loans, on bank advances, deposits, etc. There is usually a fairly definite relationship between all these rates and the rate at which the Central Bank is prepared to re-discount bills discounted by banks. This relationship however differs considerably according to whether a country is rich or poor in financial resources. In countries which possess well-established money markets the interest rates quoted in the open market are always below the Bank Rate, even though rates charged on bank loans are above it. In financially poor countries on the other hand the Bank Rate is not the maximum but the minimum rate for all types of interest rates. Since the Central Bank is only prepared to satisfy a fraction of the total credit requirements the bulk of it has to be satisfied at rates higher than those charged by the Central Bank. However this may be, what matters from the point of view of the use of the Bank Rate as a means of monetary policy is that the level of interest rates in general can be moved up or down by means of changing the Bank Rate.

The conception underlying a Bank Rate policy is that high interest rates tend to discourage borrowing while low interest rates tend to encourage it. Consequently by raising or lowering the Bank Rate the authorities are in a position to cause an increase or a decrease in the quantity of money. A higher Bank Rate tends to induce would-be borrowers to abstain from borrowing and debtors to repay their outstanding loans. It also tends to induce lenders to be more cautious in granting further loans, and even to call in existing loans, because of the possibility of a further rise of interest rates and of commercial difficulties arising from high interest rates. With the aid of high interest rates the authorities can discourage new enterprise or the expansion of existing enterprise, because high interest rates increase both cost and risk attached to business activities. The mere gesture of an increase of the Bank Rate tends to produce a psychological effect which at times is quite out of proportion to its actual material effect.

Another way in which the authorities can make themselves felt with the aid of the Bank Rate is through its effect on holders of stocks of commodities or manufactures. A high Bank Rate raises the interest charges on loans with the aid of which such stocks are carried. For this reason their holders may become more inclined to sell at a lower price rather than carry the stocks and pay high interest rates over a prolonged period. This, together with the decline of spending by producers and consumers, tends to cause a fall in prices.

Conversely a reduction of the Bank Rate, by bringing about an all-round reduction of interest rates, tends to encourage firms and individuals to borrow; it tends to stimulate new ventures and the accumulation of stocks of raw materials or finished products. Consequently it tends to increase business activity and to raise prices. This effect of the

Bank Rate is not so dependable, however, as its effect in the opposite sense. The powers of the authorities to bring about an expansion of business activities through low interest rates are not nearly as effective as their powers to reduce business activity by means of high interest rates. Even the latter powers cannot be depended upon absolutely. The Bank Rate may have to be raised to a very high level before it breaks a boom. And in a runaway inflation, such as the German inflation of 1923, even a ninety per cent Bank Rate is useless. Situations are apt to arise in which the Bank Rate, in order that it should produce the desired effect, has to be raised to a crisis level, with disastrous consequences.

Hitherto we have only been dealing with the effects of the intervention of the authorities in the sphere of interest rates on the internal economy. Its international effects are, however, equally important. The authorities may raise the Bank Rate not only for the purpose of restricting credit but also for the purpose of attracting money from abroad. In an international monetary centre such as London the use of the Bank Rate for that purpose is apt to be very effective in normal conditions. Higher interest rates tend to induce overseas banks and others to transfer their money to London in order to take advantage of the higher yield. British banks and other British residents with liquid funds abroad may decide to repatriate their money. At the same time foreign debtors may hasten to repay their short-term debts in preference to renewing them at such high interest rates. This was what happened in August 1914 when the Bank Rate was raised to ten per cent at the outbreak of the War and there was a wholesale repayment of credits by foreign debtors. A lowering of the Bank Rate tends of course to produce the opposite effect.

By means of influencing the international flow of funds with the aid of Bank Rate changes the authorities were in a position under the gold standard to influence international gold movements. By raising the Bank Rate they created a demand for sterling, which appreciated in the foreign exchange market to the point at which it became profitable

to ship gold to London. Conversely a reduction of the Bank
Rate tended to cause an outflow of funds and the resulting
selling pressure on sterling tended to depreciate its exchange
value to a level at which it became profitable to withdraw
gold from the Bank of England and sell it abroad. By means
of raising or lowering the Bank Rate the authorities were
thus in a position to raise or lower their gold reserve. This
in turn expanded or curtailed the volume of money, for
during the days of the automatic gold standard the amount
of currency and credit was determined by the size of the
gold reserve.

It was not until the managed gold standard was adopted
during the twenties that it became possible for the authorities to secure an increase or a reduction in the volume of
money to some extent independently to the size of their gold
reserve. During the thirties the quantity of money ceased to
depend on the size of the gold reserve. Even in countries
such as the United States where in theory the credit structure continued to be based on gold, in practice it is possible
to alter the volume of credit independently of the amount
of the gold reserve through enacting changes in the reserve
requirements which the banks have to observe. In the
United Kingdom the credit structure was detached from its
gold basis in the twenties when the authorities were em-
powered to increase or reduce the 'fiduciary issue'. When
there was an unwanted outflow of gold and the Bank of
England did not wish to raise the Bank Rate it advised the
Government to raise the fiduciary issue, so that the same
amount of gold could serve as a basis for a large amount of
money.

As a result of these changes the Bank Rate weapon
ceased to be essential for the purpose of bringing about
changes in the size of the metallic reserve for the sake of
preparing the way for an expansion or a contraction of
credit. The change was distinctly for the better. For the
dependence of the level of interest rates and of the domestic
credit structure on the caprices of international gold movements was a weak spot of the monetary system.

One of the sources of the difficulties had been the conflict that was liable to arise between the use of the Bank Rate weapon for internal and international purposes. On some occasions the authorities considered it advisable to raise the Bank Rate in order to discourage a boom in domestic trade. By raising the Bank Rate, however, they tended to attract gold from abroad with the result that they created a possibility of a credit expansion which tended to defeat the original object of the high Bank Rate. Likewise, their efforts to counteract a trade depression with the aid of a low Bank Rate were apt to become frustrated, because a reduction of the Bank Rate tended to cause an outflow of gold and a contraction of credit at a moment when the authorities were anxious to encourage an expansion of credit by means of cheap money.

What was even worse, the authorities were often forced to raise the Bank Rate even though conditions in domestic trade called for cheap money, in order to check an unwanted outflow of gold due to some international cause. This was what happened for instance in 1929 when the outflow of capital attracted to the United States by the Wall Street boom reduced the British gold reserve. The Bank of England felt impelled under the old rules of the gold standard to raise the Bank Rate to the crisis level of six per cent to check the outflow, even though the depressed state of British trade called for a low Bank Rate. It is well to recall such anomalies now that in face of the totally different kinds of difficulties of the present many people are inclined to idealize the past.

Another purpose for which Bank Rate changes are used is to influence the trade balance. A high Bank Rate, by causing a decline of domestic consumption and of prices, tends to stimulate exports and to discourage imports. As a result of its effect on the trade balance it tends to bring about in due course an inflow of gold in addition to the inflow caused by its effect on the movements of funds referred to above. Conversely a reduction of the Bank Rate, by causing domestic consumption to expand and prices to rise, tends to discourage exports and encourage imports leading to an outflow of gold. It takes some time, however, before these effects are produced, and they are only produced as and when the Bank Rate changes affect the price level in the desired sense.

Many economists regard the Bank Rate as the ideal weapon with the aid of which to mitigate booms and slumps. Indeed according to Hawtrey, booms and slumps could be eliminated altogether if only the authorities resorted to the necessary Bank Rate changes in good time and to a sufficient degree. Even those who deny that the Bank Rate is in a position to control the business cycle readily admit that it is an effective weapon against unsound speculative fever and overtrading.

The authorities had no unlimited power to determine the level of interest rates during the period of the automatic gold standard. Their hand was very often forced by influences which they were unable to control. If the discount market got it into its head that there was a likelihood of an increase of the Bank Rate the market rate of discount was apt to rise to the level of the Bank Rate and the Central Bank was forced to raise the Bank Rate. During a period of prolonged cheap money due to lack of demand for credit the market rates of interest were apt to lose touch with the Bank Rate which then became entirely ineffective. Under the new system of managed inconvertible currencies the authorities are much more influential in determining interest rates than they had ever been under the gold standard.

Thanks to their new techniques the authorities are in a position to change the volume of credit without having to change the level of interest rates. They can 'peg' interest rates through open market operations. This does not mean that supply and demand in the money markets are now subordinated to the official policy. The Government can determine the limit of the volume of currency and credit but it cannot determine the extent to which borrowers are willing to borrow. Admittedly the Government has the power to maintain interest rates at an artificially low level by bringing about a credit expansion that satisfies all the demand for credit at the prevailing low interest rates. This was actually done in Britain throughout the War right up to 1951. In order to maintain Treasury Bill rates at the level chosen by the monetary authorities, the official agents were prepared to buy at the official rate unlimited amounts of Treasury Bills offered for sale. In doing so, however, the authorities expanded the volume of money, thereby rendering themselves largely responsible for post-War inflation.

While technically the authorities possess the means with the aid of which they can maintain interest rates at a desired level, in practice they have to balance the advantages derived from this policy with the disadvantages of inflation. A stage may be reached – as indeed it was reached both in Britain and in the United States – at which the authorities arrive at the conclusion that it is not worth their while to maintain cheap money at such a high cost.

Hitherto we have been dealing with monetary policy as it concerns short-term rates of interest. The authorities have also to intervene, however, to influence long-term rates of interest. This form of intervention is very old because Treasuries always tried to manipulate the markets with the object of bringing down or keeping down interest rates at which they could borrow. It is only recently, however, that efforts to lower or keep down long-term interest rates have come to be regarded as forming part of the Government's monetary policy as distinct from debt management policy. The prolonged maintenance of low short-term rates of interest naturally tends to influence long-term rates in the same sense, even though the two markets can be independent of each other to a large extent. During the War most belligerent Governments were able to borrow at relatively low rates because they maintained money in plentiful supply. After the War the Governments in Britain, the United States, and other countries continued to pursue a policy of low long-term interest rates by means of artificially bolstering up the market in Government Loans. This time the main object was not to secure cheap rates for their own loan operations. Although that consideration played a part in the formulation of their policy, the main object was to keep money cheap for the requirements of trade for the sake of encouraging capital investment. The Treasuries confined their intervention to supporting the market in their own issues, but indirectly this resulted in a rise in other sections of the Stock Exchange. Owing to the very low yield on Government Loans investors were inclined to switch over to industrial and other securities and the prices of these rose in sympathy with that of Government Loans.

Intervention to check unsound Stock Exchange booms has come to be considered to form part of the duties of the monetary authorities. The Bank Rate was used on many occasions for that purpose, not only because its increase is a gesture of warning against undue optimism but also because it raises the interest charges on loans with which speculative purchases of the securities are financed. During periods of boom, however, a slight increase in interest charges is in itself not sufficient to deter most speculators from carrying their speculative positions with the aid of borrowed money. A six per cent interest rate costs only half per cent per month, and even its increase to one per cent per month would add very slightly to the cost and risk of a promising speculative operation in stocks or in commodities. Speculation on the Stock Exchange or in commodity markets can be discouraged not so much through an increase of interest rates as by a curtailment of the money of amount available for that purpose.

What is true about the limitation of the influence of interest rates on Stock Exchange speculation and on speculation in commodities is also true, though to a less extent, concerning loans for industrial and commercial purposes. If rightly or wrongly the trade takes the view that prices will continue to rise, then a slight increase in interest charges is not likely to discourage business activity financed with borrowed money. In particular, firms with a quick turnover can afford to disregard higher interest rates. If they have reason to assume that the transactions financed with bank loans liquidate themselves in three months, then an increase of interest charges by two per cent per annum will only reduce their profit by half per cent. In their case, as in the case of Stock Exchange loans, dear money is apt to be ineffective unless it is supplemented by credit restrictions. It would be unwise to assume that high interest rates necessarily reduce the volume of credit to the desired extent. So long as there is a rising tendency of prices and the business outlook appears to be favourable, the large majority of borrowers will be willing to pay the higher interest rates. Indeed in a sellers' market it is usually possible to add the interest charges to the prices of the goods, so that dear money, instead of bringing down prices, may even contribute to some slight extent to their increase.

Another consideration which has to be borne in mind is that in a period of very high taxation such as has existed in Britain since the Second World War, the deterrent effect of high interest rates is lessened by the fact that interest charges are allowable as expenses for the purposes of taxation. Those firms which are unable to add the higher interest charges to the prices of their goods may be comforted by the thought that a very large part of the additional cost will be borne by the Treasury.

While the lessons of the thirties have shown that cheap money is not all-powerful in bringing about a trade recovery and a rise in prices, the lessons of the fifties have proved the limitations of dear money in correcting excessive business expansion and consumption and in reversing the rising trend in prices. Nevertheless, it would be a mistake to underestimate the importance of the Bank Rate among the means of monetary policy. The realization of its limitations should not be regarded as an argument against its use, but merely against its exclusive and isolated use and against excessive reliance on it. Employed in conjunction with other devices the increase or reduction of interest rates can be very helpful and even indispensable for the achievement of the aims of monetary policy.

CHAPTER TWENTY-SIX

Budgetary Means

THE deliberate and systematic use of the Budget in the service of monetary policy is of very recent origin. It began during the thirties and gave rise to a variety of new policies and techniques which continued to develop after the Second World War. Until the thirties Budgetary weapons of monetary policy were almost entirely unknown. Yet from the earliest period of the evolution of State authority, public finance has played an overwhelmingly important part in the economies of most communities. Indeed at a primitive stage payments made to and by the tribal authority constituted the bulk of monetary turnover. Trading between tribesmen was based mostly on natural economy. A standardized means of payment arose very frequently from the need to pay tribute and fines to the tribal authority, which in turn rewarded those who served it by payment in the same standardized objects.

During a more advanced period taxation and expenditure decisions had very often a strong incidental bearing on monetary policy without actually serving as its instrument. Rulers were frequently confronted by the dilemma whether to raise taxation or spend less, or alternatively to cover their financial requirements out of profits on the debasement of the coinage. In some instances at any rate princes and their advisers preferred to refrain from embarking on a war rather than debase the currency. In other instances Parliament granted supplies on the condition that the king did not tamper with currency. During a more recent period Napoleon insisted on pursuing a highly orthodox fiscal policy to avoid currency inflation, as a reaction from the disastrous monetary experience of France during the Revolution.

The nineteenth century provided many instances, in

Latin America and elsewhere, of Budgetary deficits leading to currency depreciation. Most countries with inflated currencies appeared to make no conscious effort to try to safeguard the currency by means of sound Budgetary policies. The currency depreciations were attributed mostly to the adverse balance of payments, and borrowing abroad was regarded as the obvious remedy. Those responsible for the monetary policies of the countries concerned were – or pretended to be – entirely oblivious of the connexion between Budgetary deficit and adverse trade balance. It was not until the inter-War period that the close connexion between a sound Budget and sound currency came to be widely realized. The financial reconstruction schemes elaborated under the auspices of the League of Nations insisted on balanced Budgets as a means of ensuring the success of monetary stabilizations. The principle was rather vague, however. It was not until the thirties that Budgetary manipulations came to be widely adopted as a means of monetary policy – presumably because in the then prevailing conditions the use of the Budgetary weapon for monetary purposes meant unbalancing the Budgets instead of balancing them. The new policy, far from involving sacrifices, meant taking the line of least resistance. It became convenient, therefore, for Governments to believe in the connexion between the Budget and the monetary situation.

The nineteenth century idea of a sound Budgetary policy was that its aim must be simply to keep down expenditure, cover it with the aid of taxation, and, if possible, produce a revenue surplus for the gradual reduction of the public debt. When in the reconstruction schemes of the twenties balanced Budgets were insisted upon, this was done primarily with the object of inspiring confidence in the stability of currencies that had become discredited by advanced inflation. The same spirit inspired the Draconian measures adopted in Britain during the crisis of 1931. The newly-formed National Government endeavoured to restore confidence in sterling by drastic cuts in expenditure and heavy additional taxation. The material effect of these measures was bound to be a sharp contraction in the volume of money, which was bound to accentuate the prevailing economic depression. Indeed, unemployment rose to new record figures during the months that followed the adoption of the Budgetary measures. Nevertheless, it was rightly considered preferable at that time to restore the morale of the country by inspiring confidence in sterling rather than to adopt measures to stimulate trade by means of a monetary expansion which would have accentuated the prevailing distrust in sterling.

The strength of the case for supplementing conventional measures of monetary policy by Budgetary measures came to be realized during the thirties, as a result of the evidence showing that the conventional measures were largely ineffective in the prevailing conditions. One country after another tried in vain to bring about a trade revival with the aid of the time-honoured device of 'cheap money'. It was found that low interest rates signally failed to induce producers and consumers to borrow and spend. The need for direct Government intervention to stimulate trade by means of public expenditure came to be realized in many countries.

The idea was not altogether new. It was advocated from various quarters during the early post-war period and throughout the twenties. The suggestion that the Government could and should spend its way back to prosperity came to be associated with Lloyd George, whose election programme in 1929, endorsed by Keynes, advocated large-scale public works as a means for overcoming the perennial trade depression. Long before his manifesto appeared, however, the idea was strongly pressed on him without effect when he was Prime Minister. Harold Nicolson's biography of George V contains the text of a letter written by the King's private secretary, Lord Stamfordham, in 1921, urging Lloyd George to embark on public works to relieve unemployment. In 1923 in the United States one of the conclusions arrived at at the President's Conference on Unemployment was that public works should be curtailed in booms and expanded in depressions. The recommendation was forgotten, however, during the years of prosperity in the late twenties.

President Roosevelt was the first to apply the new policy on an extensive scale. One of the basic principles of the New Deal policy was large-scale Government expenditure, not only on public works but also to subsidize farmers and various classes of consumers in order to expand their purchasing power. This was done in the United States on an unprecedented scale between 1933 and the outbreak of the Second World War. These measures constituted measures of monetary policy because directly or indirectly they brought about a monetary expansion. Apart from creating additional demand as and when the Government was spending in excess of its revenue, the amounts thus spent were re-spent again and again by their recipients, so that the additional demand created by unbalancing the Budget was in the long run a multiple of the actual amount involved.

Keynes provided theoretical foundations for the new policy by putting forward his theory on the relation between saving and investment. The substance of this theory is that, if the amount of saving by the public is in excess of the amount spent on capital expenditure the demand for goods tends to fall short of supply. This means trade depression and unemployment. The remedy advocated is to increase capital investment through larger public expenditure on capital investment.

The execution of the new policy meant a deliberate unbalancing of the Budget. This was in direct contradiction to the traditional fiscal policy under which a Budgetary deficit is something which must be fought at all costs and tolerated only as matter of unavoidable necessity. This conception was not discarded altogether. Most of those favouring the new policy did not advocate a non-stop rise in the public debt through a perennial Budgetary deficit. The idea was that over a period of years Budgetary surpluses and deficits should offset each other. Budgetary policy should aim at deficits during years of depression and surpluses during years of boom.

During the thirties the Swedish Government announced that it had abandoned the idea of balancing the Budget in each financial year and that it would aim henceforth at balancing it over the entire period of a business cycle. This principle was later adopted by Congressional Committees in the United States and also by the British White Paper on Employment Policy issued by the Coalition Government in 1944. This document rejected the idea of 'a rigid policy of balancing the Budget each year regardless of the state of trade'. The Chancellor of the Exchequer was to take into account the requirements of trade and employment in framing his annual Budget. At the same time the White Paper emphasized that the Government did not contemplate any departure from the principle that the Budget must be balanced over a longer period. Dealing with practical details the White Paper suggested that capital expenditure by the Government, which in the past had generally followed the same trend as private capital expenditure – it was reduced during depressions and increased during booms – should in the future be adjusted so as to correct excessive tendencies in private capital expenditure instead of accentuating them. It should be increased when private investment is declining and should be reduced when private investment is excessive. Another suggestion was that the Government and the local authorities as large purchasers of certain types of consumer goods should vary the volume of their orders according to the general state of trade. Finally it was suggested that the rates of contribution to the proposed National Insurance Scheme should be adjusted so as to be high during periods of boom and low during periods of depression, even though the expenditure under such a scheme on unemployment benefits is apt to be high during periods of depression and low during periods of boom.

The new monetary policy bears the marks of the one-sided influence of the prolonged depression of the inter-war period. Although its advocates sometimes paid lip-service to the use of their devices also as a means to resist booms and inflations, they primarily envisaged its use as a means to expand purchasing power and stimulate trade during a depression. With the advent of the Second World War the problem to be faced was, however, one of moderating the inevitable inflation that accompanied it. There could be no question of applying Budgetary methods to counteract the inflationary trends. Owing to the heavy cost of a modern war, all belligerent countries, and even many neutral countries, had to unbalance their Budgets to an unprecedented degree. It was assumed, however, that at the end of the war history would repeat itself and that the world would experience once more a post-war slump similar to that of the early 'twenties. The White Paper on Employment Policy envisaged a two-way monetary policy in which the Budgetary weapon was to play a prominent part both as a defence against booms and as a cure for depressions, but most people expected it to be applied primarily against a post-war slump.

After the war the first Socialist Chancellor of the Exchequer, Dr Dalton, declared it to be the Government's policy that the Budget should be balanced not in each financial year, but over a period of years. Amidst the conditions prevailing immediately after the cessation of hostilities this policy was merely making virtue of necessity. It was impossible to balance the Budget for a time. The Budget remained unbalanced not from considerations of monetary policy, but because abnormal military expenditure was still running at a high figure. Nevertheless, the ease with which expenditure that was not unavoidable was authorized—Dr Dalton candidly admitted that he authorized it 'with a song in his heart' – formed part and parcel of the Government's expansionary monetary policy.

When in 1947 Sir Stafford Cripps succeeded Dr Dalton he adopted a policy of Budgetary disinflation. By that time the Budget came to be balanced, thanks to high taxation. The vicious spiral of inflation was proceeding, however, not through Budgetary deficits, but through over-full employment and the rapid extension of social services. Sir Stafford

Cripps hoped to break this vicious spiral by mopping up surplus purchasing power with the aid of an excess of revenue over expenditure. His policy was largely ineffective, however, because in spite of Budgetary disinflation, inflation was kept going by means of credit expansion and of an increase of consumers' purchasing power through rising wages and social service benefits. This situation became further aggravated during Mr Gaitskell's Chancellorship through a rise in world commodity prices. In any event, from 1951 onward it would not have been practicable to use the Budgetary device for disinflationary purposes, because the growing cost of rearmament became a major factor in the shaping of Budgets. Whatever purchasing power was mopped up with the aid of Budgetary surpluses was promptly released as a result of the increase in the volume of credit brought about by continuous intervention to support Treasury Bills.

Since the application of Budgetary devices in monetary policy is of recent origin, its full implications and details have not yet been worked out. According to an over-simplified view the monetary situation can be governed simply by producing a Budgetary surplus or deficit of the required size. In reality it makes a considerable difference whether a surplus is achieved through an increase of taxation or through a reduction of expenditure, and whether a deficit is created through an increase of expenditure or through a reduction of taxation. It stands to reason that during a period of trade depression an increase of purchasing power through tax reductions is not likely to produce the desired results because most producers and consumers are not inclined to employ their additional purchasing power. The right way of unbalancing the Budget in such circumstances is through an increase of public expenditure. Conversely, during a period of boom or inflation it would be a mistaken policy to create a Budgetary surplus by means of high taxation. Owing to the rising trend of prices a large proportion of taxpayers, whether individuals or firms, are in a position to pass on the burden of higher taxes by securing higher and yet higher wages or prices. The correct Budgetary method of resisting inflation in such circumstances is to create a Budgetary surplus by means of reducing expenditure. This was not done in Britain either under the Socialist Government or under the Conservative Government that succeeded it. During the post-war period from 1947 onward there was a rising trend of expenditure covered by an almost uninterrupted increase of the yield of taxation that was due to the inflationary increase of the national income.

Differentiation between employing the Budgetary weapon through the revenue side or the expenditure side is a step in the right direction. But it does not go far enough. A policy of using the Budget for monetary purposes must discriminate also according to the nature of the changes in revenue or expenditure. The monetary effect of an increase or reduction of revenue or expenditure varies according to the type of revenue or expenditure increased or reduced. It would be a mistake to try to fight inflation with the aid of high taxation alone. But it is both practicable and in given circumstances advantageous to use certain types of taxation for discouraging certain types of spending. The use of Purchase Tax for the discouragement of spending on luxuries may be prompted by economic and social motives; at the same time it is an anti-inflationary device because it tends to moderate wages demands. The taxation of company profits and the prohibitive rate of surtax and death duties in Britain pursued a similar combined purpose. There is, of course, another side to it. A case can be made against almost any tax on the ground that in given circumstances it tends to cause a rise in prices.

In respect of expenditure we pointed out earlier that it can serve primarily as a stimulus to production if it assumes the form of public works or primarily as a stimulus to consumption if it increases the purchasing power of large classes of consumers. The difference is not so marked, however, as some Keynesians would like us to believe. For the multiplier effect of the additional purchasing power will not be confined to the original purpose of the expenditure. Money spent on public works is liable to be respent by its recipients on consumer goods, while purchasing power created in order to stimulate consumers' demand may find its way into capital expenditure.

The use of the Budget for the purposes of monetary policy has its disadvantages and limitations. Those who believe that it could or should replace conventional methods of monetary policy take an unduly one-sided and unrealistic view. For one thing, both changes in taxation and changes in expenditure are clumsy and cumbersome devices. The Budget cannot be revised at frequent intervals. The legislative machinery that has to be set into motion is complicated and slow. As a general rule there can only be one Budget each year, and even in exceptional circumstances there are never more than two Budgets. Yet the monetary situation is liable to change suddenly and its changes are liable to call for urgent measures. It would be unwise to await the next Budget to counteract monetary trends which could easily be handled during their early stages, but which might get out of control if allowed to proceed for months. In addition to the time taken by the adoption of legislative measures needed for Budgetary changes, it usually takes further months before these measures can be actually applied and produce their full effect on the monetary situation. On the revenue side frequent changes of taxation have considerable disadvantages. On the expenditure side the volume of public works cannot always be easily adapted to the changing requirements of monetary policy. Certain kinds of public works have to go on in boom and slump alike. They cannot be arrested as soon as this appears necessary from the monetary point of view without incurring grave capital losses. Nor can they be initiated or resumed at a moment's notice. Roads cannot be neglected altogether during booms in order to be able to spend more on them during slumps.

It seems that the Budgetary weapon is only suitable for use against long-range movements which are liable to proceed for a considerable time, so that delay in the necessary adjustment of the revenue or expenditure would not matter in the long run. Pending the application of Budgetary devices and during the time-lag between their application and their effect, the authorities have to depend on other devices to cope with the situation.

One of the reasons for the unpopularity among many economists of the Budgetary devices of monetary policy is that their use has reinforced the supremacy of Treasuries over Central Banks. Ever since the First World War the influence of Treasuries has been gaining ground. The development of the use of Budgetary devices in monetary policy further increased the relative importance of Treasuries, not only as the authorities determining the ends and means of monetary policy, but also as the executing hands of monetary policy decisions. Everybody has to realize that it is impossible to put the clock back, and that the supremacy of Treasuries in the planning and execution of monetary policy is firmly established. This was due not only to the realization of the potentialities of the Budgetary device, but also to the increased importance of the part played in the monetary situation by the management of the greatly increased public debts. About this more will be said in the next chapter.

CHAPTER TWENTY-SEVEN

Treasury Operations

THE monetary trend is liable to be influenced by Treasury operations to a considerable degree. We saw in Chapter 23 that the volume of money tends to expand or contract according to the amount of Government securities bought by the authorities from the private sector of the national economy or sold to them by that sector. We saw that, when the Government sells securities to the banks, the cash reserve of the latter becomes reduced correspondingly, while the sale of securities by the banks to the authorities increases the amount of bank cash. If the securities are sold to non-banking buyers their purchasing power is reduced, and in so far as payment is made out of the bank deposits the amount of bank cash is also reduced. Conversely if non-banking sellers cash their maturing Government securities or re-sell them to the Government, their purchasing power increases and their additional bank deposits tend to increase bank cash.

This factor has a considerable importance in modern conditions owing to the almost uninterrupted rise of the public debt in most countries. Although borrowing by the State authority is a very ancient practice, its relative importance from the point of view of the monetary situation remained small so long as the loans were provided by a few wealthy bankers and the totals involved were moderate even allowing for the difference in conditions. In Britain it was not until the end of the seventeenth century that a public debt in the modern sense began to develop. Until then the public debt was considered to be the king's personal debt, and any king who died without having redeemed his loans was criticized for his improvidence. It was during the eighteenth century that the public debt came to be regarded as something permanent and its obligations came to be held widely by the public. Its amount remained relatively small until the Napoleonic Wars, and even during the greater part of the nineteenth century it was not sufficiently large for Treasury operations to play systematically a decisive part in the monetary sphere.

The sharp increase in the public debt during the two World Wars has brought about a far-reaching change in the monetary system. In Britain, Government stocks, bonds, and bills now represent a very large proportion of the assets held by the private sector of the national economy. Capital movements between the Treasury and the private sector are liable to be substantial and tend to affect the volume of money considerably. The same is true of many other countries also. Mr Snyder, Secretary of the United States Treasury in the Truman administration, in his evidence before the Joint Congressional Committee on Monetary Credit and Fiscal Policies, remarked in 1949 that the public debt is now interwoven with the financial structure of the entire economy. The importance of its management from the point of view of monetary policy is due not only to the increase of its size, but also to the broadening of its ownership. In Britain there are millions of holders of Savings Certificates, and their attitude, like that of holders of other Government securities, can react on the monetary situation.

The Treasury's rôle in influencing the monetary situation through its attitude towards the public debt is manifold. In the first place, it is the Treasury's duty to pursue policies aiming at maintaining public confidence in Government loans. This is, of course in accordance with the Treasury's own interests from the point of view of being able to borrow easily and at relatively low rates and to convert or renew maturing debts on relatively favourable terms. At the same time, however, it is of the utmost importance from the point of view of monetary stability that the Treasury should do its utmost to uphold confidence in Government loans. For large-scale non-renewal of maturing loans or withdrawal of loans subject to termination at the holders' will is liable to produce strong inflationary effects. During periods when it is inevitable that there should be a Budgetary deficit it is the Treasury's task to ensure that the purchasing power created by excess of Government expenditure over revenue is mopped up through loan operations. It is important that there should not be too long a time-lag between the creation of additional purchasing power through deficits and its mopping-up through loans. We saw in an earlier chapter that when additional purchasing power is created its repeated use is apt to multiply its effect. It is important therefore that Treasuries should mop up the additional purchasing power before it has been exercised too many times.

Nor is it a matter of indifference from the point of view of the monetary situation in what form the Treasury issues its loans to cover deficits. If they assume the form of short-term Treasury Bills they do not directly affect consumers' purchasing power. Marketable long-term securities are better from this point of view, but not nearly so good as non-marketable securities such as Savings Bonds or Savings Certificates. The latter are the ideal medium through which purchasing power inflation can be mopped up, provided that confidence in the Government's credit is maintained. Any wave of distrust is liable to induce holders to cash their Savings Certificates, thereby recovering the purchasing power they had temporarily relinquished in favour of the Government. While the sale of marketable bonds and stocks by one investor to another does not affect the volume of purchasing power, if it causes a slump in the price of Government loans the Treasury may feel impelled to intervene in order to safeguard the Government credit by buying up the bonds offered by private holders. In doing so it increases the purchasing power of the private section of the national economy.

The extent to which a wave of distrust in the Government's credit is liable to affect the monetary situation was illustrated by a letter by Mr William McC. Martin, Jr, Acting Secretary of the United States Treasury, to the Chairman of the Committee on Banking and Currency of the Senate on 4 May 1949. He pointed out that should 5 or 6 per cent of the realizable Government securities be converted into cash, the increase in bank deposits and notes would be enough to reduce the gold reserve below the legal minimum.

The Treasury is in a position to influence the monetary trend by means of a deliberate policy in the sphere of its debt management. The importance of this factor is realized in the United States to a larger extent than in Britain. In 1952 the Joint Congressional Committee on the Economic Report published in two volumes a report on monetary policy and the management of the public debt which contains a wealth of information bearing on the subject. There has been no corresponding official publication in Britain. Both the Macmillan Report and the White Paper on Employment Policy ignore the subject. According to the American Report, there is evidence that from early days United States Treasury officials were thinking about Treasury finance in relation to the money market as a whole. In 1793 in a Report to Congress on loans, Alexander Hamilton said that one reason for the timing of Government purchases of Government bonds was that 'during the winter in this country there is always a scarcity of money in the towns.' In 1857 Secretary Cobb supplied additional funds to the market by purchasing Government bonds from the public. This was done on frequent subsequent occasions and the Treasury's powers were used equally frequently also in the opposite direction.

With the emergence of the Federal Reserve System the Open Market Committee of the Federal Reserve Board developed the policy of systematic intervention to regulate the volume of credit by means of buying or selling Government securities. This policy has already been dealt with earlier. Between the wars the Bank of England developed a somewhat similar policy. By buying or selling Treasury Bills it expanded or reduced the volume of bank credit.

The Treasury is in a position to influence the volume of Government securities held by the public with the aid of devices other than open market operations. It can time its

I

new issues and repayments in accordance with the view it takes of the need for increasing or lowering the volume of money. In Britain the amount of Treasury Bills offered through the weekly tenders compared with the amount maturing during the same week largely influences the volume of credit. During the War this device was reinforced by the adoption of the system of Treasury Deposit Receipts under which the Treasury was in a position to call upon the banks to place at its disposal the amounts required.

The American monetary authorities have a totally different device at their disposal to supplement debt management and open market operations. While in Britain the Treasury keeps its account exclusively with the Bank of England – except in so far as it is necessary to use other banks for departmental requirements – in the United States it is authorized to keep an account with any commercial bank which comes under the deposit insurance scheme. Such banks are authorized to receive tax payments and the Treasury allows them to accumulate substantial deposits which are transferred to the Federal Reserve Bank when needed for the requirements of public expenditure. As we pointed out in Chapter 23, the United States Treasury is in a position to influence the volume of money by increasing or reducing its deposits with the commercial banks as a means of monetary policy. It is a most effective and subtle device.

Both in Britain and in the United States open market operations played an important part in monetary policy after the second World War. Treasury Bill rates were maintained artificially stable at a low level by means of buying unlimited amounts of bills which were offered and which would have raised the bill rates in the absence of official intervention. In Britain this policy was pursued much more rigidly than in the United States. The Treasury Bill rates were maintained rigidly pegged at $\frac{1}{2}$ per cent from 1945 till the advent of the Conservative Government in October, 1951. Intervention in the market for long-term loans was also much less subtle in Britain while it lasted. Up to 1947 the British Treasury was engaged in systematically bolstering up the market in Government loans in pursuance of Dr Dalton's policy of cheap money. With the advent of Sir Stafford Cripps to the Exchequer this policy was abandoned and Government Loans were allowed to find their own level.

In the United States the policy of supporting Government loans by official purchases through the intermediary of the Federal Reserve Banks was continued right up to 1951. It was not, however, as one-sided a policy as the one pursued in Britain between 1945 and 1947. American official intervention in the Government loan market operated both ways. When in the latter part of 1946 and early 1947 an upward trend developed in the bond market the Treasury felt impelled to intervene to counteract this trend in the interests of long-term stability of bond prices. To that end large amounts of bonds were unloaded. When in October, 1947, weakness developed in the bond market, the Treasury intervened by buying up large amounts of bonds. Although the primary object of these operations was to maintain the stability of Government bond prices, its secondary object was to maintain stability of long-term interest rates. From this point of view the American policy differed fundamentally from the British policy, which aimed at lowering long-term interest rates rather than maintaining them stable.

After the outbreak of the Korean War American intervention to prevent a rise in bond prices resulted in a heavy expansion of credit. Evidently the requirements of stability of bond prices came into conflict with the requirements of monetary stability. Eventually the latter consideration prevailed and the United States Treasury decided in 1951 to abandon the rigid support of the bond market, though it continued to afford it intermittent support at a lower level.

A great deal depends not only on the amount of the national debt, but also on its composition. It is not a matter of indifference from the point of view of the monetary situation whether the Government Loan is taken up entirely by banks or is subscribed by the general investing public. The more widely it is held by the public the larger is the extent to which it tends to immobilize purchasing power in the hands of producers and consumers. If the securities bought by the public are paid for out of bank deposits then the operation kills two birds with one stone. In addition to its direct effect on the consumers' purchasing power it also reduces the amount of bank cash and therefore leads to a reduction in the volume of credit. Both in Britain and in the United States the official policy after the Second World War aimed at placing the largest possible amount of the public debt with the general public. During the War it was inevitable that Government Loans should be financed largely by the banks. After the War it was possible to transfer a large proportion of the public debt from the banks to private investors.

Treasury operations as devices of monetary policy are not without their disadvantages. The Treasury's interests as a large debtor and borrower may conflict with the requirements of monetary policy. We saw above that when confronted with such a dilemma the British Treasury in 1947 and the United States Treasury in 1951 sacrificed considerations of debt management for the sake of those of monetary policy by allowing long-term interest rates to rise in order to avoid additional inflation. On other occasions, however, it was considerations of monetary policy which were sacrificed. Since the thirties the Treasuries of the world have discovered that as debtors and borrowers they are in the unique position of being able to determine the interest rates they pay. There is a strong temptation to use and abuse this power. Fortunately this temptation has been tempered by the extension of the Treasury's functions, which now cover not only the management of public finances but also the supreme direction of economic policy. Twenty years ago Treasuries would have been inclined to make the utmost use of their power to lower the interest rates on their debts, since in those days their principal if not only function was to safeguard the taxpayers' interest and to that end it was their duty to secure loans on the cheapest possible terms. To-day Treasuries are responsible for the economic stability and prosperity of their countries. They have to think twice before embarking on a policy which, while it assists them in keeping down the cost of public debt, increases their difficulty in performing their broader economic functions satisfactorily. This dual rôle of the Treasury is admittedly not without grave disadvantages. At the same time it has the advantage of compelling the Treasury to view its rôle from a broader standpoint, and it tends to prevent it from the misuse of its powers to determine interest rates.

Attempts have been made in various countries to reconcile the narrower interests of Treasury as borrower and debtor with its broader interests as the authority in charge of the national economy. There are various devices with the aid of which it is practicable to maintain Treasury borrowing rates at a relatively low level without having to overstimulate the private sector of the national economy by making money too cheap and too easy. It is possible for the monetary authorities to insulate interest rates on Government loans from those on private issues.

Support of the market in Government loans is one of these devices. On the face of it it might seem that if the Treasury supports its own issues while it allows private securities to find their own level the yield of the former tends to be relatively lower than that of the latter. In practice, however, an abnormally low yield on Government issues tends to divert funds towards investment in private securities, and this tends to reduce the discrepancy between their respective yields. Moreover, systematic support of the market in Government securities on a large scale produces an inflationary effect on the level of prices of private securities owing to the increase in the volume of funds available for investment.

A more effective method of insulation is the control of the market of new issues. With the aid of such control the Government is able to keep down the volume of private issues whenever the Treasury intends to appear in the market with a new issue or with a conversion operation. Under the system of control the Treasury can ensure for itself a high degree of priority over the financial resources of the country. There is no need for it to compete against the private issues by offering costlier terms.

Another device is the adoption of legislation under which banks are under obligation to hold a certain proportion of their assets in the form of Government securities. Although the main object of this system is to restrain credit expansion and to strengthen the security of desposits, it is an effective device of insulation. It is in operation in various forms in the United States, Belgium, France, Italy, the Netherlands, and Sweden. No such reserve requirements exist in Britain. British banks, however, are always willing to co-operate with the authorities in ensuring the success of Government issues.

In most countries certain assets must be held in 'trustee securities'. Even though their list may include some other types of securities, for the most part trust funds are kept in Government securities. In view of the large amount of such funds, legislation preventing their investment in most types of private securities goes a long way towards securing a considerable demand in spite of the relatively low yield of Government securities.

With the aid of these and other devices, Governments are in a position to restrict credit to the private sector of the national economy in pursuance of disinflationary policy, without having to put up with an increase of the interest rates on their own loans corresponding to that of the interest rates on private loans and credits. The discrepancy cannot, however, be increased unduly. In this, as in many other respects, the extent to which monetary policy can create and maintain artificial situations in defiance of economic trends has its limits.

Among the fiscal devices of monetary policy that of Treasury operations is distinctly more elastic and adaptable than that of Budget operations. This in spite of the fact that Treasury operations, too, have to be guided at times by considerations other than monetary policy. There can be no doubt that fiscal devices have come to stay. Even though it has become once more fashionable to advocate a reduction of the Treasury's rôle to the traditional function of collecting taxes, authorizing expenditure, and managing the public debt, it seems to be most unlikely that the clock will ever be put back. It would be impossible to revert to the system under which the sole object of Treasury operations was to cover Budgetary deficits by means of borrowing and to renew maturing debt or convert Government Loans at the lowest possible interest rates. That aspect of the Treasury's duties must of course remain prominent, in view of the importance of keeping down the burden of the greatly increased public debt. From time to time the Treasury's narrower interests are bound to be overshadowed, however, by major considerations of monetary policy which are or can be affected by the terms on which Treasury operations are arranged.

For example, even though the proportion of the floating debt is not uncomfortably high the Treasury may decide to fund some of it in pursuit of objectives of monetary policy. Although debt funding must mean an increase in the burden of the interest service, prevailing circumstances may justify the sacrifice if as a result the monetary situation is adjusted in accordance with the requirements of monetary policy. On more than one occasion in the fifties interest rates on Savings Certificates were raised, not because the Treasury found it difficult to secure the necessary funds through other channels, but because from the point of view of monetary policy it was considered expedient to mop up some of the purchasing power of the lower income groups. Many similar examples could be quoted to illustrate the extent to which Treasury operations are now based on broader principles than they were in the past.

A characteristic instance of Treasury operations inspired by considerations of monetary policy was provided by the funding of a large amount of Treasury Bills in Britain at the end of 1951. The object of this operation was to reduce the liquidity ratio of the banks – that is, the proportion of their liquid assets to their total assets – thereby discouraging excessive expansion of credit. If the banks' holding of easily

marketable Bills is reduced they would hesitate to increase
the amount of their advances, because in doing so their
liquidity ratio might decline below the traditional limit of
thirty per cent. Even though this limit is not observed as
strictly as the cash ratio – the proportion of bank cash to
bank desposits – it cannot be disregarded to any considerable extent. Hence the power of the Treasury – apart
altogether from any statutory power of compulsion – to
influence the volume of bank credits, not only by increasing or reducing the banks' cash holdings, but also by
increasing or reducing their liquid assets.

CHAPTER TWENTY-EIGHT

Influencing the Velocity of Circulation

THE ends of monetary policy may be pursued by influencing the volume of money in relation to the volume of goods in several different ways. A contraction or expansion of the volume of currency and credit may be caused either directly or by means of changing interest rates. As we shall see in a later chapter the same end may be achieved through a relative change in the volume of money as a result of increasing or reducing the volume of goods available for sale. Another alternative is to change the effect of a given amount in money by influencing its velocity of circulation. By making money circulate faster or slower the authorities are in a position to produce effects similar to those of an expansion or reduction of its quantity.

There is no need for us to enter into the highly involved controversy about the meaning of the velocity of circulation of money. For our purposes it means the average number of times money changes hands during a given period through payments for goods and services. Its turnover through purely financial transactions or through gambling does not count from our point of view. If we allowed for the use of money when it changes hands for purposes other than payments for goods and services the Principality of Monaco could claim that the velocity of circulation of her currency is many times larger than that of any other country. Since, however, the speed with which money passes from hand to hand in the Casino of Monte Carlo does not in the least affect the price level, it may be disregarded from a monetary point of view. The same is true about the velocity of circulation of money changing hands in connexion with Stock Exchange transactions. While the amount of bank balances used for that purpose is a factor, since it is not available for commercial transactions, the speed with which these balances circulate between investors, speculators, brokers, and jobbers does not affect the price level. What matters from the point of view of a monetary policy is the velocity of circulation of money in connexion with commercial transactions, that is, in its use in payment for goods and services.

In itself the quantity of money would be unable to affect the price level if its velocity of circulation were nil, as is the case with permanently hoarded money. It is through changing hands that money affects prices, and the more often it changes hands the more it is liable to affect prices. This fact was realized at a very early stage in the development of monetary theory. Writers in the seventeenth century had already a vague idea that money is only effective if it is circulated and that its effectiveness increases with its velocity of circulation. Cantillon was the first to point out clearly in the early part of the eighteenth century that an increase of the velocity of circulation produces the same effect as an increase in the quantity of money, and that a decline in the velocity of circulation is liable to counteract an increase in its quantity. He expressed the view that if an excessive supply of money raises prices too much the prince or the legislator should try to delay the circulation of money in order to avoid an undue increase in the cost of living.

To put it briefly, money is effective as a factor affecting the price level only in so far as it is used in purchases of goods and services, and the degree of its effectiveness depends on the frequency with which it is used. The authorities may be in a position to increase or reduce the quantity of money in pursuing some end of monetary policy, but their efforts are liable to be frustrated if an increase in the quantity of money is followed by a corresponding slowing down of the velocity of its circulation or if a reduction in the quantity of money is accompanied by a corresponding increase in its velocity of circulation. While the quantity of money depends on the authorities, its velocity depends first and foremost on the willingness of consumers and producers to spend. An increase in the quantity of money merely provides the means to enable producers and consumers to spend

more. If the additional money is not available they cannot
spend more, unless they increase the velocity of circulation
of the existing quantity. But if additional money is made
available they may or may not make use of the additional
facilities. If they do not spend more it means that, although
the volume of money is larger, the average number of times
it changes hands becomes smaller, and the situation is apt to
remain the same as it was before when the quantity of
money was increased.

Conversely an increase in the velocity of the circulation
means that producers and consumers spend more even in
the absence of an expansion in the volume of money. Holders of currency and of bank deposits may decide to spend
more freely because they anticipate higher prices, or for
various other reasons. Their additional spending has the
same effect as any additional spending resulting from an increase in the quantity of money. As we tried to explain in
an earlier chapter, if an amount is spent the purchasing
power it represents does not disappear but becomes available for the recipients to use again and again. Each time
the money is spent it adds to the volume of demand. In the
absence of a corresponding and simultaneous increase in the
supply of goods, the additional demand tends to cause an
increase of prices, irrespective of whether it originated
through an increase in the quantity of money or through the
faster circulation of the existing quantity. If the spirit moves
the owners of the money to spend more freely so that the
money changes hands more frequently, this increase in the
velocity of its circulation may even offset some degree of
curtailment in its quantity.

In reality what often happens is that when the quantity
of money changes its velocity of circulation also tends to
change in the same sense. A rising trend in prices caused by
an increase of the quantity of money stimulates buying, and
the larger quantity of money is liable to change hands more
frequently. Conversely, when the quantity of money is reduced the declining trend of prices thus caused tends to discourage buying so that the velocity of circulation tends to

slow down. In the absence of official intervention changes
in the velocity of circulation thus tend to accentuate an upward or downward movement of prices.

The fact that the authorities have not the same power to
determine the velocity of circulation as they have to determine the quantity of money came to be fully realized during
the thirties. The United States and many other countries
embarked on a policy aiming at stimulating trade and
causing a rise in prices by means of pumping money into
circulation. It was found, however, that the response of the
economies of the countries concerned to the increase in the
quantity of money was very disappointing. Simultaneously
with the increase in the quantity of money its velocity of
circulation declined, because consumers and producers were
not inclined to increase their spending on consumers' goods
and capital goods respectively. Indeed, since producers and
consumers were reluctant to borrow, the monetary authorities were unable to bring about the desired degree of expansion of credit through increasing the cash reserves of banks.
The only way in which they were able to add to the monetary supply of the private sector of the national economy
was by unbalancing their Budgets through additional public
expenditure. Even this device had a limited effect on the
economy because the velocity of circulation of the additional money thus created was inclined to be sluggish. Many
recipients did not re-spend the money they received, so that
the 'multiplier' effect of the purchasing power created by
the Government was relatively small.

Yet, it is well to bear in mind, it is only through the multiplier effect that an increase in the volume of money can
produce its full effect on the price level. An increase in the
quantity of currency and credit by, say 10 per cent, is not
liable to cause an increase of the price level by anything like
10 per cent unless the additional money is spent several
times. Admittedly in a sensitive market, such as are most
commodity exchanges, an increase of the demand by 10 per
cent tends to produce an instantaneous effect. On the other
hand, retail merchants do not mark up their prices by 10 per

cent merely because on a given day or during a given week or month, their turnover has increased by 10 per cent. Nor do manufacturers or wholesale merchants necessarily quote higher prices to retailers as soon as the latter increase their orders by 10 per cent. The stocks of goods held by the trade would easily absorb a once-for-all additional demand of such magnitude without any effect on prices. It is only when, as a result of the repeated re-spending of the additional money, the increase in the demand has become sufficiently persistent that merchants and manufacturers in many lines of goods may feel justified in taking advantage of it by raising their prices. It is necessary to realize this in order to appreciate the importance of the velocity of circulation among the factors affecting the price level.

The experience of the thirties gave rise to a wave of defeatism about the helplessness of monetary policy, as a reaction from the realization of the falsity of the earlier belief according to which there are practically no limits to the powers of monetary policy in influencing the trend of prices and the course of economic activities. The defeatism was largely due to the realization of the extent to which a decline of the velocity of circulation of money is liable to nullify the effects of monetary policy devices aiming at the increase of its quantity.

In reality monetary policy is by no means as helpless in the sphere of the velocity of circulation as it appeared to be by many observers in the thirties. There are various means by which the authorities are able to accelerate or slow down the velocity of circulation as an alternative to changing the quantity of money or as a means of ensuring the effectiveness of changes in the quantity of money. The following are the means which monetary policy can use for speeding up the turnover of money:

(1) *Increase of Government expenditure.* Provided that it is not offset by an increase of revenue, this has the immediate effect of increasing the quantity of money. At the same time it also tends to increase its velocity of circulation through the operation of the multiplier. It stands to reason that any additional

large-scale expenditure, whether initiated by private interests or by the Government, is apt to put new life into the economy and to stir up a certain amount of activity resulting in an increase in the velocity of circulation. If private interests are not prepared to respond to an increase of their resources available for expenditure, then it is up to the Government to initiate the process. If the Government increases the volume of money through money market operations that in itself need not give rise to any additional spending. On the other hand, if the Government increases the volume of money by embarking on additional capital expenditure or by adding to the consumers' purchasing power, without taking away the new surplus by an increase of taxation, it is liable to increase also the velocity of circulation.

(2) *Reducing Taxation.* Any reduction of direct taxes, provided that it is not accompanied by a corresponding reduction in public expenditure, tends to increase the purchasing power of the private sector of the economy. The chances are that at least part of the increase will be spent and re-spent again and again, thereby causing an increase in the velocity of circulation. A reduction of indirect taxation is apt to produce a similar effect because lower prices are apt to tempt buyers to spend. For instance, a reduction of Purchase Tax on motor cars is liable to be followed by immediate increase of demand. If some of the burden of taxation is shifted from those who are liable to save to those who are liable to spend the result is an increase in the velocity of circulation.

(3) *Repayment of Public Debt.* If the Government repays a maturing debt held largely by the public the chances are that at least some of the recipients will spend the proceeds. In addition to the increase in the volume of money its velocity is also likely to increase. No such dual effect is produced if the debt is held by banks, insurance companies, etc., though it is possible that the money thus released may be lent to people who in turn will spend it.

(4) *Lowering of Interest Rates.* This tends to increase not

only the quantity of money but also its velocity of circulation because it provides an inducement to borrow more and therefore to spend more freely. The public need not necessarily respond to this inducement, however, any more than it need respond to an increase in the volume of credit.

(5) *Moral Pressure and Propaganda.* In addition to increasing their own spending Governments can accelerate the circulation of money by encouraging the spending of others. Moral persuasion, such as official declarations to the effect that now is the time to embark on capital investments or to purchase consumer goods, may or may not meet with the expected response, but it is reasonable to assume that the public is more inclined to spend if it is officially encouraged to do so. The organization of festivities and various other devices are at the Government's disposal to reinforce its appeal.

(6) *The Provision of 'Inducement Goods'.* In a country which has experienced a period of scarcity of goods it is easy for the authorities to stimulate buying activity through arranging the reappearance of various kinds of goods which had been unobtainable for some time past. The reappearance of such goods is liable to induce consumers to spend more freely. Inducement goods are used in backward countries to tempt the population to take up industrial employment in order to be able to spend more. In such situations the effect of the increase in the velocity of circulation on prices is liable to be offset in the long run by an increase in the volume of goods.

(7) *Increased Frequency of Payments.* This is one of the means, suggested by Cantillon more than two centuries ago, by which to provide trade with more money without an increase in the quantity of money. He argued that if rents were made payable more frequently the effect would be the same as that of an increase in the quantity of money, because the change in the practice would reduce monetary requirements, at the same time as increasing the velocity of circulation. Smaller amounts would change hands more frequently. The same result could be obtained if wages and

salaries were to be paid at more frequent intervals. It is doubtful whether such an increase in the velocity of circulation would materially affect the demand.

The following are the means at the disposal of the monetary authorities for reducing the velocity of circulation of money:

(1) *Moral Pressure and Propaganda to Discourage Spending.* In the same way as some members of the public are influenced in favour of spending when encouraged by official statements, economy campaigns may also meet with response. The way the British public responded to exhortations of this kind in 1931 is an outstanding example.

(2) *Reduction of Facilities for Spending.* This can be done by means of rationing or by allowing the supplies of goods to become exhausted. As a result the public will have less opportunity for making purchases. If the amount thus saved is invested in Government loans, it reduces the quantity of money. If it is accumulated in cash or bank balances it reduces the velocity of circulation.

(3) *Fiscal Devices.* An increase in the total amount of taxation unaccompanied by an increase of public expenditure would reduce the volume of money and would not directly affect the velocity of its circulation. It is possible, however, for the Government to leave the total substantially unchanged and shift the burden of taxation from classes which are likely to spend to classes which are likely to save. In doing so the quantity of money would remain unchanged but the velocity of circulation would decline. A Budget surplus would indirectly lower the velocity of circulation in so far as it would cause a decline of prices and would tend to discourage spending. The multiplier effect would operate also in this direction. A reduction in the purchasing power of a single firm or individual could initiate a whole chain of reductions and their cumulative effect is liable to be a multiple of the amount with which the total purchasing power was originally reduced through higher taxation.

(4) *Raising Interest Rates.* At the same time as tending to lower the quantity of money higher interest rates tend to

lower its velocity of circulation. They tend to discourage borrowing and spending.

(5) *Reduced Frequency of Payments.* The suggestion to increase the velocity of the circulation of money through increasing the frequency of payments can be applied also in the reverse direction. The authorities may make their payments at less frequent intervals and may try to induce others to do the same in order to lower the velocity of circulation of money. Delays in payments on Government contracts tend to produce a similar effect. Less frequent payments of larger amounts would necessitate, however, an increase in the quantity of money, which might offset the effect of the reduction in the velocity of its circulation.

There are other more far-fetched suggestions for means to increase the velocity of circulation. During the early part of the nineteenth century Jeremy Bentham advocated interest-bearing money as a means of slowing down the velocity of circulation. A hundred years later Silvio Gesell advocated the opposite device, namely, the issue of a currency which has to be stamped every week by its holders. His idea was that in order to avoid the expense of stamping holders would hasten to spend their money and the velocity of circulation would increase.

Conceivably the increase of the denomination of the currency tends to slow down its velocity of circulation and the reduction of its denomination tends to produce the opposite effect. Adam Smith already observed that small money circulates faster than big money. Conceivably the decision of the British Government during the Second World War to withdraw all Bank of England notes in excess of £5 may have resulted in an incidental increase in the velocity of circulation.

Another factor observed by early writers on the subject is the difference in the velocity of circulation according to whether the money is held by wealthy or poor people. The former are inclined to hold larger cash balances while the latter may be under obligation to spend their money as soon as they receive it. For this reason the re-distribution of wealth making for a higher degree of equality tends to accelerate the velocity of circulation. This point was touched upon above when dealing with taxation as a device aiming at levelling down incomes.

Monetary policy in many countries aims at achieving economy in the use of notes through encouraging the banking habit. This in itself does not affect the velocity of circulation in our sense of the term. Under the modern definition of money it includes not only notes, but also bank deposits, and the substitution of payments by cheque for payment by cash leaves the velocity of circulation in our sense of the term unchanged.

CHAPTER TWENTY-NINE

The Quality of Money

HITHERTO we have been dealing with those means of monetary policy which are related directly or indirectly to the quantity of money. Monetary policy is concerned, however, also with the quality of money. In a narrower sense the quality of money means its intrinsic value, that is, its value for non-monetary purposes. In a broader sense the term covers also the buying capacity of money – which is a thing different from its purchasing power, as we propose to show below – and also the degrees of the security and liquidity of credit through which money originates under the modern system.

The monetary authorities are concerned with the quality of money either because it affects its quantity or because they accept the view that its purchasing power depends on its intrinsic value or its buying capacity. It stands to reason that if a high standard is set for the quality of the monetary object, whether it is sea-shells, or cattle, or coins, or credit, through the granting of which deposits are created, it is bound to limit the quantity. If those in charge of monetary policy are anxious to avoid inflation they can do so either by fixing direct limits to the quantity of money or by setting a high standard for its quality. At the same time those who regard money as a commodity may feel that any deterioration of its intrinsic value must necessarily entail a corresponding decline of its purchasing power, apart altogether from the inflationary effect of an increase in its quantity.

We saw in earlier chapters that from an early phase in monetary history the State authority took it on itself to protect the money of its community against depreciation through private debasements. In many instances before the adoption of metallic currency the choice of the monetary object or the confirmation of its monetary use by the State authority aimed at making its debasement difficult. Coinage was introduced for that very purpose. Nevertheless, in innumerable instances the State authority itself debased its coinage for its own benefit or for the real or imaginary benefit of the community. From an early stage debasement was regarded as a State monopoly. On the other hand, from time to time the official monetary policy aimed at raising the quality of currency by operations of re-coinage and other measures to eliminate clipped or counterfeit coins from circulation.

A policy of debasement stood to benefit the Treasuries largely because of the prolonged time-lag between the debasement and the rise in prices that followed it. It is often suggested by economic historians that debasement was a futile method from the point of view of the monarch who practised it because, having depreciated his currency, he had to accept taxation in terms of that depreciated currency. In reality, however, years had to pass before prices responded to the lowering of the quality of the coinage through debasement. For one thing, the general public was slow to notice a reduction in their metallic content. Moreover, as we pointed out before, prices, wages and other payments were very inelastic during the mediaeval period. This meant that the possession of a larger number of coins of the same denomination secured through debasement conferred on the monarch a lasting if not permanent advantage. He was in a position to finance wars or extravagant Court expenditure by increasing the number of coins minted out of the same quantity of metal. Had the price level responded spontaneously his gain would have disappeared in a very short time.

In this respect the position was substantially the same as it is under modern inflation. The increase in the volume of money assists in the financing of a war largely because there is a time-lag between monetary expansion and its effect on the price level. The moment prices have caught up with the degree of monetary inflation or debasement the advantage brought by the time-lag ceases, and the State authority can only secure further advantages by further doses of debasement or inflation. It is true the State stands to benefit by the entire additional purchasing power created through debasement or inflation incurred in connexion with a budgetary deficit, while the adverse effects of higher prices are spread between the public and private sectors of the national economy. Even so, in the long run the State stands to pay dearly for its short-lived gains.

The effect of debasement on prices would have been even slower if it had not been accompanied by an increase of the quantity of currency. Prices were rising not only because the public came to realize gradually that the intrinsic value of the coins was lower, but also because the increase of its circulation created additional purchasing power during the transition period between the increase in the quantity of coins and the full adjustment of the price level to this increase.

All but the most irresponsible princes and their advisers were most reluctant to resort to debasement. It usually encountered strong opposition and caused much discontent. In England the Rolls of Parliament are full of complaints against debasements, and the kings were often compelled to give an undertaking to abstain from tampering with the coinage. On the other hand, historians have the highest praise for kings who pursued the opposite policy by restoring the coinage to its original quality. These operations were not nearly as popular, however, in contemporary opinion as they are with the historian. They entailed grave inconveniences since they were bound to produce deflation. Producers and traders were at times almost as loud in complaining against the restoration of coinage as they had been against its debasement. When in 274 A.D. Aurelian attempted to restore the integrity of the debased Roman coinage he was faced by a dangerous insurrection, the suppression of which cost the lives of 7,000 soldiers. In a more recent characteristic instance in 1650 Stuyvesant tried to improve the quality of the wampum shell currency in New Amsterdam, but the deflation his measures entailed threatened to produce financial disaster, so that less than four months after issuing the ordinance he had to reverse it, and loose and imperfect bead-strings had to be accepted once more as legal tender.

The operation of Gresham's Law by which bad money tends to drive out good money set a limit to many attempts at improving the quality of coinage. In many instances in monetary history coins of high quality regularly disappeared through hoarding or export, in defiance of the official monetary policy. Coins of low quality remained the main circulating medium. Nevertheless, strong and sound Governments aimed at maintaining the high quality of their coinage. Roman coins during the ancient period, Byzantine coins during the Middle Ages, and sovereigns in more recent times acquired a world-wide reputation for their high quality.

Paper currency has, of course, no intrinsic value. Until recently it was widely held that its quality depended on its convertibility into gold or silver or, if it was inconvertible, on the prospects of its convertibility. The latter element was present even while the notes were actually convertible, because the size of the metallic reserves affected the prospects of being able to maintain their convertibility. Any action leading to an increase of the metallic reserve unaccompanied by an increase in the quantity of money tended to improve the quality of the notes. The proportion of the metallic reserve to the note circulation was regarded as the measurement of that quality. Once the convertibility of notes was suspended their quality was deemed to be determined entirely by the prospects of a resumption of their convertibility.

Although in some countries there is an agitation for a restoration of convertibility into gold coins, in Britain and most other countries such a change has long been considered out of the question. On the other hand, the quality of money may be considered to depend partly on the degree of its convertibility or prospects of convertibility into other currencies and partly on its buying capacity. This latter term should not be confused with purchasing power, which depends on the level of prices. The buying capacity of a money has nothing to do with the price level, but with the diversity and range of goods and services on which the money can be spent. Towards the end of the Second World War the purchasing power of money was reasonably well maintained with the aid of price controls and rationing. Its buying capacity declined, however, very considerably, because most commercial stocks were exhausted and the range of goods and services which could be bought was very limited. The position was the same in many countries.

It was one of the tasks of monetary policy in the early post-war period to raise the buying capacity of money, through the increase in the range of goods on which it could be spent, by means of production or import. This end was gradually achieved, so that while the purchasing power of money continued to decline almost incessantly its buying capacity increased materially during the early post-war years. The improvement of its quality did not prevent the depreciation of its purchasing power, though it seems reasonable to assume that had it not been for the increase of its buying capacity the fall in its purchasing power would have been even more pronounced. There would have been much less inducement to work or to sell goods in return for payment in money which could hardly buy anything beyond one's meagre rations.

The quality of credit is yet another sphere in which monetary policy can function. It is regulated primarily by the banks themselves, who lay down certain rules mainly to safeguard their own interests by making sure that the credits are well secured and reasonably liquid. In pursuing sound banking principles they improve the quality of credit and of the money it creates, at the same time as limiting its quantity. The authorities may take a hand by giving the banks guidance when this is considered necessary. Long before the advent of scientific monetary management the banking community was in the habit of expecting some degree of guidance in this sphere from the Central Bank, which was considered to be in a better position than individual banks to judge the general trend. In any case Central Banks had their own set of rules about bills which were eligible for rediscount, and these rules largely determined the requirements of all banks in this respect.

A high quality of credit money can be assured by insisting that bills and bank advances should be self-liquidating. Bills are seldom eligible for rediscount by the Central Bank unless they mature within three months. The quality of money created through bills or advances repayable in three months – during which period the goods whose production they finance may reasonably be expected to be sold – is obviously higher than that of money created in connexion with unproductive Government expenditure or even with productive long-term capital expenditure. There is, of course, no noticeable difference between notes or bank deposits created through self-liquidating credits and those created through an increase of the dead-weight debt. Nevertheless, even in the absence of an actual physical difference such as existed between full-valued and debased coins, there is bound to be some sort of intangible difference in favour of money produced through self-liquidating transactions financing the production of easily marketable goods. Any money created through long-term investment or unproductive Government expenditure remains in circulation and continues to give rise to additional demand each time it changes hands. On the other hand, money arising through self-liquidating short-term transactions is withdrawn when the credit is repaid and is re-issued again in connexion with some new productive self-liquidating transaction.

It is, or should be, the aim of monetary policy to ensure that any money created through unproductive or long-term transactions should be withdrawn at the earliest possible moment as a result of saving by the community. This end can be achieved through inducing the public to acquire newly-issued Government Loans or other long-term securities. In doing so they relinquish for some time at any rate the use of the purchasing power they possess. The ideal state of affairs is when all capital investments and Budgetary deficits are financed out of savings immediately as and when they arise. In such circumstances most money in circulation would originate through self-liquidating transactions.

Discriminatory credit policy aiming at discouraging credits to branches of industry in which there is evidence of over-trading also contributes towards maintaining the high quality of credit money, in addition to preventing an undue increase in its quantity. It prevents the development of situations in which credits originally meant to be self-liquidating become frozen.

CHAPTER THIRTY

Price Control

MEASURES affecting the quantity, price, quality, or velocity of money aim at influencing the price level by affecting one of the factors that normally determines the trend of prices. They aim at affecting the volume of demand for goods and services. In resorting to these measures monetary policy does not aim at resisting the operation of economic laws. On the contrary it seeks to employ normal economic tendencies for its purpose. We now propose to examine in this chapter devices of monetary policy which aim at defying economic laws by preventing or hampering their natural operation. It is the object or price control to prevent normal economic factors from producing their natural effect on the price level, or at any rate to moderate this effect. In this chapter we are no longer concerned with devices influencing the quantity of currency and credit in relation to the volume of goods and services. What we examine is the steps that the Governments can take in order to achieve their desired ends without resorting to such devices.

Price control is a very ancient means of monetary policy. It was already employed in the Hittite Empire during the fourteenth century B.C. An elaborate code fixed the price of domestic animals, agricultural products and other objects, and the wages of artisans, agricultural labourers, etc. An even more elaborate system of price fixing was adopted in the Roman Empire by Diocletian in the fourth century A.D. Throughout the Middle Ages highly elaborate systems of price control were in force in many communities, especially in the practically closed economies of the cities with an advanced system of guilds. It was only comparatively recently that price fixing was virtually abandoned by most Governments. The nineteenth century was the century of the free play of economic forces. During and after the two

World Wars, especially the Second World War, however, mankind reverted once more to price control on an extensive scale.

The usual object of price control is to achieve 'inflation without tears' by suppressing its natural effect on prices. This is considered necessary in given circumstances for several reasons. We saw in the previous chapter that inflation, like debasement, is liable to benefit the State to a particularly high degree during the time lag between the issue of additional money and the completion of the rise in prices it tends to produce. It is obviously to the interest of the authorities, therefore, to seek to prolong the transitional period by delaying or preventing prices from adapting themselves to the increased volume of money. Apart from this, it is to the interest of the whole community that the pace of currency depreciation should be mitigated and slowed down. Of course the community's interests would be better served if the Government, instead of suppressing the effects of inflation, refrained from inflating. But if inflation is unavoidable – for instance in the interests of national defence – there is much to be said for suppressing its effects on prices as far as possible during a critical period.

Price control pursues also social and political ends when it is largely confined to necessities and its object is to ensure adequate supplies for the poor. 'Rationing by purse' may be sound economics, but in given circumstances it may be anti-social, and it is apt to be unsound politics. Even from a purely economic point of view it is advantageous in given circumstances to keep down the prices of the essential components of the cost of living so as to avoid large-scale demands for wage increases as a result of a rise in the cost of living, provided that such an artificial state of affairs is maintained for a limited period only.

Even the most extensive system of price controls is unable to cover the whole range of goods and services available for sale. Usually it begins with a relatively small number of necessities in short supply, spreading gradually over a wider and wider range of goods and services. A discrepancy develops between the trend of the controlled and uncontrolled sections of the price level and tends to widen considerably. If, as is often the case, price control is accompanied by rationing, the public is unable to take full advantage of the artificially low prices by buying as much as it would like and could afford. Since the percentage of its inflated purchasing power that is used in the acquisition of rationed necessities thus declines, more will be available for the acquisition of uncontrolled goods and services.

The necessities are protected from the full effect of inflationary buying pressure, but that pressure exists nevertheless and becomes diverted towards the uncontrolled section of the price level. This means that while rises in the controlled section are kept lower than would be justified by the prevailing degree of inflation, rises in the uncontrolled section will tend to be more than proportionate to that degree. However, since a large part of the uncontrolled goods and services do not affect the cost of living of the wage-earners, their rise does not tend to accelerate the progress of inflation by leading to wage demands. A monetary policy which results in an unduly low price level in the controlled section of the economy and an unduly high price level in the uncontrolled section may be far from ideal, but it serves its purpose of delaying inflation. Provided that the artificial situation created is not unduly exaggerated or prolonged its results are apt to be beneficial on balance in given circumstances.

Legislation enacting price controls must contain penalty provisions in order to be effective. Since, however, the system runs counter to economic laws and to human nature even drastic penalties very often fail to discourage a large section of the public from breaking the law. In Britain the public is essentially law-abiding. Even so the operation of price controls and rationing was accompanied by the development of black markets if only on a relatively small scale. In other countries the policy of price controls was largely defeated by the extent of the black markets. In countries such as France or Italy the evasion of the law was the rule and its observance the exception. Only a fraction of the requirements and necessities could be covered on the basis of the controlled prices, so that for all practical purposes the price level in the black markets had to be regarded as the effective price level. Even in Soviet Russia and other Communist countries there have been black markets in spite of the threat of the death penalty, which was unable to ensure a watertight price control. This was realized after a while, and an officially tolerated free market in many goods was allowed to develop.

Penalty clauses in themselves are unable to ensure effective price control. They have to be supplemented by other measures such as Government trading, or trading under licence, or subsidies. One of the reasons why rationing and price control in many necessities was incomparably more effective in Britain than in other countries was that the major part of the supplies had to be imported, and it is comparatively easy to control imports. The Government secured the necessary supplies from overseas by means of bulk buying, often on long-term contracts. In order to secure the supplies produced within the country the Government had to adopt a system of subsidies. The farmers received the full price for their products in accordance with prevailing conditions. The consumers were charged considerably less and the difference was paid by the taxpayer in the form of subsidies. Likewise the Government re-sold the imported food at a loss at the taxpayer's expense.

The failure of a policy of price control through wholesale evasion has grave disadvantages from an economic, social and political point of view. It was largely responsible for the series of successive currency devaluations which France and Italy had to make after the Second World War. It was also largely responsible for the strength of the Communist Party in France and Italy. The inability of the lower income groups to meet their requirements for necessities otherwise than through purchases in the black market must have been largely responsible for the atmosphere of discontent in which subversive activities were thriving.

On the other hand the success of price control also entails grave disadvantages, because it tempts Governments to make excessive use of it in spite of the gross distortion of the economy it produces. This point is best illustrated by the effects of rent control. Rents are one of the few categories of prices the control of which can be enforced effectively not only in Britain but even in countries where price control is generally ineffective. Because of the ease with which landlords can be compelled to continue to let their premises at uneconomical rents a situation has developed in which these rents are no longer sufficient to meet the cost of essential repairs. Consequently rent-controlled property is allowed to deteriorate, and in many instances it becomes uninhabitable after prolonged rent control.

Moreover, artificially low rents tend to stimulate excessive demand for housing accommodation. Even the most effective housing drive which diverts an unduly large proportion of the nation's resources from other essential requirements is unable to keep pace with this demand. Rent control artificially stimulates the demand for something which cannot be supplied in sufficient quantity to meet the increased demand. The same thing is of course true about the price control of meat and other foodstuffs in short supply. But they at least can be rationed so as to ensure equal distribution on the basis of the artificially low prices. Since, however, rationing of housing accommodation is impracticable, the result of rent control is that those in possession enjoy the full advantages of low rents while those who are unfortunate enough to have to look for accommodation are either unable to meet their requirements or have to pay exorbitant prices.

An argument against the maintenance of rents and of the prices of food and other necessities at an artificially low level is that it stimulates demand for luxuries and necessities which are not rationed or price-controlled. The result is that the prices of such goods tend to rise considerably more than they would in the complete absence of price control. Since it is difficult if not impossible to ration and price-control certain necessities such as fresh vegetables or fruit, the cost of living of the lower income groups cannot be safeguarded altogether against the effects of inflation with the aid of price control. Since the artificially low prices and rationing of many necessities reduces the amount that can be spent on them, all but the poorest classes are liable to have a surplus purchasing power which they may employ on the purchase of luxuries. This means that in practice the taxpayers' money that is spent on subsidizing price-controlled necessities, subsidizes in reality also the purchase of luxuries such as television sets.

On the other hand it is argued that it is right that in the Welfare State necessities should be made available to all, if not free of charge, at any rate at very low prices. To that end a perpetuation of subsidized food and other necessities is favoured by many people even at the cost of economic disadvantages such as the perpetuation of high taxation. There are many other arguments for and against price controls, but it is outside our scope to deal with them.

Most economists admit that there is a great deal to be said for price control during an emergency such as a war or even in conditions such as the rearmament drive of 1950–52, provided that the artificial situation that they create is not unduly exaggerated. Against its obvious advantages it is necessary to offset the disadvantages of the disequilibrium it creates. It tends to be cumulative in character. The longer price control is applied the more artificial the situation tends to become. This does not necessarily mean that it must be condemned unconditionally as a means of monetary policy. What it means is that those applying it should be fully aware of its long-range disadvantages, instead of working under the delusion that State authority is omnipotent and is in a position to defy permanently the law of supply and demand.

Price control is apt to stimulate artificially the demand for goods the supplies of which cannot keep pace with the demand. Consumption in any given country may be raised by price control beyond the level which that country can afford. The result is an adverse balance of payments which may eventually compel the Government to apply measures by which to reduce the volume of purchasing power.

Government trading is another device by which Governments may seek to prevent or moderate a rise in prices. Its primary aim is usually outside the realm of monetary policy. The Government may embark on buying up supplies in order to secure scarce stocks or to ensure their fair distribution. It is a highly controversial point whether bulk buying by Governments makes for higher or lower prices. Long-term contracts with producing countries may have a steadying effect on the prices of imported food and raw materials and may play therefore some part in a policy of stabilizing the price level.

Yet another means by which the Government may try to intervene in order to influence the price level is legislation against monopolies and restrictive practices. One of the main arguments in support of such legislation is that it is likely to result in lower prices within the range of goods to which it applies. On the other hand it must be admitted that monopolies and restrictive practices have a steadying influence on the price level while unfettered competition is apt to cause instability. If rightly or wrongly a Government adopts price controls, their enforcement is greatly simplified by the existence of monopolies or of practices such as resale price maintenance, under which the trade associations ensure the maintenance of officially approved prices.

Monetary policy possesses devices not only for preventing a rise in prices or bringing about their reduction, but also for pursuing the opposite end. In given situations the authorities may aim at preventing falls in prices or at enforcing their rise by devices of price control. The fixing of maximum prices in general may serve the purpose of raising prices because in given circumstances maximum prices are apt to become minimum prices. By raising maximum prices the authorities may ensure favourable prices for producers.

Price controls are in some instances supplemented by controls of wages. They too can operate in both ways. The Government may fix the wage ceilings in an attempt at slowing down inflation or it may fix minimum wages. The former is an instrument of monetary policy, the latter an instrument of social policy.

K

CHAPTER THIRTY-ONE

Foreign Exchange Policy

MOST authors dealing with the subject of monetary policy consider foregn exchange policy as a thing apart. Yet the policies aiming at influencing the domestic monetary situations and those aiming at influencing the foreign exchange situation are closely interrelated. Measures affecting the volume, purchasing power, velocity of circulation, price or quality of money are liable to react on exchange rates. Conversely, any noteworthy and sustained rise or fall in the exchange rates is liable to react on the internal monetary situation. Indeed, the internal and international aspects of money are two inseparable aspects of the same thing. As a general rule anything that concerns the one is bound to concern the other. Internal price levels and exchange value are apt to be influenced by the same factors and also to influence each other reciprocally. Monetary policy may use foreign exchanges as means to pursue its ends in respect of the internal monetary situation. It may also use various monetary or non-monetary devices to influence the foreign exchange situation.

Beyond doubt exchange rates constitute the most obvious and the most sensitive barometer indicating the value of money. The metaphor, however, is not altogether correct. No barometer has ever yet been known to have influenced in the least the weather; on the other hand, movements on exchanges are liable to react sharply on the internal monetary situation. This fact has long been realized. Indeed from time to time it has been grossly exaggerated by governments guilty of the mismanagement of their currencies. It was convenient to put the blame for the deterioration of the internal monetary situation on exchange depreciation over which they claimed to have no control. The great debasement of Henry VIII in 1551, one of the most flagrant instances of currency juggling in British history, provided an early instance of that attitude. Those responsible for it were at pains to put the blame on speculators, even though the depreciation of the exchange merely expressed the debasement of the coinage. Again in Britain after the Napoleonic Wars the official view that the increase of the Bank of England's inconvertible note issue was not the cause of the depreciation of sterling in terms of gold, which was claimed to be the consequence of the adverse exchange rate, was upheld stubbornly in face of the more enlightened views put forward by Ricardo and the Bullion Committee.

However, exaggerated as the view is that the internal value of money depends on its exchange rate, it contains a sufficient degree of truth to make it evident that monetary policy, concerned with maintaining the internal stability of money, cannot afford to ignore exchange rates and that any action taken in respect of foreign exchanges has very strong bearing on the internal monetary situation.

The authorities can influence the foreign exchange position to a great extent by means of devices applied to the internal monetary position. In addition there are general devices of economic policy which can be used for influencing foreign exchanges in the sense desired. The authorities have a powerful weapon in their ability to influence international capital movements. We saw in earlier chapters how short-term capital movements respond to changes of interest rates. The same factor affects also long-term capital movements in that it influences the extent of lending and of borrowing abroad. One of the lessons which the experience of the Second World War and the post-war period taught was that monetary policy is able to influence to a hitherto unsuspected degree the level of long-term interest rates. The Government, by determining the yield of its own long-term loans through open market operations and other devices, also influences the rate of interest at which foreign borrowers can cover their requirements in the loan market. In addition it can impose official or unofficial embargoes on foreign loans as an alternative to discouraging them by means of raising the interest rates on its own loans. An un-official embargo on foreign loans was more or less in operation in Britain during the greater part of the inter-war period, as a means of safeguarding sterling against adverse pressure through overlending. It was replaced by an official embargo at the outbreak of the Second World War, and right up to the time of writing the issue or private placing of securities for the benefit of foreign borrowers requires special permission.

Yet another way in which the authorities can safeguard the exchange value of sterling against the effects of excessive lending abroad is through insisting that the proceeds must be spent within the lending country. This principle was adopted to an increasing degree during the inter-war period by Britain, as a sharp contrast to her liberal attitude before the First World War. Even the United States resorted to it in connexion with the operations of the official Import-Export Bank. In the case of Marshall Aid and U.S. military aid the rule was that a large part of the dollars received must be spent in the United States, though a certain proportion was made expendable in the receiving country or on 'off-shore purchases' in third countries.

Customs tariffs and embargoes on imports are frequently adopted not for the purpose of protecting domestic industries against foreign competition, but for the sake of protecting the national exchange against pressure through an adverse trade balance. An outstanding instance of customs tariffs adopted for that purpose was that of the McKenna Duties. They were adopted during the First World War not in order to protect the British motor industry and the other industries concerned against American and other foreign competition but in order to safeguard sterling against excessive selling pressure. Most of the discriminatory quantitative import restrictions adopted during and after the Second World War pursued a similar aim.

Hitherto we have been dealing with indirect official intervention to safeguard exchanges. The authorities have, however, a wide variety of means of influencing exchange rates also by means of direct intervention in the foreign exchange market. The object of such intervention is to keep the rate stable, or at any rate steady; or to moderate a depreciation or appreciation of the exchange; or to cause such a depreciation or appreciation, according to the ends monetary policy pursues.

The maintenance of an absolutely stable exchange rate is known as 'pegging'. It was applied extensively during both World Wars. During the First World War free dealings in the foreign exchange market were maintained, but the New York agents of the British authorities had instructions to buy all sterling offered in New York at the official rate of $4.76. Likewise the French franc was pegged for years in relation to both sterling and the dollar. During the Second World War the maintenance of fixed exchange rates was achieved not by official intervention in the foreign exchange market, but by means of instituting an official monopoly of exchange dealings at fixed official rates.

When in 1951 dealings were resumed in the foreign exchange market at London, the authorities fixed the upper and lower limits of exchange rates at which they were prepared to buy or sell dollars in order to prevent the sterling-dollar rate from rising or falling beyond those limits. Some scope was allowed for fluctuations within a narrow range so that the policy was not one of pegging but one of maintaining sterling steady around its official parity of $2.80.

From time to time during the thirties various exchange rates were maintained reasonably steady over prolonged periods by means of systematic official intervention whenever there was a tendency for the rates to depart from the approximate level at which the authorities wanted to hold them.

The aims of the official monetary policy are often more ambitious than the mere maintenance of the exchanges at a given level. The authorities often deem it necessary for a variety of reasons to intervene in order to bring about an appreciation or a depreciation of the exchange. Instances of the latter course can be found during the period of competitive currency depreciations in the thirties. More often than not the authorities did not actually intervene by operations causing their currency to depreciate. They merely abstained from supporting it against an adverse trend. This meant that while they intervened to buy up any excess of supplies of foreign exchanges, they did not intervene to make up for any deficiency of supplies but allowed the rate to find its own level at which private supply and demand balanced. Over a period this meant that they drained the market of a large proportion of the foreign exchanges, so that it was unable to meet the demand unless and until the exchange depreciated. By such means it was possible to build up a foreign exchange reserve and to bring the exchange rate to a level at which the task of supporting it became easier.

Throughout monetary history the authorities of various countries frequently intervened to prevent an unwanted depreciation by methods much more active than those practised for the purpose of holding the rate at a fixed figure. Many instances can be quoted of attempts at 'squeezing' those speculators who gambled for a depreciation of the exchanges concerned. We saw in Chapter 11 that the accumulation or defence of the gold reserve is one of the major ends of monetary policy, for the sake of which the authorities are at times prepared to put up with the disadvantages of adjustments of parities or fluctuations of exchange rates.

In the nineties there was a successful squeeze of 'bears' speculating against Russian rouble notes. The Finance Minister, Count Witte, achieved this aim by suddenly forbidding the export of rouble notes from Russia. Speculators in Berlin who had sold roubles for future delivery were unable to deliver the roubles they had sold. As a result of their efforts to buy the rate went to a high premium. The speculators were taught a sharp and costly lesson, and for a long time they kept away from the rouble. Thirty years later M. Poincaré carried out a somewhat similar 'bear squeeze' against speculators in francs in 1924. As by then speculation was no longer in notes but in exchanges, the prohibition of supplying speculators with notes was replaced by a restriction on franc credits to be granted to them. This, together with active intervention with the aid of credits raised in London and New York, brought about a sharp appreciation of the franc and gravely penalized speculators. Since French finances remained shaky speculative attacks against the franc were resumed from time to time. In 1926 Poincaré intervened once more successfully and secured stabilization for the franc for a period of ten years. During the late thirties, however, the franc came under fire again and many attempts at official intervention failed to produce a lasting effect.

It is evident that the authorities stand a better chance of effective intervention if they have scope for manoeuvring with the exchange. The scope of any manoeuvring is bound to be very limited if the rate has to be kept within a very narrow range. If the speculators know that sterling will not appreciate in any circumstances above $2.82 then their risk in speculating against it even when it is quoted at the low limit of $2.78 appears to be negligible. Many of them may consider it well worth taking on the chance of making a large profit in case the authorities should be unable to prevent a substantial depreciation. On the other hand if the upper limit of sterling exchange is not fixed then speculators are not in a position to calculate the extent of their risk, which may well be considered by many people so heavy as to offset their chances to make profit. This is one of the arguments in favour of an 'elastic' sterling. But there are many weighty considerations against it.

From an early period various Governments recognized the advantages of active intervention aimed at bringing about an appreciation of the exchange. This was done repeatedly and extensively in the sixteenth century by Gresham, who operated on behalf of his Tudor masters in the Antwerp market. In a Memorandum to Queen Elizabeth I, written some four hundred years ago, he advocated the establishment of what would be called in modern language an Exchange Stabilization Fund. The only reason why his advice was not followed was that the Government could not spare the funds required for the purpose. Even in the absence of regular resources he managed, however, to raise substantially the value of sterling on more than one occasion.

During the ensuing centuries Gresham's policy of active intervention had fallen into disuse. Official foreign exchange policy largely followed the principle he stated in paragraph 8 (1) of his Memorandum to Queen Elizabeth I: 'The waye to rayse the exchaunge for England: By making money scante in Lumbard strete.'

Throughout the nineteenth century and right up to the early thirties of the present century, the British monetary authorities largely confined themselves to influencing exchange rates by means of raising and lowering interest rates. They abstained from active intervention in the foreign exchange markets. Under the gold standard exchange rates were allowed to take care of themselves. They fluctuated freely between gold import points and gold export points.

Until recently the Bank of England did not even have a foreign exchange department of its own. It was not until the early thirties that the Bank of England assumed an active rôle in the foreign exchange market, acting on behalf of the Treasury. After some costly initial mistakes the Exchange Equalization Account became a formidable factor, and its interventions were on balance highly successful. By the middle thirties it became so efficient that speculators left sterling severely alone, and the turnover in foreign exchanges was largely confined to genuine commercial and arbitrage operations. The authorities intervened from time to time in order to prevent or mitigate the effect of seasonal or other temporary demand for dollars. Some big requirements such as those of large tobacco-importing countries were satisfied directly in circumvention of the market in order to obviate the psychological effect of the evidence of a sudden heavy demand for dollars.

Other Central Banks adopted a policy of active intervention long before the Bank of England. During the nineteenth and early twentieth centuries it was part of the functions of the Austro-Hungarian Bank to relieve the market of seasonal surpluses of exchanges and to supply the market in between export seasons. This together with resistance to speculative fluctuations has long been regarded as forming part of the normal functions of monetary policy.

During the First World War the monetary authorities of a number of countries embarked on a much more ambitious task. They attempted to defend the national currency against depreciation in defiance of the fundamental adverse trend caused by internal inflation, and the strongly unfavourable trade balance. Although prices in Britain were rising much faster than in the United States, the official policy maintained right up to 1919 the sterling-dollar rate at a discount of about 2 per cent of the pre-War parity of 4.86. This was possible so long as imports were handicapped by war-time lack of shipping space. Immediately after the War, however, lower prices in the United States resulted in heavy imports, and when the sterling dollar rate was unpegged it immediately depreciated sharply. France and Italy had a similar experience.

In the Second World War exchange stability was achieved by exchange control which, together with import control, continued during the post-War period. For this reason it was possible to maintain the exchange rate at its War-time figure up to 1949 when the Government felt impelled to devalue sterling. This experience shows that attempts at maintaining exchange at an artificial level are liable to fail in the long run even if they are supported by a system of controls which tends to isolate to a high degree the economy of country concerned from world economy.

CHAPTER THIRTY-TWO

Exchange Restrictions

EXCHANGE restrictions have a direct bearing on the international monetary situation because their main object is usually to prevent a depreciation of the exchanges which would take place in their absence. Consequently exchange restrictions have a bearing also on the internal monetary situation of the country adopting them. For, as we pointed out in the last chapter, the internal value of money is liable to be influenced considerably by exchange movements. Admittedly exchange restrictions are used occasionally for the purpose of protecting domestic producers or influencing the trend of foreign trade for its own sake rather than for the sake of producing a monetary effect. In the majority of instances, however, their object is mainly monetary.

In their origins exchange restrictions mostly assumed the form of bans on international movements of coins and precious metals. The first known instance is the prohibition of the import of coins in Sparta. The death penalty was imposed on those in possession of hoards of foreign coins. This was partly because the possession of such bonds, consisting as they did mostly of the coins of Athens or some other hostile State, were taken as evidence of treason. The main motive, however, was probably the desire to safeguard the local currency of iron bars against being discredited through the use of a more valuable and more convenient currency. Another instance of early attempts at exchange restriction was the efforts of various Roman Emperors during the period of decline to check the drain on precious metals due to the adverse balance of trade with the East.

The first legislative evidence of exchange restrictions in England is contained in the Statute of Stepney in 1299 which imposed a ban on the export of coins. Subsequent statutes confirmed this and extended it to cover the export of bullion. This restriction remained more or less in force right up to 1819. It was the manifestation of the bullionist conception which dominated economic thought during the late Middle Ages and the beginning of the modern period.

It is easy to criticize the short-sightedness of the policy trying to prevent the export of coin and bullion by means of embargoes and by compelling exporters to surrender the proceeds of their exports to the authorities. Admittedly these devices caused a great deal of inconvenience and were not easily enforceable. The alternative device to restrictions was, however, competitive debasement, which is obviously the worse of the two evils. The dilemma which confronted various Governments during the fourteenth and fifteenth centuries was substantially the same as the one that confronts many present-day Governments, namely, whether to allow their exchanges to depreciate or to bolster them up with the aid of exchange restrictions. Both solutions were resorted to during that period. Exchange restrictions were considered preferable and were almost constantly in force. They had to be supplemented, however, from time to time by debasements largely because they could not be enforced to a sufficient extent to safeguard the supply of coins and precious metals.

The Statute of Westminster in 1343 was inspired by bullionist policy. It laid down the rule that merchants exporting wool must surrender two marks of silver for each sack of wool exported. Similar measures were passed on many subsequent occasions. During the same period attempts were also made to apply the bilateralist principle of balancing trade with individual countries through the Statute of Employment under which foreign merchants selling goods in England were compelled to spend the proceeds on the purchase of English goods within a limited period.

In addition to restrictions on bullion movements and on the disposal of the proceeds of exports, restrictions on transfers of money abroad by means of bills of exchange also made their appearance at an early stage. Bills of exchange as a means for settling claims arising from foreign trade were first adopted in Italy during the thirteenth century, and became increasingly popular in England largely through the activities of Italian merchants and bankers established in London. Nor were they confined to direct payments for foreign trade transactions. They became a favourite method of transferring balances whenever this was more profitable than bullion shipments or whenever bullion shipments were forbidden. It took some time before the rulers and their advisers realized that from the point of view of their supplies of coins it makes little difference in the long run whether the proceeds of imports into their countries are remitted through the physical transfer of precious metals, in coin or bullion, or through transactions in bills of exchange. In a number of Statutes – for instance in a Statute of Richard II in 1390 – the shipment of coin and bullion is forbidden, but transfers through bills of exchange were lawful. As a result it became the regular practice of Italian merchants to secure the remittance of the proceeds of their exports to Britain by means of triangular exchange operations through the Low Countries. They employed sterling bills for the settlement of their purchases in the Low Countries, and the latter used these sterling bills in payment for wool, and later for cloth, imported from England. As a result England lost the bullion proceeds of these wool and cloth exports as effectively as if she had allowed the Italians to repatriate their balances in the form of bullion.

It took some time to realize this fact. When it was eventually realized Statutes were enacted forbidding transactions in bills of exchange except under special licence. The preamble of the Statute passed under Richard III in 1483 accused the Italians of transferring money by exchange 'to the king's great damage and to the impoverishment of his subjects'. It was repealed two years later by Henry VII, under whose efficient administration the country's monetary position became sufficiently strong to make such extreme measures of restriction superfluous. It had to be resorted to again, however, under the less prudent administration of Henry VIII. In 1531 merchants were forbidden once more to engage in exchange transactions without special licence. For the rest of the Tudor regime the granting of such licences was made the responsibility of the Royal Exchanger. Among others Sir Thomas More filled that important post for some time.

Throughout the sixteenth century lively controversy was raging around the question whether or not to prohibit exchange transactions. Gresham himself was against them because he felt confident that it was possible to safeguard the exchanges by means of intervention instead of restrictions. We saw in the last chapter that his confidence in this respect was well founded on achievement. Nevertheless he himself resorted to exchange restrictions on occasions, compelling English merchants to surrender to him the proceeds of their sales of cloth in Antwerp.

Disposal of the bullion owned by the subjects was considered a royal prerogative which was exercised by Charles I in 1640 when he seized the bullion deposits of merchants in the Tower. Under Charles II there were indications of a more liberal tendency. The re-export of foreign coins and bullion was permitted. It was not until the early part of the nineteenth century, however, that freedom of bullion movements was fully established. During the period of economic liberalism the art of exchange restrictions came to be forgotten altogether, so that when it became necessary to revert to them during the two World Wars all the rules had to be learnt from the beginning. In any case in the meantime the entire monetary system had undergone considerable changes.

Such was the reluctance to depart from liberal principles that for a long time during the First World War it remained legally possible to export gold. The Bank of England's notes remained convertible. It was not by legislative measures but by refusal of shipping space and facilities under the War Risk Insurance scheme that a *de facto* embargo on gold exports was gradually adopted. Not until after the end of the war was the export of gold made illegal. All the time the foreign exchange market remained free of restriction and was controlled by means of intervention. In other countries, on the other hand, exchange restrictions were put in operation during the war and the export of precious metals was prohibited. Most of these restrictions were removed after the stabilization of the currencies during the twenties.

During the monetary crises that followed the suspension of the gold standard in 1931 Britain retained the freedom of exchanges and bullion movements, preferring to allow sterling to depreciate rather than to hold it stable by means of restrictions. Germany, on the other hand, having had an overdose of currency depreciation after the First World War, considered restrictions the lesser evil. A number of countries in Central Europe and elsewhere followed the German example, while others got the best or worst of both worlds by adopting exchange restrictions at the same time as devaluing their currencies.

Let us now examine briefly the various types of exchange restrictions that came to be adopted by most countries after 1931, and more especially during and after the Second World War. They can be divided, broadly speaking, into two categories according to whether they aim at restricting capital movements or current trade transactions. An unofficial embargo on long-term investments abroad was in force in Britain for many years before 1939. At the outbreak of the War it was reinforced by an official ban on transfer of capital outside the Sterling Area. The British authorities went even further by ordering the surrender of existing holdings of foreign currencies and foreign investments. During the First World War it was sought to achieve the same end without applying compulsion, by imposing a special tax on the yield of securities which the Treasury wanted to secure for its own requirements. By the beginning of the Second World War liberal traditions had weakened sufficiently for the Government to adopt unhesitatingly direct official restrictions in this sphere as in the sphere of bullion exports. Most belligerent and many neutral Governments acted likewise.

It was not until some months after the outbreak of the Second World War that the British authorities realized the need for restricting the disposal of the proceeds of exports. In theory the measure compelling the surrender of foreign assets appeared to be sufficient. In practice the freedom of exporters to dispose of their assets left a very large loophole with the aid of which it was possible to build up large illicit foreign balances. To prevent this it was made compulsory for exporters to surrender the proceeds of their sales abroad. In the interests of an effective enforcement of exchange restrictions, free dealings in exchanges were suspended. Exporters and others in possession of foreign currencies had to surrender their holdings to an authorized dealer and the latter had to surrender it to the Bank of England. Importers and others requiring exchange for approved purposes had to apply for the allocation of the necessary amounts through their banks to the Bank of England. The latter became the sole source through which most foreign currencies were obtainable. It had fixed buying and selling rates with a narrow margin between them. It also sold forward exchanges to importers at fixed rates.

Although at the beginning of the War there were many loopholes through which exchange restrictions could be evaded, in the course of time the system became almost watertight. Its enforcement was made easier through Britain's insular position which obviated the need for controlling long land frontiers. War-time conditions made it comparatively easy to control traffic through the ports and also to keep an eye on communications by means of postal and telegraphic censorship. In Germany a watertight control had already been achieved before the War by the application of draconian measures which in time of peace are only possible in a totalitarian country.

The operation of exchange restrictions in various countries provided an opportunity for the adoption of a wide variety of monetary devices. In 1931, the system of 'exchange clearing' was inaugurated between Hungary and Switzerland. It was subsequently adopted by a large number of countries. In substance it is a sophisticated version of the Statutes of Employment that operated in England many centuries

earlier. The basic principle was that the proceeds of exports
had to be spent in the importing country. The system lent
itself to an almost infinite variety of methods that came to
be known as 'Schachtian devices', even though the ex-
President of the Reichsbank did not invent all of them. Substantially they were based on the principle that in a troubled
world the debtor is in a strong position to insist that creditors should go out of their way to enable him to pay his
debt. The system was grossly abused by Germany before
and during the War. Having bought large quantities of
goods from her various satellite countries in Central and
South-East Europe, they were compelled to buy from
Germany unnecessary goods – such as mouth organs and
aspirins – or goods at high prices, in order to receive payment at all. Nevertheless, the system has the advantage of
making creditor nations realize that they must import in
order to be able to export.

We said earlier in this chapter that one of the main
objects of exchange restrictions is to prevent the transfer of
capital. In Britain and other countries war-time restrictions
were imposed not in order to prevent foreigners from withdrawing their capital, but in order to prevent British
nationals from sending their capital abroad. In Germany,
on the other hand, the object of restrictions adopted in 1931
was to prevent the withdrawal of national as well as foreign
capital. Subsequently similar restrictions were also imposed
in Britain, though sterling was not blocked as a rule in the
strict sense of the term. For one thing it was always possible to transfer capital within the Sterling Area. Foreign
holders of sterling were also in a position to switch their
investment subject to certain limitations. Above all foreign
owners of sterling were permitted to sell their sterling to
residents of their own country or of the group of countries
to which their country belonged from the point of view of
British exchange regulations. Various types of sterling
accounts developed with varying degrees of transferability.
Accordingly in foreign exchange markets abroad they were
quoted at varying rates.

This system, described as 'multiple currency practice', was brought to a fine art in Germany before the war. The various types of reichsmarks held by foreign owners were allowed to be used for certain strictly defined purposes. Some of them were available to travellers in Germany; others could be spent on certain types of German goods. If the German Government was keen on stimulating the export of some goods, permission was granted for these goods to be paid for in certain types of blocked reichsmarks. Owing to their limited use these reichsmarks were quoted at a substantial discount abroad as a result of which foreign importers were able to secure the goods in question – the so-called 'additional exports' – at a low price.

Another system of multiple exchange rates was the one practised in the Argentine. Before the war exporters were compelled to surrender their foreign exchange to the Government at a rather unfavourable rate, while importers had to bid against each other at auctions to obtain the foreign exchange they needed. This practice secured considerable profit to the Argentine Government. After the war the system pursued was that of differential exchange rates according to the types of imports and exports. If the Argentine Government wanted to stimulate the import of certain goods the necessary foreign exchange was allotted to importers at a favourable rate, otherwise they had to pay much less favourable rates. Conversely if the Argentine Government wanted to encourage certain exports the exporters received more favourable rates when surrendering their foreign exchanges. It would be easy to multiply the instances of the more or less involved currency practices arising from exchange restrictions. The above instances should suffice, however, to give the reader an idea of the nature of these practices and the range they cover.

In most instances the original object of exchange restrictions was to keep down the demand for foreign currencies within the limit of the supply and to ensure that the supply available is used for approved purposes. In the course of their application, however, the purpose of exchange restrictions usually tends to broaden. From a technical device they are apt to develop into a major instrument of economic policy. Behind the shelter of exchange restrictions the domestic price level is apt to lose touch with the world level to some extent. The wider the discrepancy, the more stringent are the measures needed to bolster up the artificial position. The belief in the possibility of isolating the national economy from world economy with the aid of exchange restrictions tends to encourage the adoption of costly inflationary economic and social policies, such as a country under a liberal monetary regime could not risk in face of international competition. Beyond doubt those policies are apt to secure considerable advantages under the shielding cloak of restrictions, but only at the cost of making the situation increasingly artificial and dependent for its existence on the efficiency of isolation. Whether the result is worth the cost is largely a matter of opinion and one of degree.

In the democratic countries, it was found to be impossible for any one country to isolate effectively the national economy with the aid of exchange control from world trends. In spite of the efficiently enforced elaborate exchange control that was retained in Britain after the Second World War the trade recession in the United States during 1947 reacted sharply on her monetary position. So in a different way did the boom provoked by the Korean War, stockpiling, and the rearmament drive in 1950–51. Above all it became evident in 1949 – when sterling had to be devalued as a result of persistent speculative pressure – and to a less extent on other occasions that exchange restrictions were inadequate safeguard in face of a speculative campaign against its currency. It is true under a regime of exchange controls it is impossible to undertake speculative operations in the pre-war sense of the term. British banks are not permitted to grant credits to foreign banks so that the extent to which foreign speculators are in a position to 'go short' in sterling – that is, to sell for future delivery sterling they do not possess – is limited. There are, however, other ways in which sterling is apt to become undermined through a persistent speculative campaign. Foreign debtors in sterling may defer payment as long as possible if they anticipate a devaluation, in order to be able to repay their debts in cheaper sterling. Importers of British goods are inclined to defer their orders for fear that their competitors might be able to cover their requirements a little later with the aid of cheaper sterling and would be able therefore to sell their British goods at lower prices.

Whether or not these anticipations prove to be correct, so long as they prevail they are apt to cause a heavy drain on the gold reserve. No exchange restrictions are able to safeguard the currency against such a drain. Nor is there any way of ascertaining the potential limits of the adverse pressure. Unless the gold reserve is well above immediate requirements it might decline below danger level before the drain comes to an end.

Notwithstanding their shortcomings and disadvantages, exchange restrictions are in given circumstances the lesser evil. Inconvenient as they are, the community may have to put up with them in the interests of safeguarding the national economy from the shocks of heavy international capital movements and exaggerated speculative attacks. Nor is it possible to minimize their inconvenience by relaxing their severity. According to a popular conception the ideal solution would be to confine restrictions to capital transfers while allowing complete freedom for payments arising from current commercial transactions in the broader sense of the term. Unfortunately, freedom of commercial transactions rules out the possibility of effective control over capital transfers. Exchange restrictions are indivisible. Any substantial degree of liberalization can only be achieved at the expense of their efficient enforcement.

What is essential is that the Governments operating exchange restrictions should not work under the misconception that they possess the means by which they can isolate effectively the national economy from the world economy. They should realize the limitations of their means which are useful up to a point but are not all-powerful. Any fundamental disequilibrium that is allowed to develop behind the screen of exchange restrictions is bound to avenge itself sooner or later. Nor are exchange restrictions able to safeguard the gold reserve against the effect of developments outside the country. In 1949 a minor trade recession in the United States was sufficient to undermine the resistance of sterling. It is well to bear in mind the lessons of that experience.

CHAPTER THIRTY-THREE

Physical Controls

THE use of physical controls as means of monetary policy is one of the most highly controversial sections of a highly controversial subject. They are ignored in most pre-war books on monetary policy. In so far as post-war literature deals with them they are almost invariably treated as an expedient for which there may be an explanation and possibly even an excuse in time of war but which is something entirely abnormal and reprehensible in time of peace. Yet physical controls have been in use as a normal device of monetary policy from very early times. In particular physical control of foreign trade to safeguard or increase the monetary stocks of precious metals have been a generally adopted practice for many centuries. It was only during the liberal nineteenth century that these means of monetary policy, together with exchange control and price controls, fell into disuse in most countries. Those brought up amidst the liberal traditions of a more stable period strongly resent the revival of physical controls since the thirties of this century. They are understandably inclined to condemn the use of physical controls as an unmitigated evil in all conceivable circumstances except in time of war.

Beyond doubt there is a strong case against the perpetuation of physical controls as means of peace-time monetary policy. In given circumstances, however, there are valid arguments in their favour. In any case owing to their widespread use it is necessary to examine them. In the unsettled conditions of the post-war world some degree of physical controls has come to stay in most countries. Their use as a means of monetary policy is likely to increase whenever conditions become more difficult.

For our present purpose physical controls mean direct Government intervention to determine the volume and nature of production, distribution, consumption, and foreign trade. All such controls may be used as very effective means of monetary policy. They had already been so used extensively before the Second World War, owing to the realization that in the then prevailing conditions it was inexpedient to rely entirely on the automatic working of economic tendencies or even on conventional means of monetary policy.

Government intervention to determine production may serve non-monetary economic purposes. It may aim at raising the standard of living or the taxable capacity of the community. It may want to add to the military strength of the nation by increasing its economic strength. It may constitute a means of monetary policy if government intervention to raise the volume of production by non-monetary means aims at keeping down or lowering the price level, or at improving the exchange position by increasing the exportable surplus and by replacing imports by home production. These aims may be pursued through conscription or direction of man-power. Such intervention need not be confined, however, to an effort to raise the total output. It may aim at influencing the output of some specific categories of goods, and diverting man-power from the production of goods which are not considered essential from the point of view of the monetary policy that is pursued.

Productive capacity may be diverted from certain lines to other lines not only for reasons of monetary policy but also from considerations of social utility, or from a variety of economic considerations. Such measures may serve the purposes of rearmament. Controls of production constitute means of monetary policy only if they aim at influencing the price level or the balance of payments. Under the mercantilist system governments planned the production of their countries with the object of improving the balance of payments and thereby securing an inflow of monetary metals. This object is very much in the mind of governments in modern times also, though it does not occupy quite such a central position in their policies as it did during the days of mercantilism. Britain's post-war policy aimed at reserving much of the country's productive power for industries which are in a position to export, especially to the dollar area, or which produce goods that would obviate the need for imports, especially from the dollar area. Discrimination in the allocation of raw materials in favour of dollar-earning or dollar-saving industries clearly indicated the predominantly monetary character of the motive behind these physical controls.

Selective control of production may aim at keeping down or lowering the price level either from the point of view of the domestic monetary situation or for the sake of improving the balance of payments. To that end production is diverted from luxuries to necessities in order to keep down the prices of the latter by increasing their supply. This is essential from the point of view of keeping down the cost of living and the cost of production. Standardization is yet another method of official intervention aiming at keeping down or reducing prices. One of the main purposes of the Utility scheme operated in Britain during the Second World War and right up to 1952 was to lower the cost of production by means of mass production. This served the dual purpose of keeping down prices for the domestic consumer and increasing the competitive capacity of British producers in foreign markets. When it was found that in a buyers' market the quality of utility goods no longer satisfied Britain's overseas customers, the scheme was abandoned.

Government intervention need not necessarily aim at keeping down prices. In special circumstances it may aim at keeping up or raising prices of staple exports. It is true that the main object of 'valorization' schemes is to safeguard the interests of the substantial section of the population directly or indirectly dependent on the production of these goods. This is a non-monetary aim. But the adverse effect of unduly low export prices on the balance of paymeuts and on the monetary situation also plays an important part in the adoption of such devices. In some instances the stocks of staple products bought by the Government were kept in buffer pools to be released as and when market conditions became more favourable. Some of these supplies were eventually destroyed in the interest of maintaining high prices. This was done in the Brazilian coffee valorization scheme during the inter-war period. Alternatively the Government intervened to limit the production of the commodities concerned. Thanks to higher prices of the staple exports the terms of trade changed in a favourable sense.

Physical controls may play a very important part in the sphere of distribution. Although rationing is usually regarded as a means of social policy ensuring equal shares for all, it is at the same time a most important means of monetary policy. Combined with price controls it is aimed at suppressing the full effect of inflation on the price level. It has come to be regarded as an indispensable device in time of war, and also during difficult periods in times of peace. At the beginning of the Second World War the governments of belligerent countries had to choose between two alternative economic policies. They could have prevented an increase of purchasing power through the application of highly drastic taxation. Or they could ensure by means of rationing that in spite of the expansion of purchasing power everybody should receive a fair share of the limited supplies of essential goods. Although they went a long way towards adopting the first alternative, they could not have carried it to its logical conclusion without hampering the war effort by depriving producers of the incentive of the profit motive. For this reason, instead of embarking on a hundred per cent disinflationary policy of taxation they tolerated a certain degree of inflation as an incentive, and adopted rationing for the sake of ensuring equal distribution of necessities.

When it is considered inevitable to inflate in the interest of national defence there are two ways in which the excess of purchasing power can be dealt with, in so far as it cannot be mopped up by means of borrowing. If prices are allowed to rise in accordance with the increased purchasing power, supply and demand become balanced at a higher price level. This has the disadvantage of accelerating the pace of inflation, for in the circumstances higher prices inevitably increase the Budgetary deficit and thus lead to the creation of additional purchasing power. They also lead to wages demands. The alternative is to control prices at a relatively low level. In the absence of physical controls this would result in a rapid depletion of the supplies which on the basis of the artificially low prices are necessarily inferior to the inflated demand. For this reason it is essential that price controls should be accompanied by rationing whenever practicable. The combination of price control and rationing prevents the consumers from spending on essential goods too much of their inflated purchasing power. And since the production of luxuries is restricted by physical controls a situation may arise in which the public has to save willy-nilly a large part of its surplus purchasing power in the absence of opportunities to spend it. The nation is thus forced to save part of its earnings and the Government is able to employ a substantial proportion of the nation's financial resources and productive capacity for the economic requirements of the war effort, or of rearmament.

However necessary physical controls may be in pursuit of war-time monetary policy, their use in time of peace gives rise to much temptation to over-spend, because of the possibility of suppressing the normal effects of inflation. The idea that it is possible to have ' inflation without tears' may go a long way towards encouraging the pursuit of a policy of non-stop inflation in time of peace. While it may be intended to be moderate, such inflation is liable to gather momentum as it proceeds. The application of physical controls to suppress the visible effects of inflation on prices and on supplies is apt to create a vicious spiral. The continuation of inflation tends to make controlled prices increasingly artificial and to add to the cost of subsidies with the aid of which these prices are kept down. Larger subsidies, in turn, mean a larger inflationary Budget deficit.

Finally, physical controls in the service of monetary policy include controls over foreign trade. Historically speaking, these were the first physical controls to serve monetary ends.

The mediaeval kings in England and on the continent adopted a series of measures of direct control to ensure that imports did not exceed exports. In modern times physical controls of imports for monetary purposes include general bans on imports and the imposition of bans on imports from 'hard currency' countries. They also include the imposition of import quotas, fixing quantitative limits to certain imports from certain countries.

Needless to say, Government intervention to check imports may serve many non-monetary ends such as the protection of domestic industries in order to ensure full employment. Its essentially monetary character is particularly prominent when import restrictions are adopted in order to safeguard the balance of payments and avoid the necessity for the devaluation of an over-valued currency. Although the same effect can be achieved also by means of exchange control, very often both devices are employed at the same time in order to make the system watertight. On other occasions it is not practicable or expedient to resort to exchange restrictions, and the Government depends entirely on quantitative import restrictions for the defence of its exchange.

Physical controls are often presented as an alternative to financial controls. In given circumstances, however, they complete each other. Even those who disapprove of controls for the sake of controls must at times yield to some extent to practical necessity. Controls should not, however, be used for their own sake, only when their use is made necessary by conditions in which their absence would make it difficult or costly to achieve the legitimate ends of monetary policy solely with the aid of financial devices.

CHAPTER THIRTY-FOUR

Other Economic Devices

MONETARY policy decisions, in addition to serving immediate monetary ends, often serve broader economic ends. Conversely, measures in the sphere of economic policy often serve the purposes of monetary policy. The reciprocity of relations between monetary policy and economic policy may best be characterized by the saying, well known in golfing circles, that he who plays golf for the sake of keeping fit is wise, but he who endeavours to keep fit for the sake of playing good golf is even wiser. Monetary policy is pursued in the interests of a healthy economy, but efforts are often made to improve economic conditions for the sake of achieving sound monetary conditions.

This does not mean that all action of economic policy which tends to affect the monetary situation should be considered to come within the sphere of monetary policy. Very often the monetary effect of such action is secondary, incidental, or purely unintentional. It is only if economic action is taken at least partly for the sake of producing a monetary effect that it constitutes a device of monetary policy.

The introductory paragraph of this chapter may convey the impression that economic action taken for the sake of monetary effect is always necessarily in the right direction. Unfortunately this is by no means so. As we pointed out in an earlier chapter, a bad monetary policy is none the less a monetary policy for being bad.

The monetary situation can be influenced to a considerable extent through economic devices affecting production. Monetary inflation can be reversed either through monetary deflation or through an increase in the volume of goods to offset the excessive volume of purchasing power. A successful production drive is an effective disinflationary device, provided that it is not accompanied by an increase in the wages bill which is as large as, or larger than, the increase of the output. It is true that increasing production is usually preceded by rising prices because it is achieved through more capital investment, higher employment, and higher wages. In so far, however, as productivity is increased through a better utilization of equipment and labour and through harder work, it is definitely a very effective disinflationary device. This was one of the reasons why throughout the post-war period frequent appeals have been made to industrial workers in general and mineworkers in particular to work harder. An increase of productivity tends to produce a disinflationary effect not only by increasing the volume of goods available, but also by reducing the cost of production per unit. Any Government action taken in order to increase productivity for the sake of lowering prices or preventing their rise constitutes a monetary policy device. We saw in the last chapter that there is ample scope for such action in the sphere of physical controls. But the Government can intervene to increase the output without necessarily resorting to physical controls.

Another economic device serving monetary ends in the sphere of production is the encouragement of certain branches of production – if necessary at the expense of other branches – to increase the supply of necessities in order to keep down the cost of living. The same volume of output tends to produce a different effect on the monetary situation according to the proportion which represents necessities. This subject was already touched upon in the last chapter in connexion with the physical control of production. In this chapter we are concerned with diversion of productive efforts in the desired directions through other devices. If an unduly large proportion of productive capacity is used for the production of luxuries the volume of output of necessities tends to be inadequate in comparison with the increase in the purchasing power of consumers. Consequently the prices of necessities, in so far as they cannot be controlled, tend to rise, leading to wages demands and the accentuation of the upward movement of the inflationary spiral. To the extent to which the prices of necessities are controlled but demand for them cannot be satisfied owing to the inadequacy of the output, the surplus purchasing power is used either for the purchase of necessities at higher prices on black markets or for the increase of demand for goods the prices of which are not controlled. In either case the inadequacy of the output of necessities tends to accentuate the rising trend of prices. The remedy is, of course, a diversion of productive capacity from luxuries to necessities as a means of counteracting or moderating the rise in prices.

It is possible to divert productive capacity in the desired direction through physical controls – dealt with in the last chapter – affecting the allocation of raw materials, fuel, man-power, etc. The alternative device is the fixing of wages in accordance with the extent of the need for increasing or reducing the output in particular industries.

If it were practicable to adopt a national wages policy it would provide a method of diverting productive capacity from luxuries to necessities, thereby influencing production in a sense favourable to the requirements of anti-inflationary monetary policy. Under a national wages policy the wages in various trades, instead of being determined by the relative scarcity of labour in the trades concerned and by the level of prices that buyers of the goods concerned are prepared to pay, would be determined by the aims of economic policy to encourage the production of certain goods and to discourage the production of others. In the absence of a wages policy producers of luxuries who can afford to pay high wages are able to divert much-needed man-power from the production of necessities. With the aid of the national wages policy it would have been possible during the post-war period to secure the man-power needed for a substantial increase of the coal output without having to outbid less essential trades competing for the man-power. This would have materially improved the monetary situation in Britain after the Second World War, both through the increase in the production of necessities, the regulation of the wages spiral, and the improvement of the balance of payments. Under a national wages policy it would have been possible to liquidate redundant sections of the textile industry by fixing wages lower in comparison with those fixed in other industries which, with the aid of increased man-power attracted by higher wages, could have more effectively served the export drive and would have contributed towards the strengthening of sterling. Under a correctly conceived and efficiently executed wages policy textile wages ought to have been lowered in comparison with engineering, shipbuilding, coal mining, etc., wages, in order to provide an inducement for a voluntary transfer of labour to industries which are in a better position to contribute to the export drive. In the absence of such policy even when in 1952 large-scale unemployment developed in the textile industry it was very difficult to induce textile workers to switch over to other industries rather than remain unemployed in the hope of securing re-employment in the textile industry. The absence of a national wages policy was largely responsible for Britain's inability to build up a sufficiently large gold reserve to prevent, or at least mitigate, the bi-annual sterling crises after the Second World War.

The above example shows the importance of mobility of labour as an economic factor of monetary policy. Mobility of labour can be increased by devices other than a national wages policy. One of the objects of the housing drive is precisely to increase the mobility of labour so as to make it possible to re-employ, to the best advantage to the national economy, workers who become unemployed and who cannot find employment in their own districts. Owing to the shortage of housing accommodation the degree of mobility of workmen, especially those with families, is very low. Consequently local pockets of unemployment can exist for a long time in some districts even though other districts are able to offer employment and attractive wages. Thus the housing drive may also be regarded as serving partly monetary purposes, since its success in increasing the mobility of labour would lead to a disinflationary increase in production in general and to an increase in the production of exportable goods in particular.

Easing of the housing shortage as a means for the internal and external strengthening of sterling could be achieved not only through a housing drive aiming at satisfying the demand for accommodation, but also through a reduction of that demand by means of an increase of rents. It is largely owing to the artificially low level of rents resulting from rent control and the subsidizing of council houses that the supply of housing accommodation was unable to catch up with the demand after the Second World War. The artificial character of controlled rents became accentuated through the sharp rise in practically every other item in the cost of living. The system that operated in this sphere in Britain and in many other countries created an absurd situation, in that the State authority artificially stimulated demand for something which it was unable to supply in adequate quantities and which it was unable to ration to secure equitable distribution of the limited supply. A decontrol of rents or a substantial increase of the level of controlled rents, by reducing the inflated demand for housing accommodation, would have gone a long way towards solving the problem of housing shortage and thereby increasing the mobility of labour. On the other hand, the beneficial effect of this on the monetary situation would have been offset to a large degree by the rise in the cost of living caused by higher rents, leading to more wages demands. Moreover, the policy has distinct disadvantages from a social and political point of view. Even so, the balance of advantages is distinctly on the side of an upward adjustment of rents. In Britain the Housing Repairs and Rents Bill, introduced in 1953, was a modest first step in that direction.

An economic device which has a very close bearing on monetary policy is the Government's attitude towards the adoption of the system under which wages and salaries are adjusted to changes in the cost of living index. The Government can encourage the increasing adoption of that system by applying it in the Civil Service or by adopting legislation ensuring its application by private employers. This latter device is in operation in Australia, where there is provision to that effect in the Constitution. An article in the Australian Supplement of *The Economist* of 7 March, 1953, remarks that Australia is the only country in the world in which inflation is written into the Constitution. Minimum wages are not fixed by collective bargaining, but are adjusted each quarter by the Federal Arbitration Court on the basis of the cost of living index. Beyond doubt this system is calculated to accelerate the pace of inflation by cutting down the time-lag between a rise in the cost of living and the rise in the cost of production through higher wages. Governments and Parliaments are inclined to adopt or encourage this system, or at any rate abstain from resisting its adoption, out of sheer necessity, for social or political considerations. Nevertheless, it is not altogether unjustifiable to regard its adoption as a device of monetary policy, because it tends to mitigate the effect of inflation on the wage-earning classes and to avert troublesome industrial disputes which would produce inflationary effects throug'1 reducing the output. It is one way of reducing some of the evil social effects of inflation at the cost of accentuating the speed of its progress. Its adoption implies taking the line of least resistance as an alternative to adopting a firmer anti-inflationary policy which would resist pressure for the adoption of the index number standard.

In the sphere of foreign trade, too, economic devices can be applied as instruments of monetary policy. From this point of view it is necessary to discriminate between conditions of full employment and those of large-scale unemployment. A country which is producing to the limit of its capacity cannot increase its exports or reduce its imports without affecting the volume of goods available to satisfy domestic demand. In such countries an adverse trade balance is an anti-inflationary device because by increasing the supply of goods available it tends to prevent or mitigate the rise in trend of prices due to excessive purchasing power. Conversely in such circumstances the success of an export drive necessarily reduces the already inadequate supplies of goods available to satisfy domestic demand. It therefore tends to accentuate the rising trend of prices.

It is only in exceptional circumstances that Governments may resort to a deliberate increase of the adverse trade balance for the sake of counteracting an inflationary trend. This was done in some countries of Western Europe immediately after the Second World War. The devastation caused during the hostilities materially reduced their productive capacity, a large part of which had to be employed for reconstruction purposes. In order to satisfy the urgent requirements of consumers and thus to mitigate the bidding up of prices of the inadequate supplies of goods the Governments of these countries endeavoured during the first few post-war years to import as much as possible and to refrain as far as possible from exporting essential goods. Trade negotiations during the early post-war period were totally different from the usual trade negotiations in which the parties are trying to persuade each other to admit the largest possible quantity of each other's goods. In 1945-7 the Governments of countries which had suffered much physical devastation were at pains to persuade each other and more favourably placed Governments to export more to their respective countries without insisting on importing more unless they were prepared to accept luxuries.

When, however, there is unemployment an export surplus is an unqualified blessing. It strengthens the monetary situation by increasing the gold reserve. It does not affect domestic supplies because there is ample productive capacity to meet both domestic requirements and export requirements. As a decline in the gold reserve is liable to lead to a depreciation of the national currency, export drives and import restrictions amidst conditions of unemployment constitute devices in defence of monetary stability. There is an almost unlimited range of economic actions tending to affect the trade balance, thereby constituting act of monetary policy.

Departure from multilateral trading is an economic device which can serve the purpose of monetary policy. Its

L

object is to ensure a balanced foreign trade and thereby to safeguard the gold reserve. In addition, bilateral trading can serve monetary purposes by enabling the Government to pursue an expansionary domestic monetary policy without thereby endangering the gold reserve. Under multilateral trading any Government which expands the national currency to a higher degree than the expansion that takes place in other important countries runs the risk of losing its gold reserve and having to suffer devaluation or depreciation. By means of ensuring balanced trade with the aid of bilateral agreements and other devices such as import restrictions, exchange control, etc., the Government may feel it can inflate with impunity. The idea is to isolate the domestic economy from world economy. Any steps taken in that direction may be regarded as devices of monetary policy.

In the sphere of production diametrically opposite policies may serve monetary ends. In given circumstances a Government may find it expedient to create a scarcity of goods in order to force consumers to save part of their inflated purchasing power. On the other hand, if a Government finds that this policy acts as a disincentive and tends to discourage production, it may reverse the policy by encouraging the production of 'inducement goods' which might make workers work overtime. In either case the monetary situation is liable to be affected.

In many of the above instances economic devices are employed partly and even largely for non-monetary purposes. Nevertheless, they may be regarded as devices of monetary policy if their adoption serves to an appreciable extent the purpose of influencing the monetary situation either directly or indirectly.

PART FOUR

Conclusion

*

CHAPTER THIRTY-FIVE

International Monetary Policies

THOSE responsible for the shaping of monetary policy must have realized many centuries ago that their power to determine monetary trends in their respective countries was limited by the exercise of a similar power by the monetary authorities of other countries, or by the influence of monetary trends abroad that developed in the absence of intervention by those authorities, or through the ineffectiveness of their intervention. Clashes between the monetary policies of various countries became only too evident during the periods of frequent debasements when the advantages gained by the debasement of one currency were wiped out by the debasement of other currencies. Bullionist policies under which the export of coins or precious metals was prohibited failed to produce the desired result partly because other countries adopted similar bans. The world-wide character of price trends, in face of which monetary policies of particular countries were largely helpless, has been traced by economic historians to the period of ancient Greece. In several instances, prices in the countries of the Mediterranean civilization during the ancient period appeared to move largely in sympathy even though there is no reason to suppose that the monetary policies of these countries were uniform. The same is true in many instances about movements of world prices in subsequent periods.

It was not until the nineteenth century that the international character of some major factors affecting the monetary situation in individual countries came to be adequately realized. Economists and administrators became increasingly aware that their respective policies were largely helpless in face of major international trends, caused by such factors as changes in the world output of precious metals or decisions of other countries to change their monetary standards.

Attempts were made from time to time to influence these
international trends by means of international agreements
on subjects such as the demonetization of silver. Generally
speaking, however, the conception prevailed that the automatic working of the gold standard could be trusted to
produce the desired results in the long run.

It was considered to be part of the sovereign rights of any
independent State to determine its monetary system and
its monetary policies. The extent of international co-operation in the monetary sphere remained negligible until the
First World War. There were, it is true, some monetary
unions such as the Latin Monetary Union or the Scandinavian Monetary Union, the member countries of which
adopted identical mint parities. The practical results of such
unions were, however, modest. There was no co-ordination
of their monetary policies, and in spite of the identity of
their mint parities there were often substantial discrepancies
between their exchange rates. While the Swiss franc was on
the full gold standard, the French franc was on a 'limping
standard' and the Spanish peseta – also a currency of the
Latin Monetary Union – was inconvertible.

During the First World War close co-operation was established between the Western Allies. Britain and the United
States provided a means for maintaining the exchange rates
of France and Italy, and the United States provided the
means for maintaining sterling at a fixed rate in relation to
the dollar. Soon after the termination of hostilities the system
of monetary co-operation was brought to an end. The currency chaos that developed during the early twenties made the
world realize the need for international action to bring some
order and co-ordination in the sphere of monetary policy.

Under the gold standard up to the First World War, the
need for subordinating the monetary policy of any country
to the requirements of the monetary policies of other
countries was not very obvious. When, towards the middle
twenties, one country after another endeavoured to stabilize
its currency it became evident, however, that co-operation
was of vital importance in order to make the gold standard

work. The monetary authorities of the leading countries realized that, owing to the rise in prices since 1914, the volume of monetary gold was not adequate. For this reason, in order to prevent world-wide deflation through a scramble for the world's limited gold supplies, a number of countries, which had stabilized their currencies with the assistance of the League of Nations, were persuaded to adopt the gold exchange standard instead of the full gold standard. Their note cover was allowed to include dollars or sterling or other exchanges in addition to gold. As a result the same gold stocks served as a reserve for several countries. By such means it was hoped to reduce the world-wide demand for gold.

Close co-operation was established between a large number of Central Banks. The movement culminated in the establishment of the Bank for International Settlements at Basel, which institution had for its purpose the pursuit of systematic co-ordination of monetary policies. Before it had a chance to produce any tangible results, however, the economic crisis that followed the Wall Street slump of 1929, accentuated by the suspension of the gold standard in Britain two years later, brought the movement abruptly to a halt.

The period between 1931 and 1936 was characterized by a wave of unfettered monetary nationalism. Each country endeavoured to pursue a monetary policy that appeared to be in accordance with its immediate interest, without regard to the repercussions on other countries. The history of competitive debasements of earlier centuries repeated itself. There was a competitive currency depreciation race between a number of countries, each of which aimed at 'exporting unemployment' to other countries by depreciating its exchange in order to be able to undersell its rivals. The benefit derived by Britain through the depreciation of sterling in 1931 was largely cancelled out by the depreciation of the dollar two years later. An attempt to bring some order into the currency chaos at the World Economic Conference of 1933 failed completely, because the participating Governments were utterly incapable of seeing each other's point of view.

By that time the Sterling Area came into existence. It

provided an example for a close co-ordination of monetary policies within a group of countries whose interests were substantially identical. There was also a much looser association called the 'gold bloc', consisting of a number of Western European countries which endeavoured to maintain the gold standard and to avoid a devaluation. The United States under President Roosevelt was in favour of bold and unconventional experimenting with currency. Finally a large number of economically weaker countries – foremost amongst them Germany – adopted policies of monetary isolation with the aid of exchange control and exchange clearing. There appeared to be no common ground between them. Each country or group of countries endeavoured to work out its salvation in its own way in total disregard of the vital interests of the rest of the world.

During the years that followed the failure of the World Economic Conference the need for a co-ordination of national monetary policies came to be gradually realized. The disadvantages of unrestricted national sovereignty in the monetary sphere became increasingly evident. Looking back upon that troubled period it must now appear absurd that statesmen of standing should have imagined they could serve the fundamental interest of their respective countries by refusing to compromise in matters of monetary policy. It should have been evident to them that any action affecting the monetary situation in any one country was liable to affect other countries.

In particular it was realized that the determination of the exchange rates could not be a matter of indifference to other countries. The need for the regulation and co-ordination of conflicting rights and interests in other spheres of international relations has long been recognized. There have been many international agreements to co-ordinate matters such as air traffic regulations, or radio wavelengths, or water rights, in the interests of all concerned. Under any of these agreements the participating Governments relinquish part of their sovereignity. They renounce their right to operate on any wavelength they choose because they realize that if the other governments were to exercise their freedom to do so the inevitable result would be chaotic conditions in the ether. The same is true about monetary policies.

The realization of this truth resulted in the conclusion of the Tripartite Agreement in 1936 between the United States, Great Britain, and France. Subsequently, several other countries adhered to it. The governments concerned agreed not to engage in competitive currency depreciation and to consult each other before bringing about substantial changes in the exchange value of their currencies. This principle eventually became the basic rule of the Bretton Woods Agreement on which the world's post-war monetary system came to be founded.

During the Second World War, as during the First World War, there was a high degree of monetary co-operation between the allies. As the War appeared to be drawing near its end efforts were initiated to establish the post-war rules under which monetary policies should be co-ordinated. During 1943-44 two rival plans were under consideration. They were the British Keynes Plan and the American White Plan. Under the former an International Monetary Union was to be established with powers to create a new money of its own for the settlement of international balances. Its rules were devised in such a way as to provide an inducement to creditor countries to reduce their export surpluses and accept an import surplus.

The White Plan, too, provided for the creation of an international institution, but it was to have no power to create money. Its resources would consist of funds to be contributed towards capital by member countries. Nor did this institution provide any inducement for creditor countries to be 'good creditors'. Although the majority of countries would have preferred the Keynes Plan, in view of the overwhelming financial strength of the United States it was inevitable that the White Plan should in substance be accepted.

The Bretton Woods Agreement, concluded in 1944, stipulates that member countries should not in future change the gold value of their currencies without the consent of the

International Monetary Fund beyond the extent of ten per cent on either side of their parities. The Fund would grant its consent if in its opinion the proposed change was necessary in order to correct some 'fundamental disequilibrium'. In given circumstances the Fund is granted the right to advise member countries regarding their domestic monetary policies. It is not to have the power, however, to compel Governments to take the necessary steps for dealing either with a persistently adverse balance of payments or with a persistently favourable balance of payments. The Bretton Woods rules provide also for the removal of exchange restrictions, without, however, stipulating any date-line.

The Bretton Woods Agreement was ratified by most countries in 1946. Its ratification was preceded and succeeded by heated controversy. Experience failed to justify, however, either its critics or its supporters. Those who were afraid that the system would introduce an unduly high degree of rigidity of exchange parities proved to be wrong. After 1946 a number of member countries – including Britain – devalued or revalued their currencies with the consent of the International Monetary Fund. On the other hand those who had hoped that the Fund would be able to establish international monetary equilibrium and to provide adequate financial support to countries with adverse trade balances proved to be equally wrong. Disequilibrium continued to prevail to such an extent that the resources of the Fund were incapable of coping with the adverse balances of payments resulting from it. By 1948 the Fund practically gave up its attempt at equalizing balance of payments differences and drastically curtailed the granting of assistance.

We saw that international monetary co-operation aimed in most instances at maintaining the stability of exchanges or regulating their modifications. Obviously it is much easier to achieve international exchange stability with the aid of international co-operation than in isolation, with each country disregarding the interest of other countries. The first step in the right direction is some form of international agreement under which Governments renounced their rights for the duration of the agreement to alter their exchange rates at will. Such an arrangement is in itself, however, largely negative, unless the participating countries undertake to assist each other in the task of maintaining the stability of their exchanges. Assistance may assume various forms. The participating countries may undertake, directly or through the intermediary of an international institution, to grant financial assistance to countries which have balance of payments difficulties. Co-operation may aim at safeguarding the exchange rates against shocks or persistent pressure due to abnormal transactions.

International co-operation may also assume the form of a reciprocal undertaking not to operate in the exchanges or money markets of a country without the consent of its authorities. This form of co-operation had already reached an advanced stage before the establishment of the Bank for International Settlements. One of the rules of the co-operation between Central Banks that developed during the twenties was that the participating Central Banks agreed to transact business exclusively with each other and to close their accounts with other banks. This did not necessarily mean that they abandoned their right to carry out transactions which did not meet with the approval of the Central Bank of the country concerned. For instance during the late twenties the Bank of France decided to repatriate in gold a large part of its sterling balances in spite of the disapproval of this policy by the Bank of England. It meant, however, that all operations in the foreign exchange market and money market and all bullion shipments went through the hands of the Bank of England, which was thus in a position to mitigate the effects of such transactions through this timing and co-ordination.

Another means by which Governments were able to help each other in the maintenance of the stability of their exchanges was through co-operation in the enforcement of exchange restrictions. This form of co-operation has not reached a very advanced stage. Most Governments show themselves utterly indifferent to the infringement of the laws of other countries as far as exchange restrictions are concerned. Black markets in the currencies of countries with exchange restrictions are tolerated, and so is the misuse of various special accounts in restricted currencies. For instance no effort is made by the United States authorities to stop leaks in the British exchange control that arise through the misuse of various types of sterling of limited convertibility for indirect purchases of Sterling Area commodities for export to the United States.

The only effective way in which a large and increasing number of Governments have come to co-operate in maintaining each other's exchange restrictions has come about not for monetary but for fiscal reasons, in the form of bilateral agreements against double taxation and tax evasion. Under these agreements the contracting parties undertake to communicate to each other the incomes earned by each of its nationals in each other's country. Since 1946 there has been in existence such an agreement between Great Britain and the United States. The United States Government communicates to the British Government the American incomes of residents in the United Kingdom, and the British Government communicates to the United States Government the British incomes of residents in the United States. The main aim of this arrangement is not to prevent the evasion of the British exchange control but to prevent tax evasion. Nevertheless its effect is to make the evasion of exchange control more difficult. The number of similar agreements in operation is increasing steadily.

Above all there is scope for international assistance to maintain exchange rates in the sphere of co-ordinating domestic monetary policies. If the price level in one country is too high and the resulting adverse balance of payments threatens to undermine the stability of the exchange, this disequilibrium can be put right either through deflation in the country concerned or through inflation in other countries. Up to now there has been very little co-operation of this kind. Admittedly it would involve considerable sacrifices on the part of countries which are to adapt their monetary policies to the requirements of some other country. In his book, *The Dollar*, Harrod draws attention to one of the few instances of such co-operation. In 1927 the Federal Reserve authorities eased credit conditions in the United States mainly for the sake of assisting Britain and other countries.

Regulated adjustment of exchange parities or of actual exchange rates has been a recognized form of international monetary co-operation ever since the conclusion of the Tripartite Agreement of 1936. The object is to ensure that if and when an adjustment of exchange rates becomes inevitable it should be carried out in an orderly fashion and in such a way as to avoid competitive currency depreciations. If the price level in a country is too high and for economic, social, or political reasons its lowering through deflation is impracticable, the disequilibrium in relation to price levels of other countries has to be corrected sooner or later through devaluation. What matters from the point of view of other countries is that devaluation should merely aim at correcting the existing disequilibrium instead of creating a new disequilibrium in the opposite sense through an exaggerated reduction of the exchange value of the currency concerned. If devaluation is excessive the price level in terms of other currencies becomes unduly reduced, and this may force other countries either to deflate or to devalue. It was to avoid this that the countries participating in the Tripartite Agreement, and subsequently those who accepted the Bretton Woods system, adopted the rule not to change their exchange parities to any substantial degree without consultation with or consent of the other participating countries or, after 1946, of the International Monetary Fund.

The difficulty is to ascertain the correct exchange rates representing equilibrium. Unfortunately this is not a matter of simple arithmetic. It does not entirely depend on the ratio between the price levels of the countries concerned, nor even on the ratio between indexes based on exported and imported goods. Moreover, occasionally it is necessary and justified to devalue a currency to a higher degree than appears to be called for, on the basis of the arithmetical relation between price levels. This was the case with sterling in 1949. To restore confidence in sterling it was deliberately undervalued with the full consent and approval of the United States Government and the International Monetary Fund. It is humanly impossible to calculate the correct level, and there is apt to be a tendency to err on the safe side. What matters is that the countries concerned should endeavour to do so in a spirit of understanding towards each other's difficulties, and that they should avoid competitive currency depreciations which would be against the interests of all.

Yet another means of monetary policy in the international sphere is the mitigation of a scarcity of gold. If scarcity is due to maldistribution then the country or countries which possess an unduly large proportion of the world's stock of gold may contribute towards the solution by lending freely to other countries, or by lowering their tariff walls, thereby reducing their gold surplus. This attitude was adopted by Britain throughout the nineteenth century. In spite of a persistently favourable balance of payments, Britain never kept an unduly large gold reserve because she was willing to import the goods of her debtors and to re-lend her surpluses in the form of long-term loans and investments or short-term credits. When after the First World War the United States became the principal surplus country she did not pursue the same course to a sufficient extent. As a result she accumulated and retained an excessive proportion of the world's monetary supplies, and most other countries were left with gold reserves that were inadequate for their requirements.

There has in consequence been an almost continuous shortage in the world's monetary supply of gold outside the United States ever since the First World War. Various devices were adopted during the twenties as a result of the co-operation of the Central Banks to economize in the use of gold in order to mitigate this scarcity. The most effective if unintentional help came, however, through the unilateral action of the United States in raising its official buying price of gold to $35 an ounce in 1934.

Owing to the rise in prices that has taken place since then, and to the large-scale flow of gold to the Unites States during and after the Second World War, the monetary stocks of gold outside the United States have become less and less adequate since 1945. To remedy this situation the United States Government has been urged from various sides to raise once more substantially the dollar price of gold as part of an all-round increase of the price of gold in terms of all currencies. Such a measure was expressly provided for in the Bretton Woods scheme. In spite of this the United States has shown no inclination to make this contribution towards the solution of the world's monetary problem. Instead she prefers to assist other countries in the form of grants or loans.

The end of maintaining a stable price level is difficult to attain unless the domestic policies adopted for its sake are supplemented by international action. Unless there is virtually complete economic isolation such as exists in Communist countries all the time and in capitalist countries in times of war, the internal economy of any country is exposed to international trends to a very large extent. If there is a rising trend in world prices no single country can isolate itself from it unless it raises the exchange value of its currency. If the world trend is downward the only way in which a country can maintain the stability of its domestic prices is through a devaluation of its currency. For the sake of avoiding changes in parities while maintaining the stability of the domestic price level it is essential that a large number of countries should co-operate in reducing to a minimum the fluctuations of world prices. Progress in that direction has been negligible. It has been confined to international agreements aiming at the stabilization of a few important commodities. In order to be effective the policy would have to cover a large number of commodities and attempts at price-fixing would have to be supplemented by the creation of international buffer-pools which would remove from the markets any large surpluses and would cover deficiencies.

Although such schemes have been under discussion they belong to the realm of the distant future.

During the thirties it was imperative to reverse the prevailing deflationary trend. To that end the co-ordination of national monetary policies would have been very helpful. Instead each country endeavoured to work out its salvation independently of the others and very often at their expense. There were no co-ordinated efforts to reverse the downward trend of world prices. After the Second World War the world trend became distinctly inflationary. Again there was no co-ordinated international policy to check this unwanted trend. Even though various international organizations did their utmost to exhort the Governments to put their respective houses in order and stop their inflationary domestic policies, or at any rate to keep in step regarding the degree of their internal inflations due to the expansion of their social services, they had no power to compel sovereign States to comply with their wishes.

Exhortation appears to be still the most frequently employed means in the sphere of international monetary policy. The International Monetary Fund and the economic organizations of the United Nations and of the European movement seldom miss an opportunity to urge the member Governments to implement their various undertakings under the Bretton Woods Agreement and other agreements, and to behave in accordance with the requirements of international economic co-operation. In particular they are urged to abandon multiple exchange practices, to relax exchange controls and return to the convertibility of their currencies. The Fund itself has done very little, however, to assist member countries in carrying out these recommendations. It adopted a very narrow interpretation of its rôle of helping member countries to solve their balance of payments difficulties. Having granted them some dollar facilities during the first eighteen months of its existence, it practically stopped granting further assistance after 1948. Its substantial capital contributed by member countries remained therefore largely immobilized. In the circumstances it is hardly surprising if its exhortations met with scant response.

The truth is that so long as countries retain their political sovereignty their Governments, Parliaments and public opinion will want to exercise it in the sphere of monetary policy in accordance with what is rightly or wrongly regarded as the national interest. It is only if and when a supreme political authority should ever be recognized that the adoption of international means of monetary policy in pursuance of international ends will become a practical possibility to any considerable extent.

Meanwhile progress has been made towards the adoption of international monetary policies within limited spheres. During 1952–54 the Governments of the Sterling Area countries succeeded in co-ordinating their internal and external monetary policies to a considerable degree in order to stop the drain on the gold reserve. It was agreed to initiate disinflationary measures and to adopt drastic import restrictions. A plan for the eventual restoration of sterling convertibility was elaborated with the approval of all Sterling Area Governments. These decisions constituted a remarkable progress compared with the earlier state of affairs in which the monetary policies of these Governments were largely independent of each other, especially in the domestic monetary sphere.

Another instance of progress towards international monetary policy with a limited geographical sphere was the establishment of the European Payments Union. The rather involved multilateral payments system created in 1950 was based in some respects on the Keynes Plan under which an international institution was intended to have the means of granting credits to the member Governments to finance adverse balances of payments. Evidently even though we are still far from the goal of an international monetary policy, the distance that remains to be covered is considerably less than it was twenty years ago, when the sterling bloc, dollar bloc, and gold bloc were engaged in a bitter struggle with no quarter given or asked.

M

CHAPTER THIRTY-SIX

Monetary Theory and Monetary Policy

ALTHOUGH this book is not directly concerned with the theoretical aspects of money, it contains frequent reference to various monetary theories on which monetary policies are based. We now propose to examine very briefly the relationship between monetary theory and monetary policy. It is widely believed among laymen and even among students of economics that economic theory is expected to provide an infallible or at any rate reasonably dependable guide for the use of statesmen and administrators in the shaping of their economic policies. According to this conception, if only the Governments could be prevailed upon to accept the correct monetary theory on which to base their monetary policies, they could not go wrong.

Unfortunately things are not so simple in real life. No economic theory can be claimed to provide the full practical solution, because the chances that it covers all the factors liable to influence the economic situation are extremely remote. Any single economic theory which would try to allow for all possible factors would be so involved that it would be unintelligible to all but a few select academic economists. Most theories in the past resorted to over-simplification by limiting the range of factors to be allowed for. During the nineteenth century and the early part of this century the so-called static economic theory predominated, under which the rules were based on the assumption that the overwhelming majority of factors would remain 'neutral'. By such means it was possible to establish rules how certain factors are liable to affect the economic situation provided that other things remain unchanged. This method found application in the monetary sphere in the form of the quantity theory of money. The practical conclusions inferred from it hold good only on the assumption that factors other than the quantity of money remain the same.

The building up of such hypotheses is undoubtedly of great value provided that those who create them and those who study them constantly bear it in mind that they are broad general propositions which only operate within the limits set by the hypothesis itself, and that in a practical situation the results indicated by the theory are liable to be modified. So long as this is borne in mind monetary theories can be of great use to those in charge of managing the monetary system. If on the other hand they are interpreted in a dogmatic spirit, it is liable to lead to entirely wrong conclusions and to do much more harm than good.

During recent times an attempt was made to develop a so-called dynamic economic theory which aims at allowing for the effects of factors which have hitherto been assumed to be 'neutral' for the purposes of static economic theory. In the monetary sphere, too, dynamic theory has been gaining ground. It is undoubtedly nearer to practical requirements than the static theory. Even so, a really comprehensive watertight dynamic monetary theory which allows for every possible factor has not yet been elaborated, and it is doubtful whether it ever will be. Some essential factor is almost bound to be overlooked, partly because new factors are liable to arise or existing factors are apt to increase or decline in importance, and partly because human behaviour cannot be reduced to terms of mathematical accuracy.

In his *Capital and Employment* Hawtrey deals with the distinction between the requirements of monetary theory and economic policy. To give an idea of the difficulty about applying theory to policy we could do no better than quote his relevant observations: 'When an economic expert makes practical recommendations he passes from the theoretical plane to one in which quite different tests are necessary. In theoretical reasoning he may construct whatever hypothesis he thinks fit and proceed by deduction to general propositions as to human behaviour within the limits of the hypothesis. But as soon as he deals with a situation on the practical plane he is bound to take into account, as far as possible all actual relevant circumstances. Omniscience

being unattainable, we must in economic as in other decisions be content with an approximation in which we try
to give true weight to each element of the situation. Hypothesis which excludes any element or gives it insufficient
weight vitiates the result. For the purposes of theory the
result may have a sufficient resemblance to the truth in
that the train of reasoning contains all the requisite steps
correctly set forth, and indeed all the various practical
measures that might be called for may be separately form-
ulated. But none the less the final conclusion may for
practical purposes be fatally wrong if a distortion of the
facts at the beginning is reflected in the conclusions and
the worse is made to appear the better way.'

These views are expressed by one of the leading theoretical
monetary economists of our generation with the experience
of a lifetime in practical monetary problems gained in his
capacity of Treasury official. Hawtrey duly realizes the
limitations of the possibility of applying theory to policy. He
knows all there is to know about monetary theory, and yet
he would hesitate to recommend too close an application of
monetary theory to the management of monetary policy.
The overwhelming majority of administrators and politicians responsible for monetary policy were not nearly as familiar with monetary theory, and therefore had much more
reason for distrusting it. Indeed, as a general rule, high Treasury officials and Central Bankers are essentially practical
men with neither time nor inclination to acquire too pro-
found a theoretical knowledge. While Treasuries usually
have economic advisers, until recently those in a position to
take or influence monetary policy decisions were practical
administrators with relatively little theoretical background.
As for the politicians on whom ultimate responsibility
for major monetary policy decisions rests, they are usually
devoid of theoretical knowledge. It is only in recent times
that a generation of Treasury officials has arisen which
has due respect for economic theory and has mastered its
basic principles.

Generally speaking, it is true that theoretical monetary

economists have had relatively little share in shaping monetary policy. There were, of course, exceptions. In Britain, Goschen, one of the leading theoretical experts on foreign exchange, and the author of a standard work on its theory, became Chancellor of the Exchequer. For a time after the First World War, Hawtrey was able to influence, from a comparatively subordinate position, the trend of British monetary policy – though he would probably emphatically disclaim responsibility for much that was done in the twenties and thirties. One of the outstanding examples of monetary policy being guided by a theoretical economist was provided by the regime of Keynes at the Treasury from 1940 to 1946. In his capacity of adviser he influenced to a considerable degree the monetary policies of three Chancellors of the Exchequer. Likewise, President Roosevelt's 'Brain Trust' played a decisive rôle in shaping the monetary policy of the United States for some time after 1933. During and after the First World War the Swedish school of economists played a prominent part in shaping the monetary policies of their country. Helfferich, in his capacity of Finance Minister of the German Reich during the First World War, had ample opportunity to put his monetary theories into practice. It was the irony of fate that, even though he was one of the leading advocates of 'hard money', he had to pursue an inflationary policy that prepared the way for the great collapse of the mark in 1923.

It does not necessarily mean, however, that once a monetary economist is given an opportunity to determine monetary policy either as a Finance Minister or as head of a Central Bank or as a 'power behind the throne', he would necessarily set out to put his favourite monetary theory into operation. The moment he assumes a responsible post he gains access to a wealth of information which is liable to modify his views. Confronted with the responsibility for taking practical decisions that are liable to affect the lives of many millions of people within his country and even beyond its borders, he might be inclined to reconsider his views in the light of practical considerations which he had not hitherto encountered. During the Second World War a large number of academic economists became temporary officials for the duration. Most of them left the Civil Service with their attitude more or less modified under the influence of their practical experience. This did not necessarily mean that they came to the conclusion that their pre-war theories were wrong. What happened was that they realized the limitations of those theories as a practical guide to monetary policy. Or they may have realized that it is often politically impracticable to follow a monetary policy which would be an ideal solution from a purely economic point of view.

Notwithstanding this, in the course of monetary history monetary theory and monetary policy were proceeding on parallel courses to a remarkable degree. For centuries the mercantilist school dominated both literature on monetary theory and monetary policy. The development of credit theories coincided with the emergence of paper currency and bank credit in the modern sense. The liberal school of economists reigned supreme in monetary theory during the nineteenth and the early part of the twentieth century, which was on the whole an era of economic and monetary liberalism. So long as the gold standard reigned almost unchallenged as the theoretically ideal monetary system the monetary policies of the most advanced countries aimed at its maintenance. Managed monetary theories and policies were almost entirely unknown; they appeared simultaneously during the inter-war period.

These facts should not be regarded as necessarily indicating the overwhelming influence of monetary theory over monetary policy. The relations between the two have always been largely reciprocal. Monetary economists could not always claim credit for having guided statesmen and administrators in the shaping of monetary policy. Very often they themselves were guided by practical developments decided upon largely under the stress of practical expediency. On many occasions the rôle of economists was confined to elaborating theoretical foundations for policies which had been adopted largely independently of their influence.

A characteristic instance of the passive rôle economists were liable to play was provided by the experience of the so-called 'gold scare' in 1937. During the first half of that year the Stock Exchanges, foreign exchange markets, commodity markets, and trade in general came under the depressing influence of a growing belief that it was the intention of the United States Administration either to lower its official buying price for gold or to suspend or limit the free import of gold. Many thousands of theoretically illiterate brokers, speculators, and businessmen arrived at the conclusion, without any guidance by theoretical economists, that the United States authorities were contemplating some such action. Thereupon theoretical economists set out to provide somewhat belatedly – after the gold scare had already been in progress for months – a theoretical foundation for this assumption by producing figures and arguments in support of their contention that on the basis of the American price of $35 an ounce the world's monetary stock of gold was in excess of requirements. When it became evident that the United States authorities did not intend to change their buying price for gold or to interfere with the free influx of gold, all the theoretical reasoning in favour of such action subsided almost overnight.

An instance to show that practical monetary policy often precedes in chronological order the theoretical foundations on which it is based is provided by the policy of fighting deflation by means of public works. Keynes advocated this policy before the General Election of 1929, when he came out wholeheartedly in support of Lloyd George's electioneering programme of public works. It was not until 1936, however, that Keynes elaborated the theoretical foundation for that policy in his *General Theory*. One of the most important theoretical principles laid down in that book was that equilibrium is possible under large-scale unemployment. He endeavoured to disprove the classical theory according to which full employment is the only conceivable state of equilibrium and any unemployment constitutes temporary disequilibrium which is liable to become adjusted through the automatic working of natural economic trends. Under the classical concept any form of Government intervention to create employment was rejected as being more harmful than good. Under the principle laid down by Keynes, on the other hand, equilibrium may exist amidst large-scale unemployment, which means that no economic factors operating automatically can be relied upon for restoring full employment. Once this theoretical rule is accepted the next step is to infer from it the logical conclusion that, since full employment is not necessarily reached through the automatic working of economic tendencies, it is for the Government to intervene and create additional employment with the aid of monetary and other devices. On the basis of Keynes' theory this conclusion is unanswerable. It is worth noting, however, that he reached his conclusion in 1929 and it was not until seven years later that he elaborated the premises from which it follows. In his biography of Keynes, Harrod draws attention to this interesting point.

However, it would be idle to deny that, consciously or otherwise, politicians and administrators in charge of monetary policies are liable to come under the influence of the prevailing monetary theories. Whether or not this is a good thing depends not only on whether the theory is right or wrong, but also on the way it is applied. It is necessary to bear in mind that the same theory may serve as a basis for several different policies.

Moreover, changes in the economic situation and the other relevant circumstances are apt to affect the suitability of a monetary theory as a basis for monetary policy. There can be little doubt that nineteenth-century economic liberalism, on which the policy of maintaining the automatic gold standard was based, was in accordance with Britain's requirements between the end of the Napoleonic Wars and the beginning of the First World War. Unfortunately that classical theory continued to dominate British monetary policy even after the conditions which had justified it ceased to exist. Hence the grave mistakes made during the twenties. The theory which had been once a suitable guide for the monetary policy ceased to be suitable amidst changed circumstances.

Another instance of bad theory being responsible for bad policy occurred after the Second World War. There is every reason to believe that the mistaken popular definition of inflation was largely responsible for the inflationary policies adopted in Britain and in many other countries. Under the definition accepted in substance by most monetary theorists and by many practical men inflation was the state of affairs in which 'too much money was chasing too few goods'. From this principle politicians wishing to take the line of least resistance inferred that, provided that the rise in prices was not due to a previous increase in the volume of money, there was no inflation. This meant that if the price level rose as a result of a rise in imported raw material prices or some other reason unconnected with Government policy, and if the rise in prices resulted in pressure for an increase in the volume of currency and credit to meet increased requirements, the Government concerned did not consider it its duty to resist the trend for the volume of currency and credit to adjust itself subsequently to the higher level of prices. If only Ministers, officials, economists and the general public realized that the upward movement of the vicious spiral in which prices, cost of living, wages, cost of production, etc., are chasing each other constitutes inflation irrespective of whether the rise in prices preceded or succeeded the increase in the volume of money, there might have been more determined resistance to the expansion in the volume of money following on previous increases of prices.

Even a correct monetary theory is liable to be misused when it is applied as a basis of monetary policy. It is a fatal mistake to imagine that merely because a theory is good it necessarily provides a complete guide to practical action. As we saw from Hawtrey's quotation at the beginning of this chapter, monetary theory is only meant to apply to a hypothetical situation. It is bound to over-simplify conditions and its conclusions are always subject to the provision of 'other things being equal'. In practice other things are hardly ever equal. Those in charge of monetary policy have to allow for these 'other things' instead of merely making reservations about them in order to safeguard themselves against being blamed if forecasts based on their theories should prove to be incorrect. The trouble is that even though they and their theoretical advisers pay lip service to the reservation they are liable to come under the influence of the broad principle of the theory and are inclined to apply it as if it were a hard and fast rule.

Having said all this it is necessary to emphasize that monetary theory is indispensable as a background for monetary policy. It is, of course, conceivable that a Government may stumble on the right solution in spite of the absence of any theoretical background. The chances are, however, much more in favour of finding the right solution if they are aware of the theoretical implications, provided that the theories are applied with care and discrimination.

CHAPTER THIRTY-SEVEN

The Future of Monetary Policy

THE present generation has seen revolutionary changes in the sphere of monetary policy. In our lifetime monetary policy has become much broader and more diversified in its aim and much more scientific in its methods. Its management is no longer a task part-time amateurs, following time-honoured rules, could reasonably be expected to perform. To-day those in charge of the management of monetary policy are required to know incomparably more about it than their predecessors did. Admittedly their superior knowledge does not safeguard their communities against mistakes which are made in spite of the adoption of scientific methods – and indeed often because of it. There can be no doubt, however, that the authorities to-day are much better equipped for carrying out their difficult task. They can rely on the services of first-rate experts who are fully familiar with the theoretical background and have at their disposal a wealth of relevant factual and statistical information which did not exist until recent years.

Monetary theory itself has made remarkable progress in the past twenty years after its century of relative stagnation during the period between Ricardo and Keynes. The progress of monetary theory opened up wide possibilities for monetary policy to pursue new ends with the aid of new means.

The ends of monetary policy, like those of economic policy in general, have undergone a far-reaching change in recent years. The accent is now on social rather than economic ends. The aim is now to achieve the highest degree of welfare for the largest possible number, if necessary even at the cost of sacrificing stability. Indeed, if the economic requirements of higher productivity come into conflict with the social requirements of equalitarianism, the chances are that as often as not the latter will prevail.

The question is, are these trends in the ends and means of monetary policy likely to continue? There can be little doubt that the priority of social over economic ends will be maintained under the democratic regimes. In this respect, as in so many others, it seems to be impossible to put the clock back. Never again will public opinion in democratic countries look upon a slump brought about by orthodox monetary methods as an act of God. The electorate is not likely to endorse a policy which prefers to create large-scale unemployment rather than abandon the rigid defence of the exchange parities or the domestic purchasing power of a currency at a given level. There is room for two opinions about whether this attitude is right or wrong. It seems certain, however, that monetary policy must endeavour to conform largely to the popular view as to how to secure the highest degree of advantage for the largest number. The maintenance of the priority of social ends has become a political necessity under an electoral system based on universal suffrage.

This does not necessarily mean, however, that in the future Governments and Parliaments will always necessarily favour inflation in order to satisfy popular clamour for 'bread and circuses' – or, to translate it into modern language, for social services and television facilities. Indeed, it does not seem unreasonable to hope that in the course of time social ends will be pursued in an increasingly enlightened spirit, free of the present demagogic excesses. Not only Governments and Parliaments, but even the majority of the electorate will come to realize sooner or later that there are limits beyond which the sacrificing of economic ends for the sake of social ends is bound to react unfavourably on the latter in the long run. The largest number of people who hope to gain if monetary policy pursues exclusively social ends will discover sooner or later that they have to pay the price in the form of an ever-increasing cost of living, the absence of monetary and economic stability, and, in given circumstances, a reduction in productivity.

Social monetary policy is of too recent origin for most

people to realize its full implications, repercussions, and limitations. To-day it is still possible to work up a storm of indignation among the lower income groups over an increase in the cost of living even in instances when it is the logical, natural, and inescapable consequence of the release of additional purchasing power created for their benefit through higher wages and costlier social services. Few people appear to realize that in given circumstances the higher cost of living is just the other side of the same picture. Sooner or later the connexion between the two is bound to be realized. The next step then will be the adoption of a monetary policy which, while endeavouring to satisfy the reasonable claims of the Welfare State, will feel impelled to leave much legitimate demand unsatisfied for the sake of maintaining a reasonable degree of monetary stability. It is, of course, a matter of opinion what degree of monetary stability should be maintained even at the cost of cutting social service expenditure. Most beneficiaries probably feel that the Welfare State is worth an increase in the cost of living at an annual rate of, say, 5 per cent. Many of them would consider an annual increase of, say, 50 per cent too high a price to pay for their benefits.

When paper money first made its appearance in France in the early eighteenth century, many people were firmly convinced that this novel device had made it possible to spend unlimited amounts. Similarly to-day many people seriously believe that, thanks to the removal of the restraining influence of the gold standard, the Welfare State can be financed without limits by means of credit expansion. While disillusionment came to John Law's contemporaries in two years, it is likely to take much longer for our inflationists to realize the limitations of their policy. Sooner or later the public is bound to learn, at its cost, the need for some self-restraint in the use of credit expansion even for socially useful and economically productive purposes.

In the past monetary policy aimed at the maximum of monetary advantages in the form of monetary stability, often at the cost of general economic and social disadvantages. For a short time during a part of the inter-war period it aimed at a maximum of economic advantages in the form of higher production at the cost of social disadvantage and of monetary instability. At present it aims at the maximum of social advantages in the form of equalitarianism, at the cost of monetary and economic disadvantages. In the future it is likely to aim at achieving the optimum of social advantages – that is, the maximum compatible with vital economic interests of stability and productivity. Even the most advanced supporter of the creed that monetary policy has to be placed unreservedly at the service of social ends is bound to realize in the course of time through bitter experience that there is somewhere a limit beyond which these economic ends cannot be disregarded with impunity. The task of future monetary policy will be to ascertain where that limit is and to seek to proceed right up to that limit without exceeding it.

As for the methods and means of monetary policy there can be no doubt that scientific monetary management has come to stay, and that mankind will not revert to the automatic system. Methods which may have suited the comparatively simple situation of the nineteenth century would not stand a chance of producing satisfactory results in our incomparably more involved and less stable world in which disturbing tendencies are liable to become magnified into a major crisis that may threaten the very foundations of our economic and political system. It seems reasonable to assume that the days of *laissez-faire* are over as far as monetary policy is concerned. Conceivably gross mismanagement of monetary policy may from time to time provoke a reaction in favour of the old methods. Taking a long view, however, it is no longer considered possible to operate a system under which the volume of currency and credit is determined by the caprices of nature or by international gold movements. The extent of such movement is now liable to be much wider than it was in the nineteenth century owing to the higher degree of instability in the monetary, economic, social, and political spheres. The upheavals caused by two World Wars left a fundamentally unstable situation behind. The gold reserves provide a much too narrow safety margin for all countries, with the notable exception of the United States and one or two other fortunately placed countries. Under an automatic system most Treasuries would now be exposed to losing their gold reserves in a matter of days or at most of weeks.

This state of affairs is largely due to the unduly low dollar price of gold. While technically the United States is in a position to correct this situation and widen the margins of gold reserves, an increase in the dollar price of gold appears to be most unlikely. The gold reserves of most countries are likely to remain on the whole inadequate and at the mercy of even moderately adverse trends. To allow the volume of money to fluctuate as a result of gold movements would create an intolerable degree of economic instability. It would also handicap the monetary authorities of most countries in their task of providing for the legitimate monetary requirements of their community. Given this situation, it is absolutely necessary for the monetary authorities to take it on themselves to regulate the volume of money. They are not likely to relinquish this responsibility.

As in many other economic spheres, there has been a reaction in favour of freedom as a result of unfavourable experience in planning and of natural dislike for prolonged strict controls in time of peace. In the monetary sphere, however, all but the most fanatic believers in *laissez-faire* have realized the need for permanent scientific management. In that sphere State control has come to stay. Even the most conservative political parties have abandoned the idea of a denationalization of Central Banks. The Treasuries have also tightened their grip over the volume of credit by deposit banks and are not likely to relax their control. Although in most countries commercial banks are in private ownership, they have to submit to official requests in respect of their credit policies. There is reason to believe that the influence of the official monetary policy on the volume of bank credits and on their distribution will increase rather than decline in the future.

New methods of monetary policy are likely to continue

to be adopted. The authorities employ nowadays a much wider variety of monetary and non-monetary devices in the service of their monetary policy than before. The choice of weapons in the armoury of monetary policy is likely to widen further. Even though some of the new devices may be discarded under the influence of unfavourable experience, they are likely to be replaced by others. The authorities have much to learn regarding the technique of selective credit control. Thanks to Keynes and other reformers, new refinements have been introduced in this sphere, but the possibilities are far from having been exhausted. The adoption of fiscal means of monetary policy, too, is in its infancy and there is ample scope for development.

Above all, it is reasonably safe to expect the trend of future monetary policy to point towards an increasing degree of internationalism. Co-operation between monetary authorities is likely to make progress. Even though it may take generations before the ultimate end of the creation of an international currency can be achieved, the progress made in that direction in the past quarter of a century justifies hopes that it will continue.

Our generation has witnessed a remarkable growth in the importance of monetary policy in some directions, but it has also realized the limitations of monetary policy. In both respects progress may be expected. With further improvements in its methods monetary policy is liable to become an even more important factor in the economic system. On the other hand, intelligent realization of its limitations is likely to confine its application to within reasonable boundaries. The conception that a country's economy can be run satisfactorily with the aid of purely monetary methods, which became fashionable between the wars, is now at a discount. It is now realized that much more is needed than to take appropriate monetary measures and hope for the best. On the other hand, it is absurd to claim that our generation has witnessed the end of the rule of money and that, thanks to our more enlightened attitude, money has now become our servant instead of being our master.

In spite of its progress during the last two decades, monetary policy is always liable to remain somewhat behind in the development of the monetary situation. History in the monetary sphere seldom repeats itself exactly. There are always new factors or different combinations of the old known factors calling for original measures. Confronted with new situations, those in charge are often not in a position to apply rules elaborated on the basis of former experience. It is their task to adapt themselves to the new situations. Only too often they have to be content with being wise after the event. Even that is preferable to not being wise even after the event. Mistakes will always be made through the application of wrong devices or through the application of right devices in the wrong way. Important as it is to avoid such mistakes on the basis of accumulated experience and foresight it is even more important that the ends which monetary policy is to pursue should be correctly conceived. The solution lies in a reconciliation between social and economic ends. This may appear to involve some sacrifices from a social point of view. In the long run, however, even social interests are liable to be better served by making reasonable allowances for economic ends. It is to be hoped, in the interest of progress and stability, that, through trial and error, the correct balance between the conflicting ends will be discovered, for the lasting benefit of mankind.

Bibliography

ALSTON, LEONARD, *The Functions of Money*. London, 1932.

ANGELL, JAMES W., *The Behaviour of Money*. New York, 1936.

ARDAKAR, B. P., *The Theory of Monetary Policy*. London, 1935.

ASHTON, T. S., and SAYERS, R. S. (Editors), *Papers in English Monetary History*. London, 1953.

BAGEHOT, WALTER, *Lombard Street*. (New Edition.) London, 1931.

BALOGH, THOMAS, *Studies in Financial Organization*. Cambridge, 1947.

BAREAU, PAUL, *The Sterling Area* (2nd Edition). London, 1950.

BLOOMFIELD, A. I. *Capital Imports and the American Balance of Payments*. Chicago, 1950.

BRESCIANI-TURRONI, C., *The Economics of Inflation* (translated from Italian). London, 1937.

BROWN, W. A., *England and the New Gold Standard*. London, 1929.

BURNS, A. R., *Money and Monetary Policy in Early Times*. London, 1927.

CANNAN, EDWIN, *Money – its Connexion with Rising and Falling Prices* (8th edition). London, 1935.

CANTILLON, RICHARD, *Essai sur la nature du commerce en général*. (Translated and edited by Henry Higgs.) London, 1931.

CASSEL, GUSTAV, *Money and Foreign Exchange after 1914*. London, 1922.

The Downfall of the Gold Standard. Oxford, 1936.

CHALMERS, R., *A History of Currency in the British Colonies*. London, 1893.

CHANDLER, LESTER V., *The Economics of Money and Banking*. New York, 1948.

COLE, G. D. H., *Money, its Present and Future*. London, 1944.

CONAN, A. R., *The Sterling Area*. London, 1952.

CRAIG, SIR JOHN, *The Mint. A History of the London Mint from A.D. 287 to 1948*. Cambridge, 1953.

CROWTHER, GEOFFREY, *An Outline of Money*. (Revised Edition.) London, 1948.

CURRIE, LAUCHLIN, *The Supply and Control of Money in the United States*. Cambridge, Mass., 1934.

DACEY, W. MANNING, *The British Banking Mechanism*. London, 1951.

DILLARD DUDLEY, *The Economics of J. M. Keynes*. London, 1950.

DODWELL, D. W., *Treasuries and Central Banks*. London, 1934.

DONALDSON, JOHN, *The Dollar*. New York, 1937.

DURBIN, E. F. M., *The Problem of Credit Policy*. London, 1935.

EINZIG, PAUL, *International Gold Movements*. London, 1929.

  Exchange Control. London, 1934.

  Monetary Reform in Theory and Practice. London, 1936.

  The Exchange Clearing System. London, 1936.

  The Theory of Forward Exchange. London, 1937.

  Foreign Balances. London, 1938.

  Currency After the War. London, 1944.

  Primitive Money, in its Ethnological, Historical, and Economic Aspects. London, 1949.

  Inflation. London, 1952.

ELLIS, HOWARD S., *German Monetary Theory*. Cambridge, Mass., 1934.

  (Editor), *A Survey of Contemporary Economics*. Philadelphia, 1949.

FEAVEARYEAR, A. E., *The Pound Sterling – A History of English Money*. Oxford, 1931.

FFORDE, J. S., *The Federal Reserve System, 1915–1949*. Oxford, 1954.

FISHER, IRVING, *The Purchasing Power of Money*. (Revised Edition). New York, 1920.

  Stabilizing the Dollar. New York, 1920.

FRIEDMAN, MILTON, *Essays in Positive Economics*. Chicago, 1953.

GALBRAITH, J. K., *A Theory of Price Control*. Cambridge, Mass., 1952.

GANTENBEIN, JAMES A., *Financial Questions in United States Foreign Policy*. New York, 1939.

GAYER, ARTHUR D., *Monetary Policy and Economic Stabilization*. (2nd Edition.) London, 1937.

GOSCHEN, GEORGE J., *The Theory of the Foreign Exchanges*. (2nd Edition.) London, 1863.

GREAVES, IDA, *Colonial Monetary Conditions*. London, 1953.

GREGORY, T. E., *Foreign Exchange Before, During, and After the War*. Oxford, 1921.

  The Gold Standard and its Future. (3rd Edition.) London, 1934.

GRIEDANUS, TJARDUS, *The Value of Money*. London, 1932.

HABERLER, GOTTFRIED VON, *Prosperity and Depression*. Geneva, 1939.

HALL, N. F., *The Exchange Equalization Account*. London, 1935.

HALM, GEORGE N., *International Monetary Co-operation*. Chapel Hall, 1945.

HANSEN, ALVIN H., and CLEMENCE, R. V. (Editors), *Readings in Business Cycles*. London, 1953.

HANSEN, BENT, *A Study in the Theory of Inflation*. London, 1951.

HAMILTON, EARL J., *Money, Prices, and Wages in Valencia, Aragon, and Navarre, 1351–1500*. Cambridge, Mass., 1936.

HARRIS, S. E., *Monetary Problems of the British Empire*. New York, 1931.

(Editor), *The New Economics – Keynes' Influence on Theory and Public Policy*. New York, 1947.

HARROD, R. F., *International Economics*. London, 1933.

The Life of John Maynard Keynes. London, 1951.

The Dollar. London, 1953.

HAWTREY, R. G., *Trade and Credit*. London, 1928.

Trade Depression and the Way Out. London, 1933.

A Century of Bank Rate. London, 1938.

Currency and Credit. (4th Edition.) London, 1950.

Capital and Employment. (2nd Edition.) London, 1952.

HAYEK, F. A. VON, *Monetary Theory and the Trade Cycle*. London, 1933.

Prices and Production. (2nd Edition.) London, 1935.

Monetary Nationalism and International Stability. London, 1937.

HEILPERIN, M. A., *International Monetary Economics*. London, 1939.

HELFFERICH, KARL, *Money*, (translated from German). London, 1927.

H.M. STATIONERY OFFICE, *Report of the Committee on Finance and Industry*. London, 1931.

HICKS, J. R., *A Contribution to the Theory of Trade Cycle*. Oxford, 1950.

KEYNES, J. M., *Indian Currency and Finance*. London, 1913.

A Tract on Monetary Reform. London, 1923.

A Treatise on Money. London, 1930.

Essays in Persuasion. London, 1933.

The General Theory of Employment, Interest, and Money. London, 1936.

How to Pay for the War. London, 1940.

KINDLEBERGER, C. P., *The Dollar Shortage*. New York, 1950.

International Economics. New York, 1953.

KNIGHT, F. H., *The Ethics of Competition and Other Essays*. London, 1935.

KNAPP, G. F., *The State Theory of Money*. (Translated from German.) London, 1924.

KURIHARA, KENNETH K., *Monetary Theory and Public Policy*, London, 1951.

LAVINGTON, F., *The English Capital Market*. London, 1921.

LEAGUE OF NATIONS, *Report of the Gold Delegation of the Finance Committee*. Geneva, 1930, and 1932.

LUTZ, F. A., and MINTS, LLOYD W. (Editors), *Readings in Monetary Theory*. London, 1952.

MARSHALL, ALFRED, *Money, Credit, and Commerce*. London, 1923.

McKENNA, REGINALD, *Post-War Banking Policy*. London, 1928.

MILLIKAN, MAX F. (Editor), *Income Stabilization for a Developing Democracy*. New Haven, 1953.

MINTS, LLOYD W., *Monetary Policy for a Competitive Society*. New York, 1950.

MISES, L. VON, *The Theory of Money and Credit*, (New Edition.) London, 1953.

MYRDAL, GUNNAR, *The Political Element in the Development of Economic Theory*. (Translated from Swedish.) London, 1953.

NIEBYL, KARL H., *Studies in the Classical Theories of Money*. New York, 1946.

NOGARO, BERTRAND, *A Short Treatise on Money and Monetary Systems*. (Translated from French.) London, 1949.

PIGOU, A. C., *The Veil of Money*. London, 1949.

QUIGGIN, A. HINGSTON, *A Survey of Primitive Money*. London, 1949.

RIST, CHARLES, *History of Monetary and Credit Theory from John Law to the Present Day*. New York, 1940.

ROBBINS, LIONEL, *The Great Depression*. London, 1934.

ROBERTSON, SIR DENNIS H., *Banking Policy and the Price Level*. London, 1932.
Essays in Monetary Theory. London, 1940.
Money. (Revised Edition.) London, 1948.
Utility and All That and Other Essays. London, 1952.
Britain in the World Economy. London, 1954.

ROBEY, R. (Editor), *The Monetary Problem – Final Report of the Royal Commission to Inquire into the Relative Values of the Precious Metals, Presented to Parliament 1888*. New York, 1936.

ROBINSON, JOAN, *The Rate of Interest and Other Essays*. London, 1952.

ROOVER, RAYMOND DE, *Gresham on Foreign Exchange*. Cambridge, Mass., 1949.

ROYAL INSTITUTE OF INTERNATIONAL AFFAIRS, *The International Gold Problem*. Oxford, 1931.
Monetary Policy and the Depression. Oxford, 1933.
The Future of Monetary Policy. Oxford, 1935.

SAYERS, R. S., *Bank of England Operations, 1890–1914*. Oxford, 1936.

SHAW, EDWARD S., *Money Income and Monetary Policy*. Chicago, 1950.

SHAW, W. A., *The History of Currency, 1252 to 1894*. London. Undated.

SPEARMAN, DIANA, *The Sterling Area*. London, 1953.

STIGLER, G. J., and BOULDING, K. E., (Editors), *Readings in Price Theory*. London, 1953.

SURANYI-UNGER, THEO, *Comparative Economic Systems*. New York, 1952.

SWANN, NANCY LEE, *Food and Money in Ancient China*. Princeton, 1950.

TEW, BRIAN, *International Monetary Co-operation, 1945–1952*. London, 1952.

THOMAS, BRINLEY, *Monetary Policy and Crises – A Study of Swedish Experience*. London, 1936.

U.S. GOVERNMENT PRINTING OFFICE, *Monetary Policy and the Management of the Public Debt*. Washington, 1952.

WAIGHT, L., *The History and Mechanism of the Exchange Equalization Account*. Cambridge, 1939.

WALKER, JOHN R., *Bank Credit as Money*. New York, 1937.

WARREN, G. F., and PEARSON, F. A., *Gold and Prices*. New York, 1935.

WHITTLESEY, CHARLES R., *Principles and Practice of Money and Banking*. New York, 1948.

(Editor.) *Readings in Money and Banking*. New York, 1952.

WICKSELL, KNUT, *Interest and Prices*. London, 1936.

WILLIAMS, JOHN H., *Post-War Monetary Problems and Other Essays*. Oxford, 1949.

WITHERS, HARTLEY, *The Meaning of Money*. (6th Edition.) London, 1937.

WOLFE, MARTIN, *The French Franc Between the Wars 1919–1939*. New York, 1951.

YANG, LIEN-SHENG, *Money and Credit in China*. Cambridge, Mass., 1952.

INDEX

Index